■“十四五”应用型本科院校拓展课程规划教材

跨文化交流

主　编　陈建祥　俞　娟

副主编　盛　辉　侯昌明　裴如意

东南大学出版社
SOUTHEAST UNIVERSITY PRESS
·南京·

内容提要

本教材根据《大学英语教学指南》(2020年版)关于英语语言学习的交际应用和跨文化交际能力的要求,通过饮食、教育、神话、运动、节日、影视等12个核心话题,围绕跨文化交际意识、跨文化交际实践与跨文化交际能力评价等维度,精选具有代表性的阅读材料,设计了理解性与阐述性问题,从而帮助学习者在了解文化常识的基础上,能够自觉地进行文化比较,并进而进行文化探究和实践。

本教材集语言学习和文化熏陶于一体,有机融入思政元素,具有人文性、应用性和先进性等特点,能帮助学习者充分了解中西方文化差异、提升跨文化交际能力,并有利于在坚定文化自信的基础上促进中华文化走出去。

本书适用于普通高校通识课或拓展课程,也可供有兴趣的人士阅读借鉴。

图书在版编目(CIP)数据

跨文化交流/陈建祥,俞娟主编. —南京:东南大学出版社,2022.5(2024.12重印)

ISBN 978-7-5766-0093-3

Ⅰ.①跨… Ⅱ.①陈… ②俞… Ⅲ.①文化交流—高等学校—教材 Ⅳ.①G115

中国版本图书馆CIP数据核字(2022)第070546号

责任编辑:刘 坚(liu-jian@seu.edu.cn) **责任校对**:张万莹 **封面设计**:王 玥 **责任印制**:周荣虎

跨文化交流 Kuawenhua Jiaoliu

主　　编	陈建祥　俞　娟
出版发行	东南大学出版社
社　　址	南京市四牌楼2号(邮编:210096　电话:025-83793330)
网　　址	http://www.seupress.com
电子邮箱	press@seupress.com
经　　销	全国各地新华书店
印　　刷	广东虎彩云印刷有限公司
开　　本	787 mm×1092 mm　1/16
印　　张	16
字　　数	480千字
版　　次	2022年5月第1版
印　　次	2024年12月第5次印刷
书　　号	ISBN 978-7-5766-0093-3
定　　价	49.80元

本社图书若有印装质量问题,请直接与营销部联系,电话:025-83791830。

前 言 PREFACE

世界正面临百年未有之大变局，这是习近平同志为核心的党中央审时度势做出的英明论断。中国已然成为世界第二大经济体，国际力量对比日益均衡，多边格局逐渐形成，多样性的世界文化相互间更加开放和包容。面对如此之变局，中国不遗余力地推动全球命运共同体建设，坚持社会主义道路，坚持文化自信，在全球治理体系中争取更多的话语权，从而更好地将民族复兴与世界变局融为一体。

习近平总书记在2016年12月7日的全国高校思想政治工作会议上强调"要用好课堂教学这个主渠道，思想政治理论课要坚持在改进中加强，提升思想政治教育亲和力和针对性，满足学生发展需求和期待，其他各门课都要守好一段渠、种好责任田，使各类课程与思想政治理论课同向同行，形成协同效应"。这次大会对中国高等教育改革发展具有里程碑意义，高屋建瓴地提出了思政教育与各类课程深度融合、为社会主义事业培养接班人的新范式。2020年5月28日教育部颁布《高等学校课程思政建设指导纲要》，明确指出要切实把教育教学作为最基础最根本的工作，深入挖掘各类课程和教学内容中蕴含的思想政治教育资源，让学生通过学习，掌握事物发展规律，通晓天下道理，丰富学识，增长见识，塑造品格，努力成为德、智、体、美、劳全面发展的社会主义建设者和接班人。教育部大学外语教学指导委员会制定的《大学英语教学指南(2020版)》指出，大学英语课程要培养学生的英语应用能力，增强跨文化交际意识和交际能力，同时发展自主学习能力，提高综合文化素养，使他们在学习、生活、社会交往和未来工作中能够有效地使用英语、满足国家、社会、学校和个人发展的需要。

从服务国家战略层面上讲，跨文化交流课程致力于培养拥有全球视野、跨文化意识和交际技能，通晓国际话语体系和规则，能够参与国际磋商、具有爱国主义情操的青年人才，为促进社会经济发展，增强综合国力、提升国际形象、改革世界话语体系、参与全球治理、构建人类命运共同体提供丰富的人才储备和智力支持。从学生成长需求来看，跨文化交际课程有助于大学生汲取世界其他国家文化中的精华成分、研习领先的科学技术、吸收先进的管理理念和经验，培养他们开放、包容、进取的人文精神，葆有中国传统文化自信，尊重外国文化，开拓创新，为迎接全球化时代面临的机遇与挑战做好双语种乃至多语种交际能力上的准备。

跨文化交流课程作为大学英语素质拓展课程，具有意识形态性、现实针对性和理论批判性，极其适合承载课程思政的功能。在课程教学中深入挖掘教学内容所涉及或包含的思政元素，以社会主义核心价值观和中华优秀传统文化为中心和主线，实现语言文化教育与思政教育两翼齐飞。学生通过跨文化交流课程的系统学习，加深对国外社会与文化的理解，进行有意识的文化异同对比，提升跨文化交际能力，从而更好地服务中国文化的对外传播，向世界传输更加积极的中国国家形象。将社会主义核心价值观有机融入课程建设，立足中国文化，建立跨语言、跨文化的教学模式，帮助学生深化语言文化的学习，内化社会主义核心价值观、获得立足世界的国际视野。

本教材结合中国学生的特点，介绍中西方文化基础知识，旨在培养学生对文化差异的感知能力、理解能力和分析能力，从而帮助学生在跨文化语境中，拓宽国际视野，树立全球意识，实现有效沟通，达到特定交际目的。教材选择中西方文化核心话题，合计十二个单元，围绕跨文化交际意识、跨文化交际实践与跨文化交际能力评价三个纬度，每单元包括既互相联系又相互区别的三个专题：

1. 文化知识专题。系统介绍中国及英美等主要西方国家历史文化、文学艺术、高等教育、社会生活等，重在提高学生对中西方国家民族特性、价值观念、社会结构、人际关系、社会习俗等的认知。

2. 文化比较专题。以文化双向表达为核心，针对中西方文化在某一方面的异同进行比较与分析，旨在提高学生对文化差异的敏感性和宽容度。

3. 文化探索和实践。采用不同语境下的跨文化交际实际案例，通过讨论、演讲、辩论、项目报告等教学活动，着力培养和考查学生在言语行为层面上完成跨文化交际任务的能力。

本教材集语言学习和文化熏陶于一体，有机融入思政元素，生动多样的案例分析和课堂活动设计更增添其实用性和独特性。本教材具有以下三方面的特色：

1. 人文性：通过跨文化教育与人文教育，培养学生的跨文化交际能力，从而帮助他们树立世界眼光，增强国际交流意识，提高人文素养，提升自身综合竞争力。

2. 应用性：除了阐释跨文化交际理论、夯实基础之外，更要强调学以致用，将所学的理论运用于实践。本教材以培养跨文化交际能力为导向，切实提高学生在学术和职业领域进行交流的能力。

3. 先进性：课程思政理念深入人心，在教材中有所体现。这是与时俱进的需要，也是学生了解西方文化、思辨中西文化异同、培养跨文化意识的需求。在教材中融入正确的世界观、人生观和社会主义核心价值观，帮助学生在拓展国际视野的同时，增加家国情怀，增强文化自信。

本教材是在自编讲义基础之上改编而成，由盐城工学院教材基金资助出版。在编写过程中，盐城工学院外国语学院院长齐金花、盐城工学院外国语学院副院长叶磊、盐城工学院教务处领导和教材科领导给予了无微不至的关心和帮助；在出版过程中，东南大学出版社刘坚教授等编辑老师字斟句酌，悉心指导；在自编讲义使用过程中，同学们提出了许多有价值的意见；缪春怡和王伊宁同学为教材提供了精美的原创插图。在此一并表示感谢！

本教程在编写过程中既借鉴了现有的诸多与跨文化交流有关的教材，也有诸多自主创新之处。由于编写水平有限，不当之处，敬请各位专家、学生和读者批评指正。

本教材附有课件，读者可以通过扫描教材内页或封底的二维码链接下载，也可以从出版社网站直接下载。

陈建祥　俞娟

2022 年 4 月

INTRODUCTION

The world is in a constant and dynamic state of change. Because of fast transport and information technology, people are able to meet each other or communicate with each other instantly and conveniently. The world is becoming smaller like a village. Any country in the world cannot isolate itself, but has to conduct political, economic, and cultural exchanges with other countries. Intercultural communication is increasingly popular and becomes more frequent, and different cultures are interrelated and even interdependent due to the rapid globalization.

"The silent language" written by Edward Hall in 1959 is academically accepted as the masterpiece that launched the study of intercultural communication. Language is the carrier of culture and also the most important part of culture. Because of complexity of communication, there is no unanimous definition for culture or intercultural communication. Culture is generally considered to contain elements such as the deposit of knowledge, language, food, shelter, experience, beliefs, values, attitudes, hierarchies, religion, notions of time and space, views of life, the world and the universe, and so on. Intercultural communication involves interaction between people whose cultural perceptions and symbol systems differ enough to influence the communication event. In popular words, It refers to the communication between people from different cultural backgrounds to exchange ideas, feelings, information, etc. For example, country leaders give speeches at international summit meetings; businessmen have international trade with their overseas business partners; Chinese students chat with international students; travelers communicate with local people in a foreign country. All these are common cases of intercultural communication.

Culture exists in tangible forms and intangible forms, both of which can be passed down from generation to generation. Taking festivals for example, Chinese people attach supreme significance to Spring Festival and English-speaking countries place a high value on Christmas. These two festivals have existed for more than two thousand years. Culture can be consciously learned through school education and formal training. It can also be acquired unconsciously through proverbs, myths, legends, idioms, customs, fairy tales and bedtime stories. Therefore, each individual has a cultural identity. When people from different cultures communicate, they use interlanguage to create an inter-identity for they make endeavors to understand each other and to be closer to each other so as to carry out a smooth communication.

Even if one understands and speaks a target language well, it doesn't necessarily follow that he can communicate smoothly with people from another culture. Here is a classic example. A foreign friend praises the beauty of a Chinese hostess, and says, "You are very beautiful!" The hostess is at a loss about how to give a proper response and replies with "Where, where", which actually is a typical Chinese way to express modesty, but can confuse foreigners for it's an unexpected response. All cultures use symbols to convey meanings, but symbols they use may bear similar or different meanings. For instance, nodding heads can mean consent in some cultures while it can mean refusal in other cultures.

Because people all over the world share some universal feelings, emotions, experiences and views; there are some cultural similarities. Cultural similarities make intercultural communication possible and cultural differences may pose difficulties for communication participants. Different cultural backgrounds can lead to different understanding of cultural phenomena, even misinterpretation, hostility, confrontations and conflicts. These communication failures may result from physical barriers, emotional barriers, language barriers, barriers of attitudes, and shortage of communications skills.

Cultural differences are likely to be related to races, regions, careers, genders, ages, values, social classes and so on. Cultural differences tend to keep people apart while cultural similarities can bring people closer. Intercultural communication has effects on both sides involved. To achieve better understanding, both sides tend to abide by discursive principles such as Cooperative Principles and Politeness Principles and adopt some communicative strategies. They would even resort to formal school instructions to know about each other.

As known to all, communication is conducted based on specific contexts. In some cultures, meanings don't have to be stated directly and clearly because people have similar traditions, experiences, perceptions and societal expectations. These cultures are termed as high-context cultures. Contrary to high-context cultures are low-context cultures, where exists racial diversity. In the latter kind of cultures, people need to communicate with resort to detailed background information. Chinese culture and Japanese culture belong to high-context cultures and most western cultures are classified as the low-context cultures, but vary in degree.

China, a great country of long history, is rich in cultural heritages, which not only records the splendid historical development, but reflects traditional values, civilized conducts and artistic aesthetics. Though China encountered invasions in the last two centuries, it remains resilient and full of life and vigor and occupies a unique position in the modern world. Chinese culture is a highly homogeneous culture because Chinese people have common dreams, pursuits and faiths. Chinese people have strong cohesive force especially in case of invasions, natural disasters, global pandemic and unite together to overcome any difficulty they confront. In the world history, there were once four countries of ancient civilization, but China is the only one that still survives and thrives. In ancient times, China was once considered as the most prosperous and dominant culture in the orient and exerted great influence on Japan, Korean Peninsula, South East Asia and other regions. According to official records, China communicated with foreign cultures early in the history. In the Han Dynasty, China had economic and cultural interactions with Roman Empire through the Silk Road. In the Yuan Dynasty, Marco Polo, a world-known traveller, wrote about what he saw and what he experienced in China, producing great repercussions in the world.

Western culture can be dated back to three important sources, Christianity, ancient Rome Civilization and ancient Greek civilization. Since China adopted the opening-up policy, western culture entered China at a faster pace and affected more people, especially young university students. It is not uncommon for some people to observe western festivals but ignore and despise Chinese culture. While a handful of westerners have the stereotyped view that Chinese people have slanted eyes, some Chinese models and films even make a point of creating such images to meet this stereotype. To some extent, the negative influence of western culture cannot be neglected or ignored.

According to the *Law of China's Higher Education*, the three missions of institutions of higher learning are to cultivate talents, develop science and technology and serve the purposes of the society. Because university students are the future and backbone of China, they should develop appropriate attitudes towards Chinese culture and western culture. China's international communication aims at creating a favorable international discourse environment to win international recognition and support. To realize this aim, more college students should be cultivated to possess international visions and more textbooks should be compiled on intercultural communication from different perspectives.

This book consists of 12 chapters, food, education, mythology, sports, body language, values, movies, colours, festivals, wedding, coffee and tea, and music. When university students deal with this course, they should pay special attention to: (1) cultural similarities and cultural differences, and their influence on intercultural communication; (2) cultural shock and cultural adaptation; (3) religions, manners, rituals, customs and etiquette of both sides; (4) cultural biases, cultural stereotypes and ethnocentrism; (5) verbal communication and nonverbal communication; (6) individualism and collectivism; (7) the relations between language and culture. As a matter of course, the list of requirements is open-ended. When communicating with a foreigner, we should not be either overconfident or feel inferior. All cultures, big or small, are equal in the international community. Every culture is a treasure house in the world where people can learn from each other instead of struggling with each other.

目　录 CONTENTS

Unit One

Food

Part One

Lead-in

There is no sincerer love than the love of food.

—George Bernard Shaw

Different natural geographical environment, climatic conditions, resources, specialties, custom and unique historical development experience have created different food cultures in different countries and regions in the world. Most traditions have a recognizable cuisine, a specific set of cooking traditions, preferences and practices, which creates distinctive catering culture. Chinese Cuisine and Western cuisine are extremely diverse with each country and region boasting their unique cooking styles and typical dishes. By looking at food, the ages we are living in, the culture of different regions and the history of human beings can be better understood.

Part Two

In-Class Reading

Warm-up questions:

1. What is food culture?
2. What role does food play in your life and in your family?

The Food Chains That Link Us All

1 C. L. R James, the great Trinidadian essayist, once wrote of his favorite sport, "What do they know of cricket, who only cricket know?" The same question should be asked of food. To write about food only as food misses the point, or the many points, about the great universal human experience between birth and death. Food is not just what we eat. It charts the **ebbs and flows** of economies, reflects the changing patterns of trade and geopolitical alliances, and defines our values, status and health—for better and worse. The famous **dictum** of the early 19th century French **gastronome** Jean Anthelme Brillat-Savarin, "Tell me what you eat and I will tell you who you are," should be expanded. Tell me what you eat and I will tell you who you are, where you live, where you stand on political issues, who your neighbors are, how your economy functions, your country's history and foreign relations, and the state of the environment. By looking at food, the age we live in is better understood.

2 Once, food was defined by a very small geographic zone, prescribed by the products and traditions in that area. Where there were wars, food was modified. Arabs conquered Europe; cane sugar went with them. The Chinese entered Japan and the soybean entered the Japanese diet. Immigration left a mark, too. Jews **fleeing** Portugal brought chocolate to southwestern France. African slaves brought frying and **okra** to the Caribbean and the American South. It seemed every time a royal marriage was arranged in France, the **cuisine** gained a few ingredients and dishes. Modern historians question the influence of **Catherine de' Medici**[1] when she arrived in Paris in 1533 at the age of 14, with an extensive Italian cooking staff. The event probably did not revolutionize French cooking as is sometimes suggested, but it did bring the artichoke north. And when **Louis XVI**[2] married **Marie Antoinctte**[3] from **Lorrainc**[4], **sauerkraut**[5] became fashionable in Paris and remained popular far longer than she did.

3 Never has food been more of a global commodity than it is today. Witness the rise of

the **franchised** super chef, the **ubiquity** of **fusion fare**, and the ease with which exotic ingredients cross borders and oceans. But not all of this is a modern phenomenon. Purely local cuisines have always been rare. Take the spice trade. While fortunes were being made in Asian, African and American commerce, European food **was laced with** excessive quantities of **nutmeg**, **mace**, **ginger**, black pepper and **cinnamon**. Spanish monks put the latter in chocolate, reasoning that one **exotic** food deserved another. The slave trade brought **molasses** to New England and salt cod to West Africa and the Caribbean, while the British Navy in search of an empire carried corned beef to the Pacific as their people at home started eating curry. In the Caribbean, where history is an endless succession of migrations and conquests, there is almost nothing **indigenous** in the "local" food. Even China, **possessed** of great cuisines, is full of imports in its traditional food, such as the hot peppers the Portuguese transported from the Americas.

4 All of the processes by which cooks were introduced to new products and new ideas (and, in fact, most of history) began to speed up in the 19th century as transportation became faster—an acceleration so **relentless** that over the past 50 years the changes have seemed **bewildering**. Today trade is swift and global, and therefore food no longer reflects its place or time. No longer do you know where you are or what month it is by the food that is available. Every day organic vegetables from California, freshly caught turbots packed in dry ice from France, fresh Portuguese sardines, New Zealand oysters and smelly durian from Asia land in the airports of the world. More than ever in our history, we are now offered endless choices in food. But we may be embracing this excitement **at the cost of** the **erosion** of our own cultures.

5 Globalization has not led to equality either. Food remains **classist**. The poor still eat mostly **carbohydrates** and fats, while the rich get the protein—something that can even be seen in the difference between airline meals in first class and economy. I once had to attend a black-tie food event in New York City while on a low-carb diet. From **caviar** to fish, all of the **deluxe** fare suited my **regime**.

6 The great restaurants, with their low-carb dishes that take a paragraph to explain on a menu, prepare food that is too complicated for most people to prepare at home. It is also too expensive. Most of the great cities of the world, once **refuges** for the poor, are increasingly **enclaves** for the wealthy where cooks and even farmers can experiment without considering cost. New York City has established a much-loved system of neighborhood "farmers' markets". Originally a movement to take control back from corporate industrial agriculture, these markets, serviced by local farmers trucking in their goods, are a most fascinating **collusion** of small-scale farming and wealthy consumers. There is almost no limit to the price such farmers can ask for their produce. Farmers traditionally like to grow crops as large as

possible because the ratio of weight to effort is better. People like baby vegetables because they are cute—tiny carrots, peanut-like **squash** and bean-sized **Brussels sprouts**[6]. If the customer pays enough, the farmer will pick the vegetable when it's tiny. Precious small radish-sized potatoes from white to purple, and very **waxy** to very **floury**, sell in New York City for a price per size comparable to Manhattan real estate. The wealthy, of course, reject industrial farming, which was always intended to mass produce for the poor (and yet has failed in its greatest goal: to end world hunger). To see just how much resistance to industrial agriculture there is among the rich, travel to rural areas where wealthy **urbanites** have their vacation homes and watch them pay fees for the privilege of stooping in the field to harvest a crop.

7 But the three-star restaurants are not the ones charting the course of food. History has shown that food almost always impacts culture from the poor up, not from the rich down. The creativity of great French chefs **belies** the fact that there is less and less cooking going on in the average French home, almost none of it in any way resembling the food of restaurants; that it is becoming increasingly difficult to find good bread in France because few want to be a baker, a hard and low-paying job; that more **rarefied** crafts like chocolate making are difficult to continue because adolescents now go to school instead of **apprenticing**; and that industrial farming continues to **squeeze out** small, quality producers.

8 And yet, industrial food is out of fashion. Today there is a global market for organic fruits and vegetables, free-range birds, oysters from microbes. Technology is in. Genetically modified food offers many opportunities, not the least of which is crops that are so insect **repellent** they need no pesticides. But—to the **fury** of some farmers—some of the same people who reject **pesticides** and call for organic food are now calling for a ban on genetically modified food. The argument, though a bit **murky**, is powerful. While there is no solid proof of the evils of such food, why trust hi-tech food from the same corporations that brought us industrial food?

9 Climate change is also changing our food, particularly through its impact on that great supplier, the ocean. Water is becoming not only warmer but less salty. The oceans, however, have been **assaulted** with not only climate change, but with pollution and destructive industrial fishing. Many predictions about seafood stocks are **dire**. Will most of them be seriously **depleted** by the year 2048, as one marine biologist recently predicted? Has the number of large fish in the ocean decreased by 90% over the past 50 years, as another scientist reported? Are 31% of the 274 commercially important fish stocks in America overfished, as a 2002 U. S. government report asserted? Are 60% of the fish species studied by the U. N. **Food and Agriculture Organization** (**FAO**)[7] either fully exploited or depleted, as an FAO report claims? What is clear is that popular fish such as Atlantic salmon, cod and tuna are vanishing.

We are now eating varieties that 40 years ago were considered "trash fish". On the coast of Cornwall, in England, monkfish is the largest catch in ports that used to be known for sardines, herring and cod. But what happens if the monkfish start to vanish too? The only certainty is that the survival of the ocean's fish can no longer be assumed—something that **portends** not just a crisis for biology, but one of the most dramatic shifts in food consumption ever seen.

10 History carries tremendous burdens—the age of empire, the Industrial Revolution—that influence our lives and what we eat today. To understand the food of today, the past must be remembered. For the same reason, if future historians want to look back at what life was like in the early 21st century—the technological and information revolutions, the blessings and dangers of globalization, the challenges to the survival of a healthy planet—they would do well to look at our food. Changes in food have always been a function of changes in society. We are—and will always be—what we eat.

Mark Kurlansky[8]

New Words and Expressions

dictum /ˈdɪktəm/ *n.* a formal statement of opinion by someone who is respected or has authority 格言

gastronome /ˈgæstrənəʊm/ *n.* a person devoted to refined sensuous enjoyment (especially good food and drink) 美食家

flee /fliː/ *v.* run or hurry away 逃跑；逃离

okra /ˈəʊkrə/ *n.* long green edible beaked pods of the okra plant 秋葵;秋葵荚

cuisine /kwɪˈziːn/ *n.* the practice or manner of preparing food or the food so prepared 烹饪;佳肴

franchise /ˈfræntʃaɪz/ *v.* grant a franchise to 赋予特权;赋予公民权

ubiquity /juːˈbɪkwəti/ *n.* the state of being everywhere at once (or seeming to be everywhere at once) 到处存在;普遍存在

fusion /ˈfjuːʒn/ *n.* a combination of separate qualities or ideas 融合

fare /feə(r)/ *n.* the food and drink that are regularly served or consumed 食物

nutmeg /ˈnʌtmeg/ *n.* East Indian tree widely cultivated in the tropics for its aromatic seed; source of two spices: nutmeg and mace 肉豆蔻

mace /meɪs/ *n.* spice made from the dried fleshy covering of the nutmeg seed 豆蔻香料

ginger /ˈdʒɪndʒə(r)/ *n.* plant with a hot-tasting root used in cooking 姜,生姜

cinnamon /ˈsɪnəmən/ *n.* aromatic bark used as a spice 肉桂

exotic /ɪɡˈzɒtɪk/ *adj.* being or from or characteristic of another place or part of the world 外来的

molasses /məˈlæsɪz/ *n.* thick dark syrup produced by boiling down juice from sugar cane; especially during sugar refining 糖浆;糖蜜

indigenous /ɪnˈdɪdʒənəs/ *adj.* originating where it is found 土生土长的;本地的

relentless /rɪˈlentləs/ *adj.* continuously cruel or fierce; merciless 残酷的,毫不留情的,无怜悯心的

bewildering /bɪˈwɪldərɪŋ/ *adj.* cause to be confused emotionally 令人困惑的;使人混乱的

erosion /ɪˈrəʊʒn/ *n.* process of destroying or wearing away gradually 腐蚀;侵蚀

classist /klɑːˈsɪst/ *adj.* having bias based on social or economic class 有阶级偏见的

carbohydrate /kɑːbəˈhaɪdreɪt/ *n.* an essential structural component of living cells and source of energy for animals; includes simple sugars with small molecules as well as macromolecular substances; are classified according to the number of monosaccharide groups they contain 碳水化合物

caviar /ˈkæviɑː(r)/ *n.* salted roe of sturgeon or other large fish; usually served as an hors d'oeuvre 鱼子酱

deluxe /dəˈlʌks/ *adj.* rich and superior in quality 豪华的;高级的

regime /reɪˈʒiːm/ *n.* (medicine) a systematic plan for therapy (often including diet) 养生法

refuge /ˈrefjuːdʒ/ *n.* (a place that provides) protection or shelter from danger 避难所

enclave /ˈenkleɪv/ *n.* an enclosed territory that is culturally distinct from the foreign territory that surrounds it 一个被较大单位围住的明显划出界线的区域

collusion /kəˈluːʒn/ *n.* a secret agreement that two or more people make in order to do something dishonest 共谋,勾结

squash /skwɒʃ/ *n.* edible fruit of a squash plant; eaten as a vegetable 南瓜属植物

waxy /ˈwæksi/ *adj.* capable of being bent or flexed or twisted without breaking, smooth and lustrous 柔软的;蜡的

floury /ˈflaʊəri/ *adj.* resembling flour in fine powdery texture 粉状的;沾满面粉的

urbanite /ˈɜːbənaɪt/ *n.* people who live and work in towns and cities 都市人

belie /bɪˈlaɪ/ *v.* represent falsely 掩饰

rarefied /ˈreərɪfaɪd/ *adj.* only available to or understood by a small group of people 秘传的

apprentice /əˈprentɪs/ *v.* work for an employer for a fixed period of time in order to learn a particular skill or job 当学徒

repellent /rɪˈpelənt/	*adj.* highly offensive; arousing aversion or disgust 排斥的
fury /ˈfjʊəri/	*n.* wild and violent anger 狂怒,狂暴
pesticide /ˈpestɪsaɪd/	*n.* substance for killing insects 杀虫剂
murky /ˈmɜːki/	*adj.* complicated and difficult to understand 含糊的
assault /əˈsɔːlt/	*v.* attack something in a violent way 攻击,袭击
dire /ˈdaɪə(r)/	*adj.* fraught with extreme danger; nearly hopeless 可怕的;灾难的
deplete /dɪˈpliːt/	*v.* reduce the amount of something that is present or available 耗尽,使衰竭
portend /pɔːˈtend/	*v.* indicate by signs 预示
ebb and flow	prosperity and decline 盛衰
be laced with	have some of a quality 带有……的特点
be possessed of	have a particular quality, ability, etc. 占有,拥有
at the cost of	at the price of 以……为代价
squeeze out	do something so that someone or something is no longer included or able to continue 榨出,挤出

Notes

1. Catherine de' Medici 凯瑟琳·美第奇 Catherine de' Medici (April 13, 1519 – January 5, 1589), daughter of Lorenzo II de' Medici and of Madeleine de La Tour d'Auvergne, was an Italian noblewoman who was Queen of France from 1547 until 1559, as the wife of King Henry II. As the mother of three sons who became kings of France during her lifetime, she had extensive, if at times varying, influence in the political life of France. For a time, she ruled France as its regent.

2. Louis XVI 路易十六 Louis XVI (August 23, 1754 – January 21, 1793), born Louis-Auguste, ruled as King of France and Navarre from 1774 until 1791, and then as King of the French from 1791 to 1792. In 1789 he summoned the Estates-General to undertake fiscal reforms, an event that eventually led to the French Revolution. Louis was convicted of treason by the revolutionary government and executed in 1793.

3. Marie Antoinette 玛丽·安托瓦内特 Marie Antoinette (November 2,1755 – October 16,1793), Queen of France by marriage to Louis XIV of France. Her opposition to reform during the Revolution contributed to the overthrow of the monarchy. She was executed by guillotine at the height of the French Revolution in 1793 for the crime of treason.

4. Lorraine 洛林(法国东北部一地区) a district located in the northeast of France

5. sauerkraut 德国泡菜的一种 a German food made from cabbage that has been left in salt so that it tastes sour

6. Brussels sprout 芽甘蓝 a small round green vegetable that looks like a very small cabbage

7. Food and Agriculture Organization (FAO) 联合国粮食及农业组织 Food and Agriculture Organization is a specialized agency of the United Nations that leads international efforts to defeat hunger. Serving both developed and developing countries, FAO acts as a neutral forum where all nations meet as equals to negotiate agreements and debate policy. FAO is also a source of knowledge and information, and helps developing countries and countries in transition modernize and improve agriculture, forestry and fisheries practices, ensuring good nutrition and food security for all.

8. Mark Kurlansky 马克·克兰斯基 Mark Kurlansky (December 7, 1948) is an American journalist and writer of general interest non-fiction. He has written a number of books of fiction and non-fiction. His 1997 book, *Cod: A Biography of the Fish That Changed the World*, was an international bestseller and was translated into more than 15 languages. His book *Nonviolence: Twenty-five Lessons from the History of a Dangerous Idea* (2006) was the non-fiction winner of the 2007 Dayton Literary Peace Prize.

• Reading Comprehension

1. **Directions:** *Discuss the following questions with your classmates.*

   1) Why food was defined by a very small geographic zone?
   2) Can you give any examples to elaborate how the development of transportation sped up the changes of food in the 19th century?
   3) How do you understand "food remains classist"?
   4) Why do the rich resist the industrial farming, according to the author?
   5) What facts are covered by the seemingly thriving picture of French cooking?
   6) What is the most important opportunity provided by the GM food?
   7) How do you understand the famous dictum, "Tell me what you eat and I will tell you who you are"?
   8) How can climate change our food?

2. **Directions:** *Read the following statements carefully, and decide whether they are true(T) or false(F) according to the text.*

   (　　)1) Food charts the ebbs and flows of economies, reflects the changing patterns of trade and geopolitical alliances, and defines our values, status and health.
   (　　)2) Food was not modified by wars.
   (　　)3) China is lack of imports in its traditional food.
   (　　)4) Today trade is swift and global, and therefore food no longer reflects its place or time.

(　　)5) The poor eat mostly carbohydrates and protein.

(　　)6) Climate change is also changing our food.

3. Directions: *Fill in the form based on the information provided in Paragraph 2.*

<table>
<tr><th>Causes</th><th>Who</th><th>Food Involved</th><th>From</th><th>To</th></tr>
<tr><td>War</td><td>Arabs</td><td>cane sugar</td><td>Arabia</td><td>Europe</td></tr>
<tr><td rowspan="3">Immigration</td><td></td><td></td><td></td><td></td></tr>
<tr><td></td><td></td><td></td><td></td></tr>
<tr><td></td><td></td><td></td><td></td></tr>
<tr><td rowspan="2">Royal Marriage</td><td></td><td></td><td></td><td></td></tr>
<tr><td></td><td></td><td></td><td></td></tr>
</table>

4. Discussion

1. What are the special food and drinks in your hometown? How do these food and drinks reflect the geography, agricultural produce, and cuisine tradition of your hometown?

2. Some people argue that you can't find authentic Western food in China. What is your attitude toward the adaptation or localization of Western cuisine in China? Can you give an example of the fusion of Chinese and Western food?

After-Class Reading

Warm-up questions:

1. What is the most impressive characteristic of Chinese food in your mind?
2. Which school of Chinese cuisine do you like best? Why?

Chinese Cuisine

1 Chinese cuisine is an important part of Chinese culture. Chinese food also has a worldwide reputation due to its long-term spread from China to the other regions of the world. The famous Chinatowns in different countries are firstly known by their special service of Chinese food. Currently, Chinese food is easily found in every corner of the world, and it has become an impressive and influential symbol of Chinese culture. Chinese cuisine culture goes sophisticated as the history of China goes. There have been a multitude of cooking styles in

China due to factors such as availability of resources, climate, geography, history, cooking techniques and lifestyle. In the early Qing Dynasty, the best known and most influential cooking styles were the traditional "four major schools of Chinese cuisine"—Sichuan, Shandong, Guangdong and Jiangsu cuisines, which represent the West, North, South and East Chinese cuisines respectively. Later, four new schools of Chinese cuisine were added to form the "eight major schools of Chinese cuisine"—Shandong, Sichuan, Jiangsu, Guangdong, Fujian, Zhejiang, Hunan, and Anhui cuisines.

Main Styles of Chinese Cuisine

2 Chinese food, in general, is healthy and nutritious. Chinese people often have soybean milk(豆浆), deep-fried dough sticks(You Tiao, 油条), steamed buns(Man Tou, 馒头) or congee(粥) as breakfast.

3 Food varies within China. Traditionally there are eight main streams of Chinese cuisines, which are known as Anhui Cuisine(徽菜), Canton Cuisine(粤菜), Fujian Cuisine(闽菜), Hunan Cuisine(湘菜), Jiangsu Cuisine(苏菜), Shandong Cuisine(鲁菜), Sichuan Cuisine(川菜) and Zhejiang Cuisine(浙菜).

4 Below are eight main cuisine categories:

Cantonese Cuisine

5 Cantonese food is the most popular style outside China. Cantonese cuisine originates from the region around Canton (Guangzhou) in southern China's Guangdong Province. Cantonese cuisine is famous for its use of fresh seafood and a wide variety of meat, including pork, beef, chicken, goose, duck, etc. In traditional Cantonese cuisine, spices are used in modest amounts to avoid overwhelming the flavors of primary ingredients. Many cooking methods are used, but steaming and stir-frying are the most favored. Other methods include shallow frying, double steaming, braising and deep-frying. Condiments used in Guangdong cuisine include spring onions, sugar, salt, soy sauce, rice wine, cornflour, vinegar, scallion oil, sesame oil and so on. Traditional Guangdong dishes include Roast Goose, Steamed fish, Scalded Shrimp, Rich Noodle Rolls, and **Wonton Noodles**[1]. Guangdong cuisine is also famous for the great variety of soups such as Cantonese Seafood Soup, White Fungus Soup and Wax Gourd Soup.

Shandong Cuisine

6 Shandong cuisine is famous for its wide selection of materials and use of diverse cooking methods. The raw materials are mainly domestic animals, birds, vegetables, and seafood, such as sea cucumber, abalone and scallops. The masterly cooking methods include stewing, roasting, boiling, quick frying, quick frying with flour, and crystallizing with honey. The most famous Shandong dishes include **Man-Han Full Banquet**[2], Sweet and Sour Carp,

Braised Sea Cucumber with Spring Onions, and **Confucian Dishes**[3] such as Crystal Prawn Rings and Fried Chrysanthemum Shrimp Dumplings, which are beautifully designed and prepared with excellent cutting skills.

Jiangsu Cuisine

7 Jiangsu Cuisine, represented by Huaiyang cuisine, is very refined and is presented colorfully and artistically. The chefs of Jiangsu cuisine emphasize bringing out the distinct natural flavors in various ingredients in their dishes. It has a fresh taste, with moderate saltiness and sweetness, which is thick without being greasy and light without being thin. Meanwhile it places an emphasis on the making of soup and retaining the original taste of the ingredients. Once it was the second largest cuisine among ancient China's royal cuisines, and it remains a major part of the state banquet in China. Famous Jiangsu dishes include Wensi Tofu, Sweet and Sour Mandarin Fish, and Yangzhou Fried Rice.

Sichuan Cuisine

8 Sichuan cuisine has a long history and it is very famous throughout the world. The cuisine was originated in ancient Ba and Shu states, and then widely developed during the Tang and Song Dynasties. Sichuan style includes the tastes of Chengdu, Chongqing and some other places in the area. The typical characteristics of the style are hot, spicy and sour, thus the tastes of dishes are very strong. The strong chili taste is to stimulate the taste buds and appetite in hot and humid weather during summer, as well as to make people feel warmer during miserable winter in Sichuan and Chongqing. Well known Sichuan recipes are Sichuan beef and re-cooked pork, which is a dish of pork, cooked in boiled water, and then stir-fried in a very hot pan with cooking oil and put sauces on it finally. The most important spice in Sichuan cuisine is the Sichuan pepper with an intense, citrus-like flavor, which produces a tingly, numbing sensation in the mouth. Other commonly used spices in Sichuan cuisine are garlic, chili peppers, ginger and star anise. The cooking methods of Sichuan cuisine include stir-frying, steaming, braising, baking, and the most popular one—quick frying. There are a wide range of famous Sichuan dishes, including **Gong Bao Chicken**[4], **Mapo Tofu**[5], Dry-fried Green Beans, Sichuan Hotpot, Spicy Slices of Poached Pork, and Dandan Noodles.

Fujian Cuisine

9 Fujian cuisine is known to be light, soft and tender, with particular emphasis on an umami taste. Many diverse seafood and woodland delicacies are used, including local fish, shellfish, turtles, mushrooms and bamboo shoots. Unique seasoning from Fujian includes fish sauce and shrimp oil. The most commonly employed cooking methods in Fujian cuisine include braising, stewing, steaming and boiling. The most famous dishes in Fujian cuisine are **Fo**

Tiao Qiang[6], Fried Oysters, Lychee Meat and so on.

Zhejiang Cuisine

10 Zhejiang cuisine is dainty and refined. Many cooking methods are used in Zhejiang cuisine, including sautéing, braising and stewing. The province is traditionally noted for confections made from sugar, beans, rice, and wheat. Zhejiang dishes are fresh and soft, with the flavor of mellow fragrance. The most popular Zhejiang dishes include **Beggar's Chicken**[7], **Dongpo Pork**[8], West Lake Fish in Vinegar Gravy and so on.

Hunan Cuisine

11 Hunan Cuisine is well known for its hot and spicy flavors, fresh aroma and deep colors. Common cooking methods include stewing, frying, pot-roasting, braising and smoking. Known for its liberal use of chili peppers, shallots and garlic, Hunan cuisine is known for being "purely hot" rather than "spicy and numbing" as in Sichuan cuisine. The most popular Hunan dishes include Beer Duck, Dry-wok Chicken, Homemade BeanCurd, Mao's Braised Pork, Pearly Meatballs, **Fish Head Steamed with Chopped Chili**[9], etc.

Anhui Cuisine

12 Anhui cuisine is known for incorporating wild herbs, fungi and mushrooms from the local mountains. The chefs of Anhui cuisine use comparatively simple cooking methods (chiefly braising and stewing). However, they are particular about controlling cooking time and temperature. Famous Anhui dishes are **Li Hongzhang Hodgepodge**[10], Egg Dumplings, Steamed Stone Frog and so on.

Notes

1. Wonton Noodles 云吞面　It is a Cantonese noodle dish which is popular in Guangzhou, Hong Kong, Malaysia, Singapore and Thailand. The dish is usually served in a hot broth, garnished with leafy vegetables, and wonton dumplings. The types of leafy vegetables used are usually kai-lan also known as Chinese kale.

2. Man-Han Full Banquet 满汉全席　In the Ming and Qing Dynasties, Lu cuisine was already the main component of imperial diet served for emperors and royal families. The most famous Man-Han Full Banquet has a total of 196 courses.

3. Confucian Dishes 孔府菜　It refers to a Chinese aristocrat cuisine developed by the descendants of Confucius. The Characteristics of Confucian dishes include a wide selection of ingredients, emphasis on freshness and nutritious value, extravagant and lavish banquets in strict social stratification order, and artistic presentation of dishes. With a long history, Shandong cuisine once formed an important part of the imperial cuisine and was widely promoted in North China. Shandong is home to great philosopher Confucius, therefore, its food

style is a true embodiment of Confucianism. "No such thing as too much refinement. "(食不厌精) It is featured by a variety of cooking techniques and emphasizes purity of seasonings so as to retain the natural flavor and be tender, fragrant and crispy.

4. Gong Bao Chicken 宫保鸡丁 The dish is believed to be named after Ding Baozhen, who is a Qing Dynasty official and a governor of Sichuan Province. It is said he once visited a local restaurant and loved the dish of chicken quick-fried with peanuts. After he went back home, he asked the chef to cook for him this dish and the chef named this dish after him. His title was Gongbao. The name "Gongbao" chicken is derived from this title.

5. Mapo Tofu 麻婆豆腐 Mapo Tofu is a popular Chinese dish from Sichuan Province. It is a combination of tofu(beancurd) with fermented bean sauce and minced meat. True Mapo Tofu is powerfully spicy with both conventional"hot" spiciness and the characteristic "mala" (mouth-numbing spiciness) flavor of Sichuan cuisine. The feel of the particular dishis often described by cooks using specific Chinese adjectives: numbing, spicy, hot, fresh and delicious, tender and soft, and aromatic. The most important and necessary ingredients in the dish that give it the distinctive flavor are fermented bean sauce and Chinese prickly ash.

6. Fo Tiao Qiang 佛跳墙 In the year 1899, an official of Fuzhou entertained a governor. The official specially asked his female family members to cook dishes personally. They put more than 10 kinds of raw materials including chicken, ducks, mutton, pigeon eggs and some other seafood into a Shaoxing wine jar and then cooked them elaborately. The dish tasted marvelous. From then on, it was named Fu Shou Quan. Afterwards, it was improved by a famous chef who added more seafood and less meat into the jar. One day. Some men of literature and writing tasted the dish and intoned: "The fragrance of the dish spreads to near neighbors, which even attracts Buddha to jump off a wall and abandon deep meditation. " Since then, the dish has been named Fo Tiao Qiang (Buddha jumps over the wall).

7. Beggar's Chicken 叫花鸡 Once upon a time, a beggar caught a chicken and he was so poor to even have a pot or pan to cook with. At last he got an idea: to use soil to cover the whole chicken and put it on fire to roast. It turned out to be very delicious, even better than the ordinarily cooked chicken with seasonings. Soon the new way of cooking was scattered among the villagers.

8. Dongpo Pork 东坡肉 Su Dongpo(1037-1101A. D.), the great writer of the Song Dynasty, not only was famous for being outstanding in writing, but also for being talented as an epicure; His creation, the Dongpo Pork becomes a highly praised and popular dish. It is made by pan-frying and then braising pork. The pork is cut to around 2 inches square in dimensions, consisting of half fat and half lean meat. The mouth fell is oily but not greasy, with the

fragrance of wine. While Su Dongpo was banished to Hangzhou, he tried his best to do a lot to benefit the local people. So the local people had a better life. They knew Su Dongpo loved to eat pork, so they sent him a huge amount of pork as gifts to thank him. Su Dongpo was deeply touched by the local people and came up with an idea of cooking so much pork and then handed out the cooked pork to local people. Local people enjoyed the cooked pork very much and named it after Su Dongpo.

9. Fish Head Steamed with Chopped Chili 剁椒鱼头 It is a typical dish of Hunan cuisine. This dish uses chopped chili sauce as its main feature. Duojiao sauce or chopped chili sauce originates from Hunan cuisine, which is even spicier than Sichuan cuisine. Duojiao is made of chopped red chili pickled and has a salty and sour pickled taste.

10. Li Hongzhang Hodgepodge 李鸿章杂烩 It's a popular dish named after Li Hongzhang (1823 – 1901), a top official of the late Qing Dynasty (1616 – 1911) from Anhui Province, and a leading figure in China's relations with the Western powers. It is said that when Li Hongzhang visited the United States, he invited some American friends to have dinner. After the entree, Li mixed together all the ingredients he had left over and cooked up a new dish. All his guests praised the delicious concoction, and asked Li for its name. Li told them that the dish was called "Zasui", or "hodgepodge" in English. From then on, the dish was known as "Zasui", or "Li Hongzhang Hodgepodge", and became popular in both the U. S. and China. Its main ingredients include sea cucumber, fish maw, squid, bamboo shoots, dried beans, chicken, ham, egg yolk pudding, and pigeon eggs, liver and so on.

- **Reading Comprehension**

1. **Directions**: *Read the passage quickly and match each of the dishes with the school of cuisine it belongs to.*

________Wonton Noodles	A	Shandong cuisine
________Li Hongzhang Hodgepodge	B	Sichuan cuisine
________Confucian Dishes	C	Jiangsu cuisine
________Fo Tiao Qiang	D	Guangdong cuisine
________Gong Bao Chicken	E	Fujian cuisine
________Dry-wok Chicken	F	Zhejiang cuisine
________Dongpo Pork	G	Hunan cuisine
________Wensi Tofu	H	Anhui cuisine

2. **Directions**: *Complete the following table with the missing information based on the text.*

Schools of cuisine	Materials	Cooking methods	Characteristics
Shandong			
Sichuan			
Jiangsu			
Guangdong			
Fujian			
Zhejiang			
Hunan			
Anhui			

Part Three

Topic-Related Activities

1. Case Study

Dinner with Friends

1 Janice is a young American engineer working for a manufacturing joint venture near Nanjing. She and her husband George, who is teaching English at a university, are learning Chinese and enjoying their new life. They have been eager to get to know Chinese people better so were pleased when Liu Lingling, Janice's young coworker invited them to her home for dinner.

2 When Janice and George arrived, Lingling introduced them to her husband Yang Feng, asked them to sit down at a table containing 8 plates of various cold dishes, served them tea and then disappeared with her husband into the kitchen. After a few minutes Lingling came back and added water to their tea. Janice offered to help in the kitchen but Lingling said she didn't need help. She invited the couple to look at their firsthand CD player and their color TV and then disappeared again.

3 A half-hour later she came back and sat down and the three began to eat. Yang Feng came in from time to time to put dish after hot dish on the table. Most of the food was

wonderful but neither George nor Janice could eat the fatty pork in pepper sauce or the sea cucumbers, and there was much more than they could eat. They kept wishing Yang Feng could sit down so they could talk to him. Finally he did sit down to eat a bit, but quickly turned on the TV to show them all its high-tech features. Soon it was time to go home.

4 George and Janice felt slightly depressed by this experience, but returned the invitation two weeks later. They decided to make a nice American meal and felt lucky to find olives, tomato juice, crackers and even some cheese in the hotel shops. They put these out as appetizers. For the main course they prepared spaghetti and a salad with dressing made from oil, vinegar, and some spices they found in the market.

5 When Liu Lingling and Yang Feng arrived, they were impressed by the apartment and asked the price of the TV, video player, vacuum cleaner and other things. Janice politely refused to answer their questions. They took small tastes of the appetizers and seemed surprised when both George and Janice sat down with them. They ate only a little spaghetti and did not finish the salad on their plates. George urged them to eat more but they refused and looked around expectantly. Janice and George talked about their families and jobs and asked the Chinese couple about theirs. After a while, George cleared the table and served coffee and pastries. Yang Feng and Lingling each put four spoons of sugar into their coffee but did not drink much of it and ate only a bite or two of pastry.

6 After they left, George said that at least they had a chance to talk, but Janice was upset. "We left their place so full that we couldn't walk and they're going to have to eat again when they got home. What went wrong?"

Questions

1) What is the difference in terms of food culture?

2) What is the Chinese understanding of the host-guest relationship?

3) What is the American couple's attitude towards friendship?

4) Can you give some advice to both couples to help them further their friendship?

2. Critical Thinking & Cultural Exploration

Step One

Directions: *Ask students to discuss special dishes or traditional food their families prepare for holidays or celebrations.*

Step Two

Directions: *Please work in pairs and match the food in Column A with relevant holidays in Column B.*

Column A		Column B
zongzi		Mid-autumn Day
moon cake		The Double Seventh Festival
dumpling		The Dragon Boat Festival
tangyuan		The Spring Festival
chocolate		The Lantern Festival
turkey and pudding		Thanksgiving Day
egg		Christmas
candy		Valentine's Day
turkey and pumpkin pie		Easter
chocolate		Halloween

Step Three

Directions: *Is there any folklore behind the holidays and the traditional food? Choose one you are interested in and make a presentation about it.*

3. Translation

Directions: *Translate the passage into English.*

很多人喜欢中餐，在中国，烹饪不仅被视为一种技能，而且也被视为一种艺术。精心准备的中餐既可口又好看。烹饪技术和配料在中国各地差别很大。但好的烹饪都有一个共同点，就是要考虑到色泽、味道、口感和营养(nutrition)。由于食物对健康至关重要，好的厨师总是努力在谷物、肉类和蔬菜之间取得平衡，所以中餐美味又健康。

Unit Two

Education

Part One

Lead-in

Better be unborn than untaught, for ignorance is the root of misfortune.

—Plato (Ancient Greek philosopher)

Education is the whole process of training the new generation who is ready to engage social life, and also a key link in the process of human social production experience to carry on, mainly refers to the process of school training to school-age children, the young and the youth. Education is not an end, but a means to an end. As soon as we realize this fact, we will understand that it is very important to choose a good way of education. In this unit we look at some different types of education, giving you the chance to consider which you prefer.

Part Two

In-Class Reading

Warm-up questions:

1. What is education?
2. What is the function of education?

Education in the United States

1 As might be expected, educational institutions in the United States **reflect** the nation's basic values, especially the ideal of equality of opportunity. From elementary school through college, Americans believe that everyone **deserves** an equal opportunity to get a good education.

2 From the beginning, when Americans established their basic system of public schools in 1825, they **reaffirmed** the principle of equality by making schools open to all classes of Americans, and financing the schools with tax money collected from all citizens. Those who favored these public schools believed that these institutions would help reduce social class **distinctions** in the United States by educating children of all social classes in the same "**common schools**[1]", as they were known at the time.

3 Alexis de Tocqueville, a French aristocrat, arrived in the United States in 1831. He found a great deal of enthusiasm about the new and growing public elementary schools. He also noted that American public education had a strong practical content that included the teaching of vocational skills and the duties of citizenship. Thus, public education not only gave Americans the desire to better themselves, but it also gave them the practical tools to do so. Moreover, the material abundance of the United States provided material rewards for those who took full advantage of the opportunity for a public education.

4 During the next century and a half, public schools in the United States were **expanded** to include secondary or high schools (grades 9 – 12) and colleges and universities, with both undergraduate and graduate studies.

The Educational Ladder

5 Americans view their public school system as an educational ladder, rising from elementary school to high school and finally college undergraduate and graduate programs. Most children start school at age five, by attending kindergarten, or even at age three or four

by attending pre-school programs. Then there are six years of elementary school and usually two years of middle school (or junior high school), and four years of high school. Not all school systems have kindergarten, but all do have twelve years of elementary, middle school, and senior high school. School systems may **divide** the twelve years **up** differently—grouping sixth, seventh, and eighth graders into middle school, for example. After high school, the majority of students go on to college. Undergraduate studies lead to a bachelor's degree, which is generally what Americans mean when they speak of a "college". The word college is used in several different ways. It is generally used instead of university to refer to the education after high school, as in the expressions "go to college", and "get a college education". It is also used to refer to the school, as in "Where do you go to college?" Often people use the word "college" to refer to a small school that does not offer graduate degrees, and university for large schools that offer both undergraduate and graduate degrees. The bachelor's degree can be followed by professional studies, which lead to degrees in such professions as law and medicine, and graduate studies, which lead to master's and doctoral degrees. American public schools are free and open to all at the elementary and secondary level (high school), but public universities charge tuition and have competitive entrance requirements.

6 The educational ladder concept is an almost perfect reflection of the American idea of individual success based on equality of opportunity and on "working your way to the top". In the United States there are no separate educational systems with a higher level of education for the wealthy and a lower level of education for the masses. Rather, there is one system that is open to all. Individuals may climb as high on the ladder as they can. The abilities of the individuals, rather than their social class background, are expected to determine how high each person will go.

7 Although the great majority of children attend the free public elementary and high schools, some choose to attend private schools. There are a number of private religious schools, for example, that **are associated with** particular churches and receive financial support from them, though parents must also pay tuition. The primary purpose of these schools is usually to give religious instruction to children, which cannot be done in public schools. The most **numerous** of these, the **Catholic schools**[2], have students whose social class backgrounds are similar to the majority of students in public schools.

8 There are also some **elite** private schools, which serve mainly upper-class children. Students must pay such high tuition costs that only wealthier families can afford them. Parents often send their children to these schools so that they will associate with other upper-class children and **maintain** the upper-class position held by their parents, in addition to getting a good education.

9 Unlike private religious schools, elitist private schools do **conflict with** the American ideal of equality of opportunity. These schools often **give** an extra educational and social **advantage to** the young people whose families have the money to allow them to attend. However, because these schools are relatively few in number, they do not **displace** the public school as the central educational institution in the United States. Nor does the best private school education protect young people from competition with public school graduates for **admission** to the best universities in the nation.

10 There is another area of inequality in the American education system. Because of the way that schools are funded, the quality of education that American students receive in public schools varies greatly. More than 90 percent of the money for schools comes from the local level (cities and counties), primarily from property taxes. School **districts** that have middle class or wealthy families have more tax money to spend on education. Therefore, wealthier school districts have beautiful school buildings with computers and the latest science equipment, and poorer school districts have older buildings with less modern equipment. The amount of money spent on education may vary from $7,000 per child in a wealthy suburb to only $ 1,200 per child attending an inner-city school, or one in a poor rural area. Although the amount of money spent per child is not always the best **indicator** of the quality of education the child receives, it certainly is an important factor.

Attending an American University

11 Money is also increasingly a factor in a college education. All university students must pay tuition expenses in the United States. Because tuition is much lower at public universities than at private ones, wealthy students have more choices. There are a number of financial aid programs in the form of loans and scholarships **available** at both public and private schools. However, the expenses of buying books and living away from home make it increasingly difficult for many students to attend even the less expensive public universities.

12 **Ironically**, it may be the middle-class family that suffers the most from the rising tuition costs. The family income may be too high to qualify for financial aid, but not high enough to afford the $15,000 to $35,000 per year (or more) needed for a private college education. At present, 80 percent of all college students attend public universities, where expenses are usually closer to $10,000 a year. Many students must work during their college years to help meet even these costs. A number of students who cannot afford to go away to college attend **community college**[3] programs for two years in their hometowns. These two-year programs often **feed into** the state university systems and offer educational opportunities to large numbers of students who ordinarily would not be able to attend a university.

13 Despite its costs, the percentage of Americans seeking a college education continues

to grow. In 1900, less than 10 percent of college-age Americans entered college. Today, over 60 percent of Americans ages 25 to 39 have taken some college courses, and over 20 percent of all Americans have attended four years or more. There are about 15 million students attending college now, about six times more than 50 years ago, and there are roughly 3,000 different colleges and universities to choose from. Today, many parents who were not able to attend college when they were young have the satisfaction of seeing their sons and daughters attend.

14 Even the formerly elitist private universities have **yielded** a great deal **to** public pressure for greater equality of opportunity in education. **Harvard**[4], a private university considered by many to be one of the nation's most **prestigious**, provides a good example. Before World War II, the majority of Harvard students came from elite private **preparatory** schools. Now, the majority of them come from public high schools. As equality of opportunity came to Harvard, the competition that **accompanies** it also increased dramatically. Before World War II, Harvard admitted about 90 percent of those who applied. Now, Harvard admits only about 16 or 17 percent of its applicants.

The Money Value of Education

15 The American definition of success is largely one of acquiring wealth and a high material standard of living. It is not surprising, therefore, that Americans value education for its monetary value. The belief is widespread in the United States that the more schooling people have, the more money they will earn when they leave school. The belief is strongest regarding the **desirability** of an undergraduate university degree, or a professional degree such as medicine or law, following the undergraduate degree. The money value of graduate degrees in "nonprofessional" fields such as art, history, or philosophy is not as great.

16 In recent years, there has been a change in the job market in the United States. In the past, it was possible to get a high-paying factory job without a college education. Workers with skills learned in vocational schools or on the job could do work that did not require a college education. These were among the jobs that new immigrants were often able to obtain. Increasingly, however, the **advent** of new technologies has meant that more and more education is required to do the work. Many of the new jobs in the United States either require a college education, even a graduate degree, or they are low-paying jobs in the service sector of the economy, such as fast-food restaurants, small stores, and hotels.

Educating the Individual

17 American schools tend to **put** more **emphasis on** developing critical thinking skills than they do on acquiring quantities of facts. American students are encouraged to express their own opinions in class and think for themselves, a reflection of the American values of individual freedom and self-reliance. The goal of the American education system is to teach

children how to learn and to help them reach their maximum potential.

18 The development of social and interpersonal skills may be considered as important as the development of intellectual skills. So to help students develop these important skills, schools have added a large number of **extracurricular** activities to daily life at school. These activities are almost as important as the students' class work. For example, in making their decisions about which students to admit, colleges look for students who are "**well-rounded**". Grades on high school courses and scores on tests like the **SAT**[5] (Scholastic Aptitude Test) are very important, but so are the **extracurricular activities**[6]. It is by participating in these activities that students **demonstrate** their special talents, their level of **maturity** and responsibility, their leadership qualities, and their ability to get along with others.

19 Some Americans consider **athletics**, frequently called competitive sports, the most important of all extracurricular activities. This is because many people believe it is important for young people, particularly young men, to learn how to compete successfully. Team sports such as football, basketball, and baseball are important because they teach students the "winning spirit". At times, this athletic competition may be carried to such an extreme that some students and their parents may place more importance on the high school's sports program than its academic offerings.

20 Student government is another extracurricular activity designed to develop competitive, political, and social skills in students. The students choose a number of student government officers, who compete for the votes of their fellow students in school elections. Although these officers have little power over the central decisions of the school, the process of running for office and then taking responsibility for a number of student activities if elected is seen as good experience in developing their leadership and competitive skills, and helping them to be responsible citizens.

21 Athletics and student government are only two of a variety of extracurricular activities found in American schools. There are clubs and activities for almost every student interest—art, music, drama, debate, foreign languages, photography, volunteer work—all aimed at helping the student to become more successful in later life. Many parents watch their children's extracurricular activities with as much interest and concern as they do on their children's intellectual achievements in the classroom.

Multicultural Education

22 The changing populations of students in American schools has brought some changes in what is taught in the schools as well. Ethnic and racial minorities have criticized schools and textbooks for focusing too much on the literature and historical events of Anglo-Europeans or white males. They believe that schools have almost ignored the contributions of African-

Americans, Latinos, and Native Americans. More seriously, some have charged that American history has been told from the **perspective** of Anglo-Europeans rather than exploring historical events from the various perspectives of those involved. For example, the westward movement has been presented more from the perspective of **descendants** of white settlers than from the perspectives of the descendants of the Native Americans who were moved in the process.

23 During the 1990s, schools began to examine seriously their curricula and to try to **incorporate** more varied cultural information and perspectives into education. These **attempts** to provide multicultural education have ranged from simply adding information and literature to the current textbooks and curricula to more **sweeping** attempts to **transform** the basic curriculum into one that is more reflective of the **diversity** of the students who will study it. Many schools have adopted history or social studies textbooks that include more information about African-Americans, Hispanic-Americans, and other **minorities**, and American literature texts that include poetry and fiction written by Americans of all ethnic backgrounds. In some colleges, the traditional set of Western great books, sometimes called the canon, has been replaced by a much broader set of literary texts, reflecting the experiences and backgrounds of the students who will be reading them.

24 Not all Americans support multicultural education, however. Some fear that replacing the Western civilization and literary traditions, which have been the basis of American education, with a much broader historical and literary discussion will result in **fragmentation** of American society. Schools have traditionally been the place where students of all ethnic, religious, and racial backgrounds have learned "American" history, literature, and values. With so many competing views of history or sets of values in the school, some fear that it will be difficult for the country to remain "American". It is a serious question: Can a country as diverse as the United States have schools that reflect that diversity and still retain a core national identity and culture?

George S. Counts[7]

New Words and Expressions

reflect /rɪˈflekt/ — *v.* express, make clear, or be a sign of; show 表达,反映

deserve /dɪˈzɜːv/ — *v.* have earned by one's actions or character; be worthy of 应受,应得,值得

reaffirm /ˌriːəˈfɜːm/ — *v.* affirm once again 重申;再确认

distinction /dɪˈstɪŋkʃn/ — *n.* the fact of being distinct; clear difference 区别,明显差别,特征

abundance /ə'bʌndəns/ *n.* quantity that is more than enough; plenty 大量,充足

expand /ɪk'spænd/ *v.* to become larger in size, number, or amount, or to make something become larger 使……膨胀;详述;扩张;增加;张开

numerous/'njuːmərəs/ *adj.* very many; being or existing in great quantity 很多,许多

elite /eɪ'liːt/ *n.* a group or class of persons enjoying superior intellectual or social or economic status 出类拔萃的人,精英
adj. selected as the best 精英的;优秀的

maintain /meɪn'teɪn/ *v.* keep up; retain; continue 保持; 继续

displace /dɪs'pleɪs/ *v.* take the place of; put sth./sb. else in the place of 替换,取代

admission /əd'mɪʃn/ *n.* a statement saying or agreeing sth. is true 承认,供认

district /'dɪstrɪkt/ *n.* part of a country or town having a particular quality 地区,区域

indicator /'ɪndɪkeɪtə(r)/ *n.* a number or ratio (a value on a scale of measurement) derived from a series of observed facts; revealing relative changes as a function of time 指标

available /ə'veɪləbl/ *adj.* obtainable or accessible and ready for use or service 可利用的;可得到的;有空的;有效的

ironically /aɪ'rɒnɪkli/ *adv.* in a way that is interesting, strange, or funny because of being very different from what you would expect 讽刺地;说反话地

prestigious /pre'stɪdʒəs/ *adj.* having an illustrious reputation; respected 享有声望的;声望很高的

preparatory /prɪ'pærətri/ *adj.* preceding and preparing for something 预备的;准备的;初步的
n. 预备学校;预科(在美国指为升入大学做准备的学校)

accompany /ə'kʌmpəni/ *v.* happen or appear with sth. else; exist or appear at the same time or same place as 伴随; 与……同时发生

desirability /dɪˌzaɪərə'bɪləti/ *n.* the quality of being worthy of desiring 称心如意的人(东西);有利条件

advent /'ædvent/ *n.* the coming of an important event, person, invention, etc. 出现; 来临; 降临

extracurricular /ˌekstrəkə'rɪkjʊlə/ *adj.* outside the regular academic curriculum 课外的;业余的

well-rounded /'wel'raʊndɪd/ *adj.* well-planned for proper balance 成熟的;全面的

demonstrate /'demənstreɪt/ *v.* show clearly by giving proofs or examples 证明; 演示

maturity /məˈtʃʊərəti/ *n.* state of being mature; full development 成熟

athletics /æθˈletɪks/ *n.* the general name for a particular group of sports in which people compete, including running, jumping, and throwing 体育运动;田径

perspective /pəˈspektɪv/ *n.* point of view 观点,想法

descendant /dɪˈsendənt/ *n.* a person considered as descended from some ancestors or race 后裔;子孙;后代

incorporate /ɪnˈkɔːpəreɪt/ *v.* make into a whole or make part of a whole 合并

attempt /əˈtempt/ *v.* make an effort at; try to do sth., especially without succeeding 试图;尝试

sweeping /ˈswiːpɪŋ/ *adj.* comprehensive and wide-ranging 广泛的

transform /trænsˈfɔːm/ *vt. & vi.* change the shape, appearance, quality or nature of 改变

diversity /daɪˈvɜːsəti/ *n.* the state or quality of being different or varied 多样性;差异

minority /maɪˈnɒrəti/ *n.* a small part of a population which is different from the rest in race, religion, etc. 少数民族,少数信仰不同的人

fragmentation /ˌfrægmenˈteɪʃn/ *n.* the disintegration of social norms governing behavior and thought and social relationships 分裂

divide up to divide and dole out portions of something 瓜分;分配

be associated with to connect or involve with a cause, group, or partner 与……相联系

conflict with to interfere or clash with something 抵触;与……冲突

give advantage to to give privilege to 给予某人优待、特权

feed into to insert or input something into something 注入(流入,装进)

yield to to submit or give in to someone or something 向……屈服

put emphasis on to emphasize something 把重点放在;着重于;强调

Notes

1. common school 美国公共学校 A common school was a public school in the United States during the 19th century. Horace Mann (1796 – 1859) was a strong advocate for public education and the common school. In 1837, the state of Massachusetts appointed Mann as the first secretary of the State Board of Education where he began a revival of common school education, the effects of which extended throughout America during the 19th century.

2. Catholic school 天主教学校 A Catholic school is a parochial school or education ministry of the Catholic Church. As of 2011, the Catholic Church operates the world's largest non-governmental school system. In 2016, the church supported 43,800 secondary schools,

and 95,200 primary schools. Catholic schools strive to cultivate a humane, Christian, and humanitarian ethos, while also participating in the evangelizing mission of the Church, integrating religious education as a core subject within their curriculum.

3. community college 社区大学 In the United States, community colleges, sometimes called junior colleges, technical colleges, two-year colleges, or city colleges, are primarily two-year public institutions providing lower-level tertiary education, also known as continuing education. They grant certificates, diplomas, and associate degrees. After graduating from a community college, most students transfer to a four-year liberal arts college or university for two to three years to complete a bachelor's degree. Before the 1970s, community colleges in the United States were more commonly referred to as junior colleges. That term is still used at some institutions. However, the term "junior college" is generally applied to private two-year institutions, whereas the term "community college" is used to describe publicly funded two-year institutions. Community colleges primarily attract and accept students from the local community, and are often supported by local tax revenue. They may also work with local businesses to ensure students are being prepared for the local workforce.

4. Harvard 哈佛大学 Harvard University is a private Ivy League research university in Cambridge, Massachusetts. Established in 1636 and named for its first benefactor, clergyman John Harvard, Harvard is the oldest institution of higher learning in the United States and among the most prestigious in the world. The university is composed of ten academic faculties plus the Radcliffe Institute for Advanced Study. Arts and Sciences offers study in a wide range of academic disciplines for undergraduates and for graduates, while the other faculties offer only graduate degrees, mostly professional. Harvard has three main campuses: the 209-acre Cambridge campus centered on Harvard Yard; an adjoining campus immediately across the Charles River in the Allston neighborhood of Boston; and the medical campus in Boston's Longwood Medical Area. Harvard's endowment is valued at $41.9 billion, making it the largest of any academic institution. Endowment income helps enable the undergraduate college to admit students regardless of financial need and provide generous financial aid with no loans. The Harvard Library is the world's largest academic library system, comprising 79 individual libraries holding about 20.4 million items. Harvard has more alumni, faculty, and researchers who have won Nobel Prizes (161) and Fields Medals (18) than any other university in the world and more alumni who have been members of the U. S. Congress, MacArthur Fellows, Rhodes Scholars (375), and Marshall Scholars (255) than any other university in the United States. Its alumni also include eight U. S. presidents and 188 living billionaires, the most of any university. Fourteen Turing Award laureates have been Harvard affiliates. Students and alumni have also won 10 Academy Awards, 48 Pulitzer Prizes, and 108 Olympic medals (46

gold), and they have founded many notable companies.

5. SAT (Scholastic Aptitude Test) 美国大学本科标准入学考试 The SAT is a standardized test for most college admissions in the United States. The SAT is owned, published, and developed by the College Board, a nonprofit organization in the United States. It was formerly developed, published, and scored by the Educational Testing Service which still administers the exam. The test is intended to assess a student's readiness for college. It was first introduced in 1926, and its name and scoring have changed several times. It was first called the Scholastic Aptitude Test, then the Scholastic Assessment Test.

6. extracurricular activity 课外活动 An extracurricular activity (ECA) or extra academic activity (EAA) is an activity, performed by students, that falls outside the realm of the normal curriculum of school, college or university education. Such activities are generally voluntary (as opposed to mandatory), social, philanthropic, and often involve others of the same age. Students and staff direct these activities under faculty sponsorship, although student-led initiatives, such as independent newspapers, are very common. However, sometimes the school principals and teachers also bring in these activities in the school among the students.

7. George S. Counts 乔治・康茨 George S. Counts, in full George Sylvester Counts (born December 9, 1889, near Baldwin City, Kansas, U. S.; died November 10, 1974, Belleville, Illinois), American educator and activist who, as a leading proponent of social reconstructionism, believed that schools should bring about social change. After graduating (1911) from Baker University, Counts earned a doctorate (1916) in education with a minor in sociology at the University of Chicago under Charles Hubbard Judd and Albion W. Small. He subsequently taught at various universities before joining the faculty of Teachers College, Columbia University, in 1927. Early in his career Counts studied the influence of powerful social and economic forces in American education. In *The Selective Character of American Secondary Education* (1922) and *The Social Composition of Boards of Education* (1927), he argued that the interests of upper-class elites dominated high schools and school boards, thus belying equality of opportunity, particularly for immigrant and African American children. After study tours in the Soviet Union in 1927 and 1929, he published *The Soviet Challenge to America* (1931). Impressed by Soviet efforts at social planning, he attributed the social and economic devastation of the Great Depression to the lack of planning in the United States. Hoping to spread his ideas, Counts and several colleagues launched a journal of social and educational commentary, *The Social Frontier*, in 1934. Under his editorship (1934–37) the journal became the voice of the educational theory called social reconstructionism, which was based on the theory that society can be reconstructed through education. By that time Counts

had also come to admire the work of historian Charles A. Beard, whose progressive interpretation of history and emphasis on economics affected Counts' social and educational theory. Also at this time he published *The Social Foundations of Education* (1934) and *The Prospects for American Democracy* (1938). Counts served as president of the American Federation of Teachers (AFT) from 1939 to 1942. Counts retired from Teachers College in 1956, but he continued to teach at various universities until 1971.

• Reading Comprehension

1. **Directions**: *Discuss the following questions with your classmates.*
   1) What is the difference between college and university?
   2) What is the difference between public and private schools in the United States?
   3) Are there any areas of inequality in the American education system? Illustrate your points with instances.
   4) Why the middle-class family suffers the most from the rising tuition costs?
   5) What other skills American schools emphasize besides intellectual skills? Why?
   6) What are the major characteristics of education in America?
2. **Directions**: *Read the following statements carefully, and decide whether they are true (T) or false (F) according to the text.*

   ( ) 1) American public education had a strong practical content that included the teaching of vocational skills and the duties of citizenship.

   ( ) 2) There are six years of elementary school and usually three years of middle school (or junior high school), and three years of high school.

   ( ) 3) Elitist private schools displace the public school as the central educational institution in the United States.

   ( ) 4) Nowadays, it is impossible to get a high-paying factory job without a college education.

   ( ) 5) American schools tend to put more emphasis on developing critical thinking skills than they do on acquiring quantities of facts.

   ( ) 6) All Americans support multicultural education.
3. **Directions**: *Choose the correct answer to each of the following questions.*

   ( ) 1) Which of the following subjects are not offered to elementary school students?

   A. Music and physical education. B. Politics and business education.

   C. Mathematics and languages. D. Science and social studies.

   ( ) 2) What most Americans like most about higher education is ________.

   A. its cultural value B. its moral value

   C. its monetary value D. its technical value

( )3) The expenditure in American public schools is guided or decided by ________.

A. students B. headmasters

C. boards of education D. teachers

( )4) Which of the following would not be considered an extracurricular activity?

A. The student government of a school. B. A classroom research project.

C. A school baseball team. D. A music club.

( )5) Both public and private universities depend on the following sources of income except ________.

A. investment B. government funding

C. student tuition D. endowments

( )6) Which of these statements is true?

A. In the United States there are separate educational systems with a higher level of education for the wealthy and a lower level of education for the masses.

B. There are a number of financial aid programs in the form of loans and scholarships only available at public schools.

C. Nowadays, the majority of Harvard students come from elite private preparatory schools.

D. American public education had a strong practical content that included the teaching of vocational skills and the duties of citizenship.

• **Discussion**

1. What do you think is the difference between home schooling and studying at school?

2. What do you think the real value of education is? Is it monetary? Is it intellectual? Is it social?

After-Class Reading

Warm-up questions:

1. Is it necessary to take a national examination to get into a university? Why?

2. What was the purpose of the Imperial Examination in ancient China?

Education in China

1 Education in China is primarily managed by the state-run public education system, which falls under the command of the Ministry of Education. All citizens must attend school for a minimum of nine years, known as nine-year compulsory education, which is funded by the government. Compulsory education includes six years of primary education, typically starting at the age of six and finishing at the age of twelve, followed by three years of junior secondary education (junior middle school). Some provinces may have five years of primary schooling but four years for junior middle school. Junior middle schooling is followed by three years of senior middle school, by the end of which secondary education is completed.

2 In 2019, the Ministry of Education reported an increase of 1.5611 million students entering into compulsory education. In 1985, the government abolished tax-funded higher education, requiring university applicants to compete for scholarships based on their respective academic capabilities. In the early 1980s, the government allowed the establishment of the first private institution of higher learning, thus increasing the number of undergraduates and people who hold doctoral degrees from 1995 to 2005. In 2003, central and local governments in China supported 1,552 institutions of higher learning (colleges and universities), along with their 725,000 professors and 11 million students.

Basic Education

3 China's basic education involves pre-school, nine-year compulsory education from elementary to junior high school, standard senior high school education, special education for disabled children, and education for illiterate people. China has over 200 million elementary and high school students, who, together with pre-school children, account for one sixth of the total population. For this reason, the Central Government has prioritized basic education as a key field of infrastructure construction and educational development.

4 In recent years, senior high school education has developed steadily. In 2004 enrollment was 8.215 million, 2.3 times that of 1988. Gross national enrollment in senior high schools has reached 43.8 percent, still lower than that of other developed countries. The government has created a special fund to improve conditions in China's elementary and high schools, for new construction, expansion, and the re-building of run-down structures. Per-capita educational expenditure for elementary and high school students has grown greatly, teaching and research equipment, books, and documents being updated and renewed every year. Government's aim for the development of China's basic education system is to approach or attain the level of moderately developed countries by 2010. Graduates of China's primary

and secondary schools test highly in both basic skills and critical thinking skills.

History

5 China's ancient education was one of the most splendid components of ancient Chinese culture. Chinese education has a long history dating from the Xia, Shang and Zhou dynasties thousands of years ago.

6 In the Shang Dynasty (16th – 11th century BC), formal schools emerged with the names like "Xiao" (school), "Xue" (study) and "Daxue" (higher school). Teachers then were all government officials and students were all children of the nobility, so that was the earliest "Guan Xue" (government school). Education became more popular by the Spring and Autumn/Warring States Period. Confucius became the earliest founder for "Private Education". This type of private school education is often known as "Si Xue".

7 From Han till Qing Dynasty, the formation of government institution had been well-established. All the teaching materials and educational training were geared towards the preparation for Imperial Examination. After receiving a title in the Imperial Examination, one might receive a post in the state bureaucracy. At the same time, private schools were also developing. Most of the famous philosophers and scientists originated from private schools. Apart from schooling, "family education" began to play an important role. Many of the famous historical figures grew up under the education and strict "teaching" by their parents or other senior family members, and they studied hard in order to become successful. For instance, it was well documented that Mencius's mother had moved three times with her son before she eventually found a proper neighborhood for her son's education. After the Han Dynasty, because of the increased status of Confucianism and its influence, the teaching of "poetry and rites" became the basic content for family education. Loyalty, Filial Piety, Benevolence and Righteousness were core values taught in family education.

8 In ancient Chinese education, there was another form of education system known as "Xue Shu Jiao Yu". This belongs to neither an institute education nor a family education. These are generally "primary schools for the folks". Sometimes, they were called "Meng Guan" (primary education hall), "Si Shu" (private school), "Zu Xue" (extended family school), etc. Most students would first learn how to read characters, and then they would learn *The Three Character Classic*, *The Hundred Family Surnames*, and *The Thousand Character Classic*. Then they would learn the "**Four Books**[1]". In addition, they would also learn Chinese calligraphy and couplets. In this type of school, the rules and regulations were especially strict.

9 There were other methods such as Academies, and Directorate of Education. They all formed a unique way of knowledge teaching and became an important system for the

development on "study of knowledge" "teaching method", etc. All of these formed the basis for today's Chinese education.

Confucianism

10 Confucius, the fifth century BC Chinese philosopher whose *Analects of Confucius* deeply shaped Chinese society, is familiar to many in the West, who see him as among the most accessible, anodyne aspects of Chinese culture. Confucianism has transcended the East to become well-known to the West, making the philosopher's name a prime tool for cultural diplomacy. The Chinese government has invested heavily in molding Confucius's image and projecting it to an international audience. Confucius Institutes and Classrooms are clustered in English-speaking nations, particularly in the United States. They provide the place for foreigners to learn Chinese culture.

11 The historical importance of education in Chinese culture is derived from the teachings of Confucius. The connection between Confucius and the official Chinese educational system thus became permanently linked right into the present time. Confucius broke the rule of "Xue Zai Guan Fu". He encouraged "learning for all hierarchical levels and for all ages", and opened the door of education to the commoners. He established his own school and started to spread his teaching, thoughts and views. He became the earliest founder for "Private Education".

12 In ancient Chinese education, whether they were government schools or private schools, they all placed a great emphasis on humanities and cultural education, which focused on the teaching of morality and the development of wisdom. It covered philosophy, language, literature and other cultural subjects. The curriculum at the Great Academy was based on the Confucian **Five Classics**[2].

13 Confucius taught his students morality, proper speech, government, and the refined arts. He emphasized the "**Six Arts**[3]"—ritual, music, archery, chariot-riding, calligraphy, and computation. Other than placing a strong emphasis on morality education, Confucius also emphasized greatly on learning and teaching methods and principles. Confucius's main educational thoughts were to teach students according to their aptitude, to treat students equally and to inspire thinking. His pedagogical methods were striking. He posed questions, cited passages from the classics, or used apt analogies, and waited for his students to arrive at the right answers.

14 The status of education remains high in Confucian heritage cultures in East Asia. Beyond that, translations of Confucian texts influenced European thinkers of the period as well, particularly among the philosophical groups of the Enlightenment who were interested in the integration of the system of morality of Confucius into Western civilization.

Four Great Academies

15 China Ancient Academy, also called Shu Yuan, was a type of school in Imperial China. Unlike national academies and district schools, Shu Yuan were usually private establishments built away from cities or towns, providing a quiet environment where scholars could engage in studies and contemplation without restriction and worldly distractions.

16 Shu Yuan originated in 725 during the Tang Dynasty. They were places where scholars could teach and study the classics, and where books collected from around the country could be preserved. By the late Tang Dynasty, private academies had appeared all over China. During the Northern Song (960 – 1127), many academies were established with government encouragement. Each academy had its own teaching and administrative structure and was economically independent. They made great contributions to the succession and popularity of Chinese culture as well as diversities of theories and heritages. A lot of ancient thinkers were educated in such a form of educational sectors.

17 The most famous four ancient Chinese academies include: Yuelu Academy, White Deer Grotto Academy, Yingtian Academy and Songyang Academy.

• Yuelu Academy

18 The Yuelu Academy (岳麓书院) is on the east side of Yuelu Mountain in Changsha, Hunan Province, on the west bank of the Xiang River. As one of the four most prestigious academies over the last 1,000 years in China, Yuelu Academy has been a famous institution of higher learning as well as a centre of academic activities and cultures since it was formally set up during the Northern Song Dynasty. The academy was converted into Hunan Institute of Higher Learning in 1903. It was later renamed Hunan Normal College, Hunan Public Polytechnic School, and finally Hunan University in 1926. Yuelu Academy was once the center for the pursuit of Chinese ancient learning and idealism in China's feudalist era. The academy has witnessed more than a thousand years of history and is the only one of the ancient Chinese academies of Classical Learning to have evolved into a modern institution of higher education.

• White Deer Grotto Academy

19 The White Deer Grotto Academy (白鹿洞书院) is a former school at the foot of Wulou Peak in Lushan Mountain, now in Jiujiang, Jiangxi Province. It was one of the Four Great Academies of China, and today it is maintained as an important landmark. The academy had its beginnings as a place for the pursuit of learning by the Tang Dynasty poet Li Bo when he was living in retirement. As Li Bo kept a white deer, he was known as the White Deer Teacher and the school premised themselves as the White Deer Grotto. In the years 937 –942, when the area was under the control of the Southern Tang, a school was officially established here under the name "Lushan Guoxue" by Li Shandao. In the early years of the Northern Song

Dynasty, which began in 960, the Lushan Guoxue was transformed into an academy known as the White Deer Grotto Academy. Having fallen into ruin, the academy was rebuilt and expanded by Zhu Xi during the Southern Song Dynasty. The new academy opened its doors to students and scholars in 1180. It was involved in instruction, the collection and preservation of books, religious sacrifices, the development of curricula, and lectures by famous scholars, including Lu Jiuyuan and Wang Yangming. The academy continued to flourish for eight centuries. The rules of the academy as set down by Zhu Xi had a profound and lasting influence on the subsequent development of Confucianism.

- Yingtian Academy

20 The Yingtian Academy was one of the oldest private educational institutions in China. The first designation is derived from the Tang Dynasty (618 – 907) for the sake of the name of the city of Shangqiu, where the academy was located. In 1006 Shangqiu was elevated to the status of prefecture with the name of Yingtian, and in 1014 it was given the designation of Southern Capital (Nanjing). The beginnings of the academy reached back to the times of the Later Jin (936 – 947), one of the Five Dynasties (907 – 960), when a certain Yang Que , who was fond of education and teaching, was able to gain the support of general Zhao Zhi to organize regular lessons for students in an institution called Nandu Xueshe (School of the Southern Capital). After Yang Que's death his disciple Qi Tongwen (903 – 976 or 912 – 985) continued the lectures and raised the funds necessary to provide scholarships for students. The famous writer and politician Fan Zhongyan (989 – 1052) had also visited the Yingtian Academy. After Qi Wentong's death in 976, the wealthy book collector Cao Cheng decided to take over the responsibility of financing the academy and had erected a building with more than 150 rooms, and a vast library. In 1009 he was granted the allowance to open the academy with public support, and the emperor bestowed the institution an official board inscribed with the name of the academy. During the reign of Emperor Renzong (1022 – 1063), the writer Yan Shu (991 – 1055) was appointed prefect of Yingtian. He asked Wang Zhu (997 – 1057) to become a teacher at the academy, as successor of Sun Fu. During Wang's professorship the number of students increased considerably, and the Yingtian Academy became the most important educational institution in Northern China. Its curriculum included the Confucian Classics, historiography, the "masters and philosophers", Yin-Yang teaching, astronomy, and philology. In 1035 the academy was transformed into a prefectural school. In 1043 the institution was made the Directorate of Education of the Southern Capital. It occupied an important role in the educational system of the Northern Song Dynasty (960 – 1127). In 1126 the buildings were destroyed by Jurchen troops during their invasion of Northern China, and the school fell into decay. Only during the Ming Dynasty (1368 – 1644), in 1531, censor Cai

Ai reorganized the school and gave it the name Yingtian Academy. It ceased to function as a school soon thereafter 1579.

- Songyang Academy

21 Songyang Academy is located on the southern side of Songshan Mountain in Dengfeng City, Central China's Henan Province. According to records, the academy was first built during the Northern Wei Dynasty (386–534). Songyang is famous for its rationalistic Confucian philosophical school. It was originally built for Buddhism activities, and then changed to a Taoism site by Emperor Yang of the Sui Dynasty. It was renamed Songyang Academy by Emperor Renzong in 1035. Since then, it has been a place for eminent scholars to teach. Famous academics in the Song Dynasty, such as Cheng Hao, Cheng Yi, Sima Guang, Fan Zhongyan and Zhu Xi once lectured there. Historically Songyang Academy was jointly an institution of Buddhism and Taoism at first, but later dedicated itself to Confucianism exclusively. Cheng Hao and Cheng Yi, two great masters of the Luo School of Confucianism, spread their theories to hundreds of students there. Songyang Academy is an institution of higher education in ancient China and is regarded as a representative of Confucian culture.

22 Only when China's academies' history and culture have been learned by more and more people, will people realize the great value of those ancient institutions and reaccept them gradually.

Notes

1. Four Books 四书 Four Books are Chinese classic texts illustrating the core value and belief systems in Confucianism. They were selected by Zhu Xi in the Song Dynasty to serve as the general introduction to Confucian thought, and they were, in the Ming and Qing dynasties, made the core of the official curriculum for the civil service examinations. They are:

Great Learning《大学》 Originally it is one chapter in the *Book of Rites*(礼记). It consists of a short main text attributed to Confucius and nine commentary chapters by Zengzi, one of the disciples of Confucius. Its importance is illustrated by Zengzi's foreword that this is the gateway of learning. It is significant because it expresses many themes of Chinese philosophy and political thinking, and has therefore been extremely influential both in classical and modern Chinese thought. Government, self-cultivation and investigation of things are linked.

Doctrine of the Mean《中庸》 Another chapter in *Book of Rites*, attributed to Confucius' grandson Zisi. The purpose of this small, 33-chapter book is to demonstrate the usefulness of a golden way to gain perfect virtue. It focuses on the Tao(道) that is prescribed by a heavenly mandate not only to the ruler but to everyone. To follow these heavenly instructions by learning and teaching will automatically result in a Confucian virtue. Because Heaven has laid down what is the way to perfect virtue, it is not that difficult to follow the steps of the holy rulers of old if one only knows what the right way is.

Analects《论语》 A compilation of speeches by Confucius and his disciples, as well as the discussions they held. Since Confucius's time, the *Analects* has heavily influenced the philosophy and moral values of China and later other East Asian countries as well. The Imperial Examinations, started in the Sui Dynasty and eventually abolished with the founding of the Republic of China, emphasized Confucian studies and expected candidates to quote and apply the words of Confucius in their essays.

Mencius《孟子》 It is the collection of conversations of the scholar Mencius with kings of his time. In contrast to the sayings of Confucius, which are short and self-contained, the *Mencius* consists of long dialogues with extensive prose.

2. Five Classics 五经 They are five pre-Qin Chinese books that form part of the traditional Confucian canon. Several of the texts were already prominent by the Warring States Period. Mencius, the leading Confucian scholar of the time, regarded the Spring and Autumn Annals as being equally important as the semi-legendary chronicles of earlier periods. During the Western Han Dynasty, which adopted Confucianism as its official ideology, these texts became part of the state-sponsored curriculum. It was during this period that the texts first began to be considered together as a set collection, and to be called collectively the "Five Classics". They are:

Classic of Poetry《诗经》 A collection of 305 poems divided into 160 folk songs, 105 festal songs sung at court ceremonies, and 40 hymns and eulogies sung at sacrifices to heroes and ancestral spirits of the royal house.

Book of Documents《尚书》 A collection of documents and speeches alleged to have been written by rulers and officials of the early Zhou period and before. It is possibly the oldest Chinese narrative, and may date from the 6th century BC. It includes examples of early Chinese prose.

Book of Rites《礼记》 It describes ancient rites, social forms and court ceremonies. The version studied today is a re-worked version compiled by scholars in the third century BC rather than the original text, which is said to have been edited by Confucius himself.

Book of Changes《易经》 The book contains a divination system comparable to Western geomancy or the West African Ifá system. In Western cultures and modern East Asia, it is still widely used for this purpose.

Spring and Autumn Annals《春秋》 It is a historical record of the State of Lu, Confucius's native state, 722–481 BC.

3. Six Arts 六艺 The Six Arts formed the basis of education in ancient Chinese culture. During the Zhou Dynasty (1046 - 256 BCE), students were required to master the Six Arts: Rites (礼), Music (乐), Archery (射), Charioteering (御), Calligraphy (书), Mathematics (数). Men who excelled in these six arts were thought to have reached the state of perfection, a perfect gentleman. The Six Arts were practiced by scholars and already existed before Confucius, but became part of Confucian philosophy. The Six Arts were practiced by the 72 disciples of Confucius. The Six Arts concept developed during the pre-imperial period. It incorporated both military and civil components. The civil side was later associated with the Four Arts (qin playing, chess, calligraphy and painting). However, the latter was more a leisure characteristic for the late imperial time. It evidently overlaps with the Six Arts, since the qin epitomized music, the chess related to the military strategy, while calligraphy dealt with the aesthetics of writing and the character cultivation.

- **Reading Comprehension**

1. **Directions**: *Complete the following table with the missing information based on the text.*

Notable Ancient China Academies

Names of Academy		Location	Time of Foundation
Chinese	English		
岳麓书院			
白鹿洞书院			
应天书院			
嵩阳书院			

2. **Directions**: *Translate the following passage into English.*

儒家的创始人是孔子(公元前551—前479),他提出了一套道德规范,基于五种美德:仁、义、礼、智、信。其中“仁”被认为是他的哲学理念的基石,代表着忠诚、孝道(filial piety)、宽容和善良。他还提倡人与人之间和谐相处,按照行为规范标准建立生活社区。他的追随者之一孟子(公元前372—前289)不断地向统治者们游说,试图说服他们修身养德,为人典范,以仁政赢得人民的尊重。

Part Three

Topic-Related Activities

1. Case Study

1 Karen had been teaching high school English in the United States before she accepted a teaching job at a teacher's college in China. She found her new environment and her new teaching assignment exciting. Both her students and her colleagues seemed a bit shy of her, but Karen was sure that in time they would all come to be friends.

2 In the classroom, however, Karen was very frustrated. When she asked a question, the class was silent. Only if she called on a particular student would she get an answer, often a very good one. She could not understand why they wouldn't volunteer when they obviously knew the answers. They were very quiet when she was speaking in front of the class, and never asked questions, let alone interrupted with an opinion, but as soon as the class ended, they would cluster around her desk to ask questions one-by-one. They would also offer their suggestions about the lesson at this time.

3 Karen often asked her students to work in small groups during class, especially when they were editing each other's writing. They were slow to move into groups and when they did, they often simply formed a group with the people sitting next to them. Finally she devised her own system of forming groups to get them to interact with students sitting in another section of the classroom.

4 Most frustrating of all, after she taught her class how to edit essays, she found that the students were likely to write vague and not very helpful remarks on their classmates' papers. They would say nice things about the essays and correct small grammatical errors, but seemed unwilling to criticize them in a way that would help another student revise the essay. They usually accepted her criticism of their writings with good spirits and promises to improve. In fact they frequently asked for more correction of their English from her than she wanted to give. She felt that one hundred percent grammatical correctness was not as important as learning how to correct what they had written on their own and with the help of others. After all, they would not always have a teacher to tell them what was good and not so good about their English writing.

Questions

1) What do you think of Chinese students' behavior in class?

2) Do you think Confucianism will affect Chinese students' verbal behavior in communication?

2. Critical Thinking & Cultural Exploration

Step One

Directions: *Ask students to discuss whether Confucianism is still a powerful influence in China and what we should do with it as one of our cultural resources.*

Step Two

Directions: *The class is to be divided into two groups and debate on the two different views on studying abroad. State your point of view clearly and support your argument with convincing and substantial evidence.*

Topic: Is studying abroad a good choice for young people?

For: Studying abroad is a good choice for young people.

Against: The value of foreign diploma has depreciated.

Step Three

Directions: *Nowadays more and more people tend to send their children to a private academy for traditional education. What are the pros and cons of a private academy in your opinion? Discuss with your classmates about this issue and write a composition of more than* 200 *words to state your point of view.*

3. Translation

Directions: *Translate the passage into English.*

随着中国经济的蓬勃发展,学汉语的人数迅速增加,汉语成了世界上人们最爱学的语言之一。近年来,中国大学在国际上的排名也有了明显的提高。由于中国教育的巨大进步,中国成为最受海外学生欢迎的留学目的地之一就不足为奇了。2015 年,近 40 万国际学生蜂拥来到中国留学。他们学习的科目不再限于中国语言和文化,还包括科学与工程。在全球教育市场上,美国和英国仍占主导地位,但中国正在迅速赶上。

Unit Three

Mythology

Part One

Lead-in

The creation of myth is on the basis of reality.

—Maxim Gorky

Every nation has its own culture including belief, art, literature, philosophy, etc. But cultures vary greatly from one nation to another. If we trace their cultures back further, we would find something very interesting, mythology, in which there are the gods, demigods, and legendary heroes, even the origin of human beings. Conversely, in the mythology, we also see the origin of the belief, art, literature, philosophy of a nation.

Part Two

Reading Passage

In-Class Reading

Warm-up questions:

1. Do you know the story *Da Yu Governed the Flood*?
2. Do you know any other stories about flood?

Noah's Ark

1 And when **Noah**[1] was five hundred years old, he became the father of Shem, Ham, and Japheth.

2 And after a time, when men were increasing on the earth, and had daughters,

3 The sons of God saw that the daughters of men were fair; and they took wives for themselves from those who were pleasing to them.

4 And the **Lord** said, "My Spirit will not be in man for ever, for he is only flesh; so the days of his life will be a hundred and twenty years."

5 There were men of great strength and size on the earth in those days; and after that, when the sons of God had connection with the daughters of men, they gave birth to children: these were the great men of old days, the men of great name.

6 And the Lord saw that the **sin** of man was great on the earth, and that all the thoughts of his heart were **evil**.

7 And the Lord had **sorrow** because he had made man on the earth, and **grief** was in his heart.

8 And the Lord said, "I will take away man, whom I have made, from the face of the earth, even man and **beast** and that which goes on the earth and every bird of the air; for I have sorrow for having made them."

9 But Noah had **grace** in the eyes of God.

10 These are the generations of Noah. Noah was an **upright** man and without sin in his generation: he went in the ways of God.

11 And Noah had three sons, Shem, Ham, and Japheth.

12 And the earth was evil in God's eyes and full of violent ways.

13 And God, looking on the earth, saw that it was evil: for the way of all **flesh** had become evil on the earth.

14 And God said to Noah, "The end of all flesh has come; the earth is full of their violent doings, and now I will put an end to them with the earth.

15 "Make for yourself an ark of **gopher wood** with rooms in it, and make it safe from the water inside and out.

16 "And this is the way you are to make it: it is to be three hundred **cubits** long, fifty cubits wide, and thirty cubits high.

17 "You are to put a window in the ark, a cubit from the **roof**, and a door in the side of it, and you are to make it with a lower and second and third floors.

18 "For truly, I will send a great flow of waters over the earth, for the destruction from under the heaven of all flesh in which is the breath of life; everything on the earth will come to an end.

19 "But with you I will make an agreement; and you will come into the ark, you and your sons and your wife and your sons' wives with you.

20 "And you will take with you into the ark two of every sort of living thing and keep them safe with you; they will be male and female.

21 "Two of every sort of **bird and cattle** and of every sort of living thing which goes on the earth will you take with you to keep them from destruction.

22 "And make a store of every sort of food for yourself and them."

23 And all these things Noah did; as God said, so he did.

24 And the Lord said to Noah, "Take all your family and go into the ark, for you only in this generation have I seen to be upright.

25 "Of every clean beast you will take seven males and seven females, and of the beasts which are not clean, two, the male and his female;

26 "And of the birds of the air, seven males and seven females, so that their **seed** may still be living on the face of the earth.

27 "For after seven days I will send rain on the earth for forty days and forty nights, for the destruction of every living thing which I have made on the face of the earth."

28 And Noah did everything which the Lord said he was to do.

29 And Noah was six hundred years old when the waters came flowing over all the earth.

30 And Noah, with his sons and his wife and his sons' wives, went into the ark because of the flowing of the waters.

31 Of clean beasts, and of beasts which are not clean, and of birds, and of everything which goes on the earth,

32 In twos, male and female, they went into the ark with Noah, as God had said.

33 And after the seven days, the waters came over all the earth.

34 In the six hundredth year of Noah's life, in the second month, on the seventeenth day of the month, all the **fountains** of the great deep came **bursting through**, and the windows of heaven were open;

35 And rain came down on the earth for forty days and forty nights.

36 On the same day Noah, with Shem, Ham, and Japheth, his sons, and his wife and his sons' wives, went into the ark;

37 And with them, every sort of beast and cattle, and every sort of thing which goes on the earth, and every sort of bird.

38 They went with Noah into the ark, two and two of all flesh in which is the breath of life.

39 Male and female of all flesh went in, as God had said, and the ark was shut by the Lord.

40 And for forty days the waters were over all the earth; and the waters were increased so that the ark was lifted up high over the earth.

41 And the waters overcame everything and were increased greatly on the earth, and the ark was resting on the face of the waters.

42 And the waters overcame everything on the earth; and all the mountains under heaven were covered.

43 The waters went fifteen cubits higher, till all the mountains were covered.

44 And destruction came on every living thing moving on the earth, birds and cattle and beasts and everything which went on the earth, and every man.

45 Everything on the dry land, in which was the breath of life, **came to its end**.

46 Every living thing on the face of all the earth, man and cattle and things moving on the face of the earth, and birds of the air, came to destruction: only Noah and those who were with him in the ark, were kept from death.

47 And the waters were over the earth a hundred and fifty days.

48 And God kept Noah in mind, and all the living things and the cattle which were with him in the ark: and God sent a wind over the earth, and the waters went down.

49 And the fountains of the deep and the windows of heaven were shut, and the rain from heaven was stopped.

50 And the waters went slowly back from the earth, and at the end of a hundred and fifty days the waters were lower.

51 And on the seventeenth day of the seventh month the ark came to rest on the mountains of **Ararat**[2].

52 And still the waters went on falling, till on the first day of the tenth month the tops of

the mountains were seen.

53 Then, after forty days, through the open window of the ark which he had made,

54 Noah sent out a **raven**, which **went this way and that** till the waters were gone from the earth.

55 And he sent out a **dove**, to see if the waters had gone from the face of the earth;

56 But the dove saw no resting-place for her foot, and came back to the ark, for the waters were still over all the earth; and he put out his hand, and took her into the ark.

57 And after waiting another seven days, he sent the dove out again;

58 And the dove came back at evening, and in her mouth was an **olive**-leaf **broken off**: so Noah was certain that the waters had gone down on the earth.

59 And after seven days more, he sent the dove out again, but she did not come back to him.

60 And in the six hundred and first year, on the first day of the first month, the waters were dry on the earth: and Noah took the cover off the ark and saw that the face of the earth was dry.

61 And on the twenty-seventh day of the second month the earth was dry.

62 And God said to Noah,

63 "Go out of the ark, you and your wife and your sons and your sons' wives.

64 "Take out with you every living thing which is with you, birds and cattle and everything which goes on the earth, so that they may have **offspring** and be **fertile** and be increased on the earth."

65 And Noah went out with his sons and his wife and his sons' wives;

66 And every beast and bird and every living thing of every sort which goes on the earth, went out of the ark.

67 And Noah made an **altar** to the Lord, and from every clean beast and bird he made burned offerings on the altar.

68 And when the sweet smell came up to the Lord, he said in his heart, "I will not again put a **curse** on the earth because of man, for the thoughts of man's heart are evil from his earliest days; never again will I send destruction on all living things as I have done."

69 While the earth goes on, seed time and the getting in of the grain, cold and heat, summer and winter, day and night, will not come to an end.

—Excerpt from the Genesis[3] of Bible[4]

New Words and Expressions

Ark /ɑːk/ *n.* (also called Noah's Ark) (in the Bible) a large wooden ship built by Noah in order to save his family and a male and female of every type of animal when the world was covered by a flood(《圣经》中的)诺亚方舟

Lord /lɔːd/ *n.* (in the Christian religion) God or Jesus Christ(基督教的)主,上帝,耶稣

sin /sɪn/ *n.* the offence of breaking, or the breaking of, a religious or moral law (违反宗教戒律或道德规范的)罪,罪过

evil /ˈiːvəl/ *adj.* morally bad, cruel, or very unpleasant 道德败坏的;邪恶的,恶毒的;讨厌的

sorrow /ˈsɒrəʊ/ *n.* (a cause of) a feeling of great sadness 悲痛,伤心,悔恨;伤心事,不幸

grief /griːf/ *n.* very great sadness, especially at the death of someone(尤指某人之死引起的)悲痛,悲伤,悲哀

beast /biːst/ *n.* an animal, especially a large or wild one(尤指大型或野生的)动物;野兽

grace /greɪs/ *n.* approval or kindness, especially (in the Christian religion) that is freely given by God to all humans(尤指上帝赐予人类的)恩典,恩宠

upright /ˈʌpraɪt/ *adj.* honest, responsible, and moral 诚实的;负责的;正直的

flesh /fleʃ/ *n.* a person or animal 人或动物

gopher wood /ˈgəʊfə(r) wʊd/ specially refer to the wood that makes the Noah's Ark

cubit /ˈkjuːbɪt/ *n.* an ancient unit of length based on the length of the forearm 肘尺,腕尺(古代长度单位,约 45 厘米,或自肘至指尖的长度)

roof /ruːf/ *n.* the covering that forms the top of a building, vehicle, etc. 屋顶;车顶;顶部;盖子

bird and cattle a creature with feathers and wings, usually able to fly and the other animals that walk on the earth 飞禽走兽

seed /siːd/ *n.* refers to the descendant of the animals that in the Ark

fountain /ˈfaʊntɪn/ *n.* a stream of water that is forced up into the air through a small hole, especially for decorative effect, or the structure in a lake or pool from which this flows 喷泉

raven /ˈreɪvən/ *n.* the largest bird in the crow family, with shiny black feathers 渡鸦,乌鸦

dove /ˈdəuv/	a bird of the pigeon family, usually is used as a symbol of peace 鸽子
olive /ˈɒlɪv/	*n.* a small bitter green or black fruit that is eaten or used to produce oil, or a Mediterranean tree on which this fruit grows 橄榄;橄榄树
offspring /ˈɒfsprɪŋ/	*n.* the young of an animal 动物子嗣
fertile /ˈfɜːtaɪl/	*adj.* be able to produce (a lot of) young or fruit (动物或植物)可繁殖的,能生育的,能结果的
altar /ˈɔːltər/	*n.* a type of table used in ceremonies in a Christian church or in other religious buildings 圣坛,祭坛
curse /kɜːs/	*v.* to say magic words that are intended to bring bad luck to someone 说咒语,施魔咒
burst through	to break open and come out 迸出
come to its end	refers to that the flood is gone 指洪水消退
go this way and that	refers to that the raven goes and looks around 指乌鸦四处查看
break off	to become detached 折断

Notes

1. Noah 亚当生赛特,赛特生以挪士,以挪士生该南,该南生玛勒列,玛勒列生雅列,雅列生以诺,以诺生玛土撒拉,玛土撒拉生拉麦,拉麦生诺亚 who built the ark in which he, his family, and living creatures of every kind survived the flood; Noah's father is Lamech, Lamech's father is Methuselah, Methuselah's father is Enoch, Enoch's father is Jared, Jared's father is Mahalaleel, Mahalaleel's father is Cainan, Cainan's father is Enos, Enos's father is Seth, Seth's father is Adam

2. Ararat 阿勒山;亚拉腊山;阿拉腊山,位于土耳其东部 mountain 16,946 feet (5,165 meters) in Eastern Turkey near the border with Iran. Ararat is traditionally thought to be the landing place of Noah's Ark

3. Genesis《创世记》(《圣经》首卷,描述上帝如何创造世界) the first book of the Bible, which describes how God made the world

4. Bible 基督教《圣经》(包括《旧约》和《新约》);犹太教《圣经》(包括《律法书》《先知书》《圣录》) (a copy of) the holy book of the Christian religion consisting of the Old and New Testaments, or the holy book of the Jewish religion consisting of the Law, the Prophets, and the Writings

- **Reading Comprehension**

1. Directions: *Discuss the following questions with your classmates.*

1) What can be chosen to the Noah's Ark and how many of them?

2) Give a brief description of the Noah's Ark.

3) What happened on the earth and in the heaven in the six hundredth year of Noah's life?

4) What happened to the rest living creatures that weren't be chosen to the Noah's Ark?

5) How many days did the Noah's family stay in the Ark?

6) At the second time what did the dove come back with in her mouth and what does it mean?

7) When the sweet smell came up to the Lord, what did he do?

2. **Directions:** *Read the following statements carefully and decide whether they are true(T) or false(F) or (N) not mentioned according to the text.*

( )1) And when Noah was six hundred years old, he became the father of Shem, Ham, and Japheth.

( )2) And the Lord said, "My Spirit will be in man for ever, for he is not only flesh."

( )3) The Lord wanted to destroy all the living creatures on the earth, because they are evil in heart.

( )4) After the raven went away, Noah sent out a dove, to see if the waters had gone from the face of the earth.

( )5) The olive tree grew out from the seed that dropped out from the Noah's Ark.

( )6) The Lord will not destroy the living things again.

3. **Directions:** *Fill in the blanks based on the information provided in the article (what happened on the date?).*

1) In the six hundredth year of Noah's life, in the second month, on the seventeenth day of the month

____

____

2) And for forty days the waters were over all the earth

____

____

3) And the waters were over the earth a hundred and fifty days

____

____

____

4) On the seventeenth day of the seventh month

____

____

5) In the six hundred and first year, on the first day of the first month

____

____

- **Discussion**

1. How to explain that the flood existed in both eastern and western mythology?
2. Can you find some paradox in the mythology?
3. How to explain the existence of the mythology?

After-Class Reading

Warm-up questions:

1. What is the most impressive character of Chinese mythology in your mind?
2. Which story of Chinese mythology do you like best? Why?

Chinese Myth: The Creation of the World and Mankind

1 According to Chinese legend, the world was created by **Pangu**[1], a giant who splited the chaos with his strength and axe.

2 It may seem that every culture has its own tale about the creation of the world and the beginnings of mankind—and China is no different. The ancient Chinese story of the beginning of the universe is replete with chaos and mythic heroes who rise above it to create order and the world as we know it.

Pangu Created the World

3 According to Chinese lore, in the beginning there was nothing in the universe but a dark, formless chaos. The mythic hero Pangu, who had been sleeping in the chaos for 18,000 years, woke up. When he realized that he was confined to this dark and chaotic environment, he decided to break out. He mightily swung his giant axe to smash through the chaos. This caused the lighter parts of the universe to rise up and become the sky, while the heavier parts sunk down and became the earth. In order to keep the sky and earth separated, Pangu stood between them and exerted himself to push up the sky. With each day the sky grew higher and the earth grew wider.

4 After another 18,000 years immersed in the nascent universe, Pangu thought his job was done and he lay down to rest. Then his breath became wind and cloud; voice became thunder; his left eye became the sun and right eye, the moon; his hair became stars in the sky; his blood became the rivers and lakes; his muscles became the fertile lands; his bones became minerals; his sweat fell as rain; and his fur became forests and grasslands.

5 That's the beginning of the world.

Nüwa[2] Created Mankind and Repaired the Sky

6 Nüwa is a goddess in ancient Chinese legend known for creating mankind and repairing

the sky. It is said that Nüwa existed in the beginning of the world and created men from yellow clay. At first, she sculpted each human individually. But she found that she needed a more efficient way to make more people. So she dipped a rope in clay and flicked it. Then blobs of clay landed everywhere and each of these blobs became a person.

7 But later there was a fight between the god of water **Gonggong**[3] and the god of fire **Zhurong**[4]. When Gonggong lost the fight, he smashed his head against **Mount Buzhou**[5] out of fury. Since Mount Buzhou was a pillar holding up the sky, the sky began to fall and caused a lot of damage. Because of that, people's lives became miserable. Nüwa was really concerned about her people so she picked out colorful stones in **Mount Tiantai**[6] and used them to seal the broken sky. In this way peace and happiness returned to mankind.

Dayu[7] Tamed the Flood

8 When **Yao**[8] was in power, there was a great flood in the Yellow River valley. Crops were flooded, houses were destroyed, and people had to move to higher places. In many places, there are poisonous snakes and beasts that hurt people and animals and make people unable to live.

9 Yao held a tribal alliance meeting to discuss water control. He asked the tribal leaders of the Quartet for their advice, "Who should be sent to deal with the floods?" The chiefs recommended Gun.

10 Yao didn't trust Gun very much. The chiefs said, "There's no one stronger than Gun now. Give it a try!" Yao reluctantly agreed.

11 Gun spent nine years harnessing the water and did not contain the flood. Because he only knew how to cover the water with earth and build dikes and dams. As a result, the floods broke down the dikes and made the floods worse.

12 After **Shun**[9] succeeded Yao as the leader of the tribal alliance, he personally visited the place where water was harnessed. When he found out that Gun could not do anything well, he killed Gun and let his son Yu go to treat the water.

13 Shortly after his marriage, in order to control the water, Yu traveled everywhere and passed through his home many times without entering. On one occasion, his wife Tu Shanshi gave birth to his son Qi. The baby was crying wow. Yu passed by the door. He heard the crying, but he did not enter.

14 Yu changed his father's way of draining and dredging rivers to divert the flood into the sea. He worked with the common people, wearing hats and shovels, and took the lead in digging and picking soil. He was so tired that he polished the hairs on his calves.

15 After 13 years of hard work, the flood was eventually diverted to the sea, and the ground could be used for planting crops.

16 All descendants praised Yu's achievements in water control and honored him as Dayu.

The Cowherd and the Weaving Girl

17 Long, long ago, there was an honest and kind-hearted fellow named Niu Lang (Cowherd). His parents died when he was a child. Later he was driven out of his home by his sister-in-law, so he wandered the old cattle to go to a piece of barren mountain, lived lonely.

18 He treated the old cattle very well. But his cattle was a magic cattle. One day, he spoke. He spoke to Niu Lang how to get a wife.

19 At the same time, the youngest of the seven celestial(天上的) princesses had grown tired of the privileged but secluded life in the heavenly palace. She longed for a mundane life she often saw down beneath her. That was a very pervert idea to cherish in heaven. Yet, determined to pursue what she deemed to be her own happiness, she sneaked out and descended onto the earth and fell in love with Niu Lang.

20 They married and had a lovely boy and a girl. While the Cowherd worked in the fields with his old pal the cattle, the heavenly princess weaved at home to help support the family. Villagers all admired her excellent weaving skill and started learning from her. She was now well-known as the Weaving Girl.

21 The family lived moderately but peacefully and happily until the girl's celestial royal (皇室) family found her missing and traced her to the village. By the way, it is popularly believed that a day in heaven accounts for years on the earth. The years she had spent with the Cowherd was but a day or so by the celestial calendar.

21 The Celestial Empress was in such a wrath that she gave her daughter only two choices: to go back home or see her husband and children destroyed. She had no choice but to leave.

22 The old cattle suddenly began to speak to the bereaved and now astonished young man, saying that he was dying in no time and asking him to use his hide as a vehicle to catch up with his wife. And off he sailed to heaven taking his young son and daughter in two baskets carried by a shoulder pole.

23 Fearing that the young man would catch up, the Empress took out her hair spin and drew a big river across the sky, known to the Chinese as the Silvery River. She wanted to separate the family forever.

24 However, all the magpies in the world, deeply touched by the story, came to their rescue. Each year, on the seventh day of the seventh month, tens of thousands of magpies came to build a bridge so that the family may enjoy a brief reunion.

25 The Empress was eventually moved and allowed them to meet each year on the 7th of the 7th lunar month. Hence their meeting date has been called "Qi Xi" (Double Seventh).

Notes

1. Pangu 盘古 Chinese mythic hero, who separates the sky and the earth and creates the world

2. Nüwa 女娲 Chinese mythic hero, whose upper body is human being alike and the under part is a snake tail

3. Gonggong 共工 Chinese mythic hero, the god of water

4. Zhurong 祝融 Chinese mythic hero, the god of fire

5. Mount Buzhou 不周山 a mountain to the northwest of Kunlun Mountain, also a pillar holding up the sky

6. Mount Tiantai 天台山 It is universally acknowledged that the Mount Tiantai is located in She County, Hebei Province. There are many other mountains in China named after Tiantai.

7. Da Yu 大禹 Chinese ancient hero, who tamed the flood, also called Emperor Yu

8. Yao 尧 also called Emperor Yao, Chinese ancient emperor, who initiated Shanrangzhi, according to which the leadership of the tribe should be handed down based on the successor's talent and personal character rather than blood.

9. Shun 舜 Chinese ancient emperor, who was respected for his family filial piety, also called Emperor Shun

• Reading Comprehension

1. **Directions:** *Read the following statements carefully, and decide whether they are true(T) or false(F) according to the text.*

( )1) According to Chinese legend, the mighty Nüwa, broke through the chaos with his strength and axe to create the world as we know it.

( )2) When the god of fire lost the fight, he smashed his head against Mount Buzhou out of fury.

( )3) When Shun was in power, there was a great flood in the Yellow River valley.

( )4) The chiefs recommended Gun and Yao trusted Gun very much.

( )5) Yu changed his father's way of draining and dredging rivers to divert the flood into the sea.

( )6) After twelve years of hard work, the flood was eventually diverted to the sea, and the ground could be used for planting crops.

2. **Directions:** *Fill in the blank according to the passage about the Cowherd and the Weaving Girl.*

Long, long ago, there was an honest and ____1____ fellow named Niu Lang

(Cowherd). After his parents died he was ___2___ of his home by his sister-in-law, so he wandered the old cattle to go to a piece of barren mountain, lived lonely. But his cattle was a magic cattle and helped Niu Lang get a wife who was the youngest of the seven celestial princesses. His wife had grown tired of the ___3___ life in the heavenly palace. She ___4___ a mundane life she often saw down beneath her. They married and had ___5___ and a girl. While the Cowherd worked in the fields with his old pal the cattle, the heavenly princess weaved at home to help support the family. The family lived ___6___ and happily until the girl's celestial royal family found her missing and traced her to the village. The Celestial Empress was ___7___ that she forced the Weaving Girl to leave. The old cattle helped Niu Lang to catch up with his wife. ___8___ the young man would catch up, the Empress took out her hair spin and drew a big river across the sky, known to the Chinese as the Silvery River. However, all the ___9___ in the world, deeply touched by the story, came to their rescue. Each year, on the seventh day of the seventh month, tens of thousands of magpies came to build a bridge so that the family may enjoy a ___10___. The Empress was eventually moved and allowed them to meet each year on the 7th of the 7th lunar month. Hence their meeting date has been called "Qi Xi" (Double Seventh).

Part Three

Topic-Related Activities

1. Case Study

12 Greek Gods and Goddesses

1 Cruel and fickle, passionate and vindictive, jealous and insecure, petty and insane: the inhabitants of Mount Olympus represent an attempt by the ancient Greeks to explain the chaos of the universe through human nature. Thus, like every deity invented before and since, these gods and goddesses are embodiments of human solipsism. (Of course lightning is caused by a giant, angry man in the sky... obvi. I mean, what else could it be?) The stories of their battles, bickering, and sexual conquests have indelibly influenced the course of Western language and narrative. Here is a selection of some of the A-list names of the Greek pantheon.

Zeus

2 With the assistance of Hades and Poseidon, Zeus overthrew his father, Cronus, king of the Titans, and became the chief deity in a new pantheon comprising mostly his siblings and children. In addition to controlling the weather, Zeus was noted for his chronic infidelity to his

sister-wife, Hera. Among the results of his weakness for comely mortal women was Helen of Troy. His Roman equivalent was Jupiter.

Poseidon

3 Poseidon is best known as the Greek sea god, but he was also the god of horses and of earthquakes. (Thus, many of his temples were inland.) And he had some seriously strange children. Though humanoid, he fathered both the winged horse Pegasus (by Medusa, no less) and the Cyclops Polyphemus, who is blinded by Odysseus and his crew in the *Odyssey*. His Roman equivalent was Neptune.

Hermes

4 Like many gods in the Greek pantheon, Hermes presided over multiple spheres. He was a pastoral figure, responsible for protecting livestock, and was also associated with fertility, music, luck, and deception. In the *Odyssey*, he is depicted as a messenger god. His Roman equivalent was Mercury.

Hera

5 Thequeen goddess of Olympus, Hera was both sister and wife to Zeus. Though she is often depicted as reserved and austere, she was mercilessly vindictive when it came to her husband's (many) extramarital adventures. Unfortunately for the objects of Zeus's godly affections, Hera tended to torment the "other women" (and their offspring, including Heracles) rather than Zeus himself. Her Roman equivalent was Juno.

Hades

6 Hades ruled the world of the dead, with which he was sometimes synonymous. The chilly lord of the underworld was among the few Greek gods to come across as dispassionate. He was not the ultimate judge of the souls that wandered his domain nor did he mete out their punishments for sins committed during their mortal lives. He was, however, cunning; he tricked Persephone into eating enchanted pomegranate seeds so that she would have to remain with him for a portion of the year. His Roman equivalent was Pluto or Orcus.

Dionysus

7 Dionysus was a son of Zeus born to a mortal mother. When Zeus accidentally killed her, he sewed the young Dionysus into his thigh and, when the young god emerged, passed him to the care of the maenads. The cult of Dionysus revolved around intoxication, sex, and savage ritual sacrifice. He was often symbolized by a bull due to his association with the sacrificial animal. Elements of his character are seen in the Roman god of wine, Bacchus.

Dcmctcr

8 Demeter, an agricultural goddess, was mother to Persephone, who was abducted by the underworld god Hades to be his bride. While searching for her stolen daughter, she

accepted the hospitality of the royal family of Eleusis. The Eleusinian Mysteries, perhaps the most important religious rites in ancient Greece, are attributed to her teachings. Her Roman equivalent was Ceres.

Apollo

9 The twin brother of Artemis, Apollo was among the most important (read: feared) of the gods. Son of Zeus, he disseminated the will of his divine compatriots through various means, notably oracles. The Oracle at Delphi was his mouthpiece; a 2001 study determined that the oracle was likely hallucinating due to ethylene gas rising from the rocks beneath the temple.

Ares

10 Ares was the god of bloodlust. (His half-sister Athena represented the more "noble" aspects of combat and civil conduct during war.) Though his fellow deities weren't particularly fond of him, the Spartans had no problems, er, donating some prisoners of war to his worship. And sacrificing dogs... yeah, that's right, Ares liked dead puppies. Jerk. His Roman equivalent was Mars.

Artemis

11 Artemis was the fleet-footed goddess of the hunt. Often depicted in painting and sculpture with a deer or a hunting dog, she was both huntress and protectress of the living world. Her Roman equivalent was Diana.

Athena

12 Athena was the goddess of reason, wisdom, and war. She famously sprung fully formed from the forehead of Zeus. A major figure in the *Odyssey*, in which she instructed Odysseus, she also guided Perseus and Heracles through their trials. The Parthenon was her chief temple in Athens, which is named in her honor. Her Roman equivalent was Minerva.

Aphrodite

13 Aphrodite was the goddess of love, sex, and beauty. Unsurprisingly for a love goddess, she was said to have emerged from the foam generated when the severed testicles of her father, Uranus, were thrown into the sea by his son, the Titan Cronus. (Or is that surprising?) Kind of makes Botticelli's surreally lovely *Birth of Venus*—which depicts Aphrodite's Roman counterpart emerging from the waves—a little more visceral, doesn't it?

Questions

1) Can you name the 12 gods of Greek and Rome separately? Who are they? Is there any difference from that you thought before?

2) Why the gods have the same shortcomings as human beings in the Western mythology?

3) Have you noticed that some gods' names sound like some planets? Can you give some examples?

4) Try to make a comparison between the gods from Western and Chinese mythology.

2. A Matching Game

Step One

Directions: *Ask students to interview each other about the 12 gods in Greek and Rome mythology separately.*

Step Two

Directions: *Please work in pairs and match the gods in Column A and Column B. Search on the Internet and find out their differences.*

Column A		Column A
Zeus		Minerva
Poseidon		Pluto, Orcus
Hermes		Apollo
Hera		Mercury
Hades		Venus
Dionysus		Neptune
Demeter		Mars
Apollo		Jupiter
Ares		Diana
Artemis		Bacchus
Athena		Juno
Aphrodite		Ceres

Step Three

Directions: *Since the Western mythology influences their culture greatly, please give some examples to illustrate, for example the literature works.*

3. Translation

Directions: *Translate the passage into English.*

在特洛伊(Troy)建成之前,战火已弥漫了十年。一位预言家说:只要雅典娜(Athena)的神像受人民的爱戴,特洛伊城就永远不会衰灭。为了将神像偷出城,一天夜里,奥德修斯和狄俄墨得斯(Odysseus and Diomedes)乔装改扮潜入首都,这一切只有海伦知道。这个可恶的女人把他们介绍给特洛伊皇后赫克犹巴(Hecuba),奥德修斯立刻跪倒在她的面前乞求怜悯。皇后答应了他们的要求,在海伦的帮助下,拂晓前,他们成功地带着雕像回到希腊营地。

Unit Four

Sports

Part One

Lead-in

Life lies in movement.

—Voltaire

Nowadays sports is a hot topic. People enjoy all kinds of games through the mass media, reading newspaper sports news, watching games live on the internet, etc. But don't forget to go outside and do some sports by yourself. In the morning or the evening, you can go out jogging in your community or a park nearby; at the weekend you can invite some friends to play the ball games together; and in the holidays you can go for a mountain climbing and so on. Sports can help you to keep fit, fresh you from hard work and depression mood, and bring you some new friends.

Part Two

Reading Passage

In-Class Reading

Warm-up questions:

1. What sport do you like? Are you good at it? How much time do you spend in exercising?
2. How much do you know about the Ancient Olympic Games?

Welcome to the Ancient Olympic Games

1 From boxing contests with no weight **classifications** or point scoring to **chariot** racing where danger **lurked** on every corner, it is easy to see why the Ancient Games **enthralled** the Greeks for so long. Here, we give you the essential **lowdown**, highlight our favorite facts.

2 Full of blood, passion and extraordinary feats of **athletic endeavor**, the Olympic Games were the sporting, social and cultural highlight of the Ancient Greek calendar for almost 12 centuries.

3 "It is hard for us to exaggerate how important the Olympics were for the Greeks," Paul Christesen, Professor of Ancient Greek History at Dartmouth College, USA, said.

4 "The classic example is that when the **Persians**[1] **invaded** Greece in the summer of 480 (BC) a lot of the Greek city states agreed that they would put together an allied army but they had a very hard time getting one together because so many people wanted to go to the Olympics. So, they actually had to delay putting the army together to defend the country against the Persians."

5 The threat of invasion or not, the Games took place every four years from 776**BC**[2] to at least 393**AD**[2]. All free Greek males were allowed to take part, from farmhands to royal heirs, although the majority of Olympians were soldiers. Women could not compete or even attend. There was, however, a **loophole** to this **misogynistic** rule—chariot owners, not riders, were declared Olympic champions and anyone could own a chariot. Kyniska, daughter of a **Spartan**[3] king, took advantage of this, claiming victory **wreaths** in 396BC and 392BC.

6 At their heart, the Games were a religious festival and a good excuse for Greeks from all over the **Mediterranean basin** to gather for a **riotous** barbeque. On the middle day of the festival a vast number of cows were slaughtered in honour of Zeus, King of the Greek Gods—

once he had been given a small taste, the rest was for the people.

7 For the first 250-plus years all the action took place in the **sanctuary** of **Olympia**[4], situated in the north-western **Peloponnese**[5]. Pock-marked by olive trees, from which the victory wreaths were cut, and featuring an altar to Zeus, it was a hugely scared spot.

8 The Games lasted a full five days by the fifth century BC and saw running, jumping and throwing events plus boxing, wrestling, **pankration**[6] and chariot racing. At least 40,000 spectators would have packed the stadium each day at the height of the Games' popularity, in the second century AD, with many more selling their wares outside.

9 But first, here are our 10 favourite facts to get you started:

- All athletes competed naked.
- Wrestlers and pankration (a sort of mixed martial art which combined boxing and wrestling) competitors fought covered in oil.
- **Corporal** punishment awaited those guilty of a false start on the track.
- There were only two rules in the pankration—no biting and no **gouging**.
- Boxers were urged to avoid attacking the on-display male genitals.
- There were no points, no time limits and no weight classifications in the boxing.
- Athletes in the combat sports had to indicate their surrender by raising their index fingers—at times they died before they could do this.
- Boxers who could not be separated could opt for climax, a system whereby one fighter was granted a free hit and then vice-versa—a toss of a coin decided who went first.

Pankration

10 "No biting and no gouging"—but all else fair game in "brutal" pankration. A combination of boxing and wrestling with barely any restrictions, pankration was the wild, no-holds-barred center of the Ancient Olympic Games. Boasting huge men of incredible strength, it became a fountain of **wondrous** stories and stirring myths.

11 Pankration was a magnificently simple sport.

12 "You could do pretty much anything you could possibly imagine in order to **incapacitate** your opponent," Paul Christesen, Professor of Ancient Greek History at Partmouth College, USA, explained.

13 "And the Greeks thought this was the coolest thing ever."

Boxing

14 Honor rules despite tough nature of boxing at Ancient Games. With no weight classifications, no scoring system, no time limit and death a real possibility, boxing at the Ancient Olympic Games appears to have been a brutal and barbaric affair. But in reality,

honor, respect and fair play were always at the **fulcrum** of this noble art.

15 It is no accident that Diagoras of **Rhodes**[7] was one of the most celebrated **pugilists** of ancient times. The victor at the 79th Olympiad in 464BC is said to have never **ducked**, stooped, or sought to **evade** a single punch. Instead the crowd favorite stood face on and took all that his opponent could throw at him while searching for his own knockout blow.

16 This sense of dignity is one that modern Olympians recognize.

Running

17 "Run Leonidas Run": meet the stars of the track at the Ancient Olympic Games.

18 From completing three marathons in one day—post Olympic title—to chasing down a live hare, the achievements of the running idols at Olympia were remarkable.

19 Leonidas of Rhodes is not just the greatest runner of the Ancient Olympic Games, he is arguably the most impressive Olympian of all-time. The man's feats were so extraordinary that he was deified by his countrymen in his own lifetime, and, were it not for the hard, indisputable historical evidence, his records would likely be dismissed as **embellishment** at best.

20 Undefeated, Leonidas won both **premier sprint** events and the race in armor at four consecutive Olympic Games, running 164BC to 152BC. Twelve victories in twelve years, with the final three coming at the age of 36—even **Usain Bolt**[8] cannot match that.

Discus

21 The discus has a long tradition in the Greek world, first mentioned by **Homer**[9]. Strangely, it also has a close connection with death in Greek mythology. Both **Apollo** and **Perseus**[10] accidentally killed loved ones with **errant** throws.

22 Often engraved with picturesque scenes or poetry, discuses were made first of stone and later of iron, lead or even bronze. It seems that the set weight of the discus varied from Games to Games, with discoveries ranging from weights of 1.3–6.6kg and diameters of 17–32cm. Launched in a similar manner to that employed by modern athletes, there is a record of **Phayllos of Kroton**[11] throwing 95ft/28.9m.

Chariot Racing

23 Thrills, spills and crashes were guaranteed at the ancient chariot races. Chariot racing is one of the most thrilling, **visceral** and danger-filled sports ever invented by man. Present at the Ancient Olympic Games from 680BC, it continues to capture our attention and fuel our imagination more than two-and-a-half thousand years later.

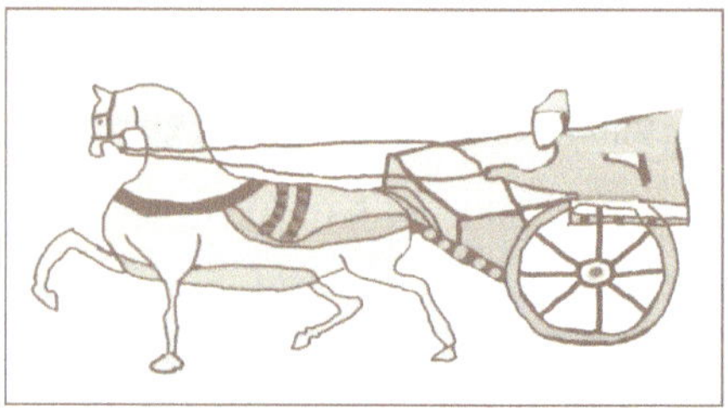

24 The four-horse chariot race was the most popular, prestigious and long-lasting event on the **equestrian** programme at the Ancient Games. With the driver **perched** on a wooden-wheeled, open-backed chariot, which rested on its own back **axle**, teams would funnel into an ingenious starting gate in Olympia's specially-constructed **Hippodrome**[12]. The mechanism was the shape of a ship's **prow**, facing down the track. At the sound of a trumpet an **imperious** eagle would rise at the point of the prow as a dolphin fell, this movement would **precipitate** the rising of the ropes holding in the back markers at either side. As these chariots emerged and drew level with the ones in front the ropes holding them in fell and so on. Eventually, all the chariots would be level, hurtling down the track together.

25 Among others are long jump, **javelin** and so on.

26 For over one thousand years, the Greeks, and later the Romans, met at Olympia to celebrate the festival in honour of Zeus and ensure that the Games remained an important event. We now know that the Games were still being organized in the 4th century AD. In 393 AD, the Christian emperor **Theodosius I**[13] forbade the celebration of **pagan** cults, which included the Games. Nonetheless, the popularity of sports contests and cultural festivities continued in many Greek-influenced provinces of the Roman empire as late as the 6th century AD.

New Words and Expressions

classification /ˌklæsɪfɪˈkeɪʃən/ *n.* a group that something is divided into 类别,等级,门类

chariot /ˈtʃæriət/ *n.* a two-wheeled vehicle that was used in ancient times for racing and fighting and was pulled by a horse or horses(古时用于比赛或战争的)双轮马车

lurk /lɜːk/ *v.* to wait or move in a secret way so that you cannot be seen, especially because you are about to attack someone or do something wrong(尤指为攻击某人或做坏事而)潜伏,隐蔽,悄悄移动

enthrall /ɪnˈθrɔːl/ *v.* to keep someone completely interested 迷住,使着迷;吸引住

lowdown /ˈləʊdaʊn/ *n.* the most important facts and information about something 真相,实情;重要信息

athletic /æθˈletɪk/ *adj.* strong, healthy, and good at sports 强壮的;擅长运动的

endeavor /enˈdevər/ *n.* an attempt to do something 尝试;努力

invade /ɪnˈveɪd/ *v.* to enter a country by force with large numbers of soldiers

	in order to take possession of it 入侵,侵略(名词形式 invasion)
loophole /ˈluːphəʊl/	*n.* a small mistake in an agreement or law that gives someone the chance to avoid having to do something(协议或法律的)漏洞,空子,破绽
misogynistic /mɪsɒdʒɪˈnɪstɪk/	*adj.* showing feelings of hating women or a belief that men are better than women 厌恶女性的
wreath /riːθ/	*n.* an arrangement of flowers and leaves in a circular shape, used as a decoration or as a sign of respect and remembrance for a person who has died 花环;花圈
Mediterranean /medɪtəˈreɪniən/	*n.* the sea between southern Europe and North Africa 地中海
basin /ˈbeɪsən/	*n.* an open, round container shaped like a bowl with sloping sides, used for holding food or liquid 盆;水盆
riotous /ˈraɪətəs/	*adj.* very loud and uncontrolled, and full of energy 热闹的;喧闹的;放纵的
sanctuary /ˈsæŋktʃʊəri/	*n.* protection or a safe place, especially for someone or something being chased or hunted 庇护,保护;避难所,庇护所
corporal /ˈkɔːpərəl/	*adj.* of or relating to the body 身体的,肉体的
gouge /gaʊdʒ/	*v.* to make a hole in something in a rough or violent way 凿,挖
wondrous /ˈwʌndrəs/	*adj.* extremely and surprisingly good 极棒的,绝妙的
incapacitate /ˌɪnkəˈpæsɪteɪt/	*v.* to make someone unable to work or do things normally, or unable to do what they intended to do 使无能力(正常工作或做事);使无法(做想做之事)
fulcrum /ˈfʊlkrəm/	*n.* the point against which a lever is placed to get a purchase, or on which it turns or is supported(杠杆的)支点,支轴
pugilist /ˈpjuːdʒɪlɪst/	*n.* a boxer or fighter 拳击手;斗士
duck /dʌk/	*v.* to move your head or the top part of your body quickly down, especially to avoid being hit(尤指为避免被击中而)猛低头,猛弯腰
evade /ɪˈveɪd/	*v.* to avoid or escape from someone or something 逃脱,躲开;回避,逃避
embellishment /ɪmˈbelɪʃmənt/	*n.* something added to make another thing more beautiful or

	interesting, or the process of doing this 装饰,修饰
premier /ˈpremiər/	*adj.* best or most important 首位的,首要的
sprint /sprɪnt/	*v.* to run as fast as you can over a short distance, either in a race or because you are in a great hurry to get somewhere 短距离快速奔跑,冲刺
errant /ˈerənt/	*adj.* behaving wrongly in some way, especially by leaving home(尤指离家出走而)犯错的,行为不当的,出格的,出轨的
visceral /ˈvɪsərəl/	*adj.* based on deep feeling and emotional reactions rather than on reason or thought 发自内心的;发自肺腑的
equestrian /ɪˈkwestriən/	*adj.* connected with the riding of horses 骑马的;骑术的
perch /pɜːtʃ/	*v.* to sit on or near the edge of something 坐在……(的边缘)上;栖息于;停留于
axle /ˈæksəl/	*n.* a bar connected to the centre of a circular object such as a wheel that allows or causes it to turn, especially one connecting two wheels of a vehicle 轴;车轴
prow /praʊ/	*n.* the front part of a boat or ship 船头
imperious /ɪmˈpɪəriəs/	*adj.* unpleasantly proud and expecting to be obeyed 专横的,跋扈的
precipitate /prɪˈsɪpɪteɪt/	*v.* to make something happen suddenly or sooner than expected 促成;使突如其来地发生;加速……的发生
javelin /ˈdʒævlɪn/	*n.* a long stick with a pointed end that is thrown in sports competitions 标枪
pagan /ˈpeɪgən/	*adj.* belonging or relating to a religion that worships many gods, especially one that existed before the main world religions 多神教的

Notes

1. Persian 波斯;波斯人;波斯语 a person from Iran or the main language spoken in Iran

2. BC, AD 公元前和公元 Before Christ and Anno Domini (a Latin phrase meaning "in the year of the Lord", which is used when referring to a year after Jesus Christ was born)

3. Spartan 简朴的,清苦的;斯巴达式的 simple and severe with no comfort(Sparta is the second powerful city-state of the Ancient Greece)

4. Olympia 希腊南部平原的一个城市,位于伯罗奔尼撒的西北。它是古代用以祭拜宙斯的宗教中心，又是古代奥林匹克运动会的遗址。 a plain in south Greece, in the NW Peloponnese; in ancient times a major sanctuary of Zeus and site of the original Olympic Games

5. Peloponnese 伯罗奔尼撒 the peninsula of Greece, joined to central Greece by the Isthmus of Corinth; chief cities in ancient times were Sparta and Corinth, now Patras.

6. Pankration 古代奥林匹亚竞技大会的一项技击性项目，是一种可以同时使用拳击与角力技巧等全面性技术的一种搏斗比赛。 ancient Greek form of no-holds-barred wrestling and boxing

7. Rhodes 罗德岛，在爱琴海的东南部。 a Greek island in the SE Aegean Sea

8. Usain Bolt 尤塞恩博尔特，牙买加短跑运动员。 a Jamaican sprinter

9. Homer 荷马，公元前 8 世纪左右希腊诗人。 Greek poet in 800BC to whom are attributed the Iliad and the Odyssey; Almost nothing is known of him, but it is thought that he was born on the island of Chios and was blind.

10. Perseus 珀耳修斯，宙斯和阿尔戈斯王阿克里西奥斯女儿达那厄之子。 (Greek mythology) a son of Zeus and Danaë

11. Phayllos of Kroton 来自科罗顿的法洛斯(在奥林匹亚戴上胜利者的王冠不少于6次，出生在意大利南部，在那里有许多希腊殖民地)。 a sportsman, born in the southern Italy, won the first place at least 6 times in the Ancient Olympic Games

12. Hippodrome 露天跑道 (in ancient Greece or Rome) an open-air course for horse and chariot races

13. Theodosius I 狄奥多西大帝一般指狄奥多西一世。 called the Great. ? 346 – 395 AD, Roman emperor of the Eastern Roman Empire (379 – 395) and of the Western Roman Empire (392 – 395)

- **Reading Comprehension**

1. **Directions**: *Discuss the following questions with your classmates.*

   1) Try to describe the Ancient Olympic Games with some words in the text.

   2) How long history does the Ancient Olympic Games have?

   3) Why the Ancient Greece held the Games?

   4) Who is Kyniska and what did she do in the Games?

   5) Where is the Olympia and why the ancient Greek held the Games there?

   6) How many facts do you know about the Games and what are they?

2. **Directions**: *Read the following statements carefully and decide whether they are true(T) or false(F) according to the text.*

   (　　)1) Pankration was a magnificently simple sport. Boasting huge men of incredible strength, it became a fountain of wondrous stories and stirring myths.

( ) 2) In "brutal" pankration one can bite and gouge because there were no restrictions.

( ) 3) With strict weight classifications, but no scoring system, no time limit and death a real possibility, boxing at the Ancient Olympic Games appears to have been a brutal and barbaric affair.

( ) 4) Diagoras of Rhodes is not just the greatest runner of the Ancient Olympic Games, he is arguably the most impressive Olympian of all-time.

( ) 5) The discus has a long tradition in the Greek world, first mentioned by Homer.

( ) 6) There were only five games in the Ancient Olympic Games: Pankration, Boxing, Running, Discus and Chariot Racing.

3. Critical thinking

1) What is the difference between the ancient and modern Olympics? Why?

2) Would the ancient Greece hold the Olympic Games if there were no threat from Persians?

After-Class Reading

Warm-up questions:

1. What is the most impressive traditional Chinese sport in your mind?
2. Which kind of traditional Chinese sport do you like best? Why?

Some Traditional Sports in China

Cuju

1 Cuju is an ancient ball game which is played in China. It is a ball sport which involves kicking a ball through an opening into the net. Using your hands are not allowed in this game. It is said that the game can be dated back to the **Warring States Period**[1].

2 Cuju was done as an entertainment in the folks and also at feasts which will celebrate the emperor's birthday or international events. In Han Dynasty Cuju was an item for military training. In this type, two teams play with 12 to 16 players each. Cuju went popular in the **Song Dynasty**[2]. In this type, scoring goals used methods like playing in a field enclosed using thread, and the players alternately kick the ball within the set limit

3 The winner is decided depending on the number of fouls of a player and the team with the most points. Points are deducted for some faults, for example, when a ball is not passed far enough to reach the other member. Low points are scored when the ball is kicked too low or kicked at the wrong moment.

Wushu (Kung Fu)

4 Wushu, or Kung Fu, is a general term for Chinese martial arts. Wushu actually means martial arts in Chinese: Wu means military or martial, and Shu means art. The sport of Wushu was developed from Chinese martial arts in the 1940s. The goal was to standardize the practice of traditional martial arts.

5 Wushu is also a combination of performance elements and martial arts. Wushu focuses on striking, grappling, throwing, quickness, explosive power, and relaxed movement. Contemporary Wushu includes a lot of Chinese martial art styles.

6 There are two Wushu disciplines, taolu (forms) and sanda (sparring):

- Taolu is a combination of martial art styles and movements in which competitors are assessed and scored according to rules. Taolu consists of basic movements: stances, kicks, punches, balances, jumps, and throws. Contemporary Taolu may be done with bare hands, short weapons, or long weapons.
- Sanda (sometimes called Sanshou) is a contemporary fighting style influenced by Chinese boxing. Sanda is more like **Muay Thai**[3], but it has grappling techniques.

7 Professional Sanda matches are conducted in boxing rings and fighters do not wear any protective gear. Scoring is based on strikes, but the points awarded for moves vary based on which organizing body conducts the tournament.

8 Sanda is also extensively practiced as a part of Wushu. Many **MMA**[4] fighters also use Sanda moves in fights and have been very successful.

Chinese Archery

9 For millennia, Chinese archery has played a pivotal role in Chinese society. In particular, archery featured prominently in ancient Chinese culture and philosophy: archery was one of the **Six Noble Arts**[5] of the Zhou Dynasty (1146 –256 BCE); archery skill was a virtue for Chinese emperors; **Confucius**[6] himself was an archery teacher; and **Liezi**[7] (a Daoist philosopher) was an

avid archer. Because the cultures associated with Chinese society spanned a wide geography and time range, the techniques and equipment associated with Chinese archery are diverse. The improvement of firearms and other circumstances of the 20th century China led to the demise of archery as a military and ritual practice, and for much of the 20th century only one traditional bow and arrow workshop remained. However, at the beginning of the 21st century, there has been a revival in interest among craftsmen looking to construct bows and arrows, as well as a practice technique in the traditional Chinese style.

Lion Dance

10 The Lion Dance is one of the most widespread folk dances in China. The lion is the king of animals. In Chinese tradition, the lion is regarded as a mascot, which can bring good luck. The dance has a recorded history of more than 2, 000 years. During the **Tang Dynasty**[8], the Lion Dance was already introduced into the royal family of the dynasty.

11 In the dance usually two people act as a lion: one waving the lion head and the other waving the lion body and tail; or one performer acts as a cub, while the other holds a silk ball to play with it. They dance in tempo to the musical melody.

12 Ancient people regarded the lion as a symbol of braveness and strength, which could drive away evil and protect humans and livestock. Therefore, performing the lion dance at the **Lantern Festival**[9] and other festive occasions became a custom where people could pray for good luck, safety, and happiness.

Dragon Boat

13 Every year during the Duan Wu Jie, also known as the Dragon Boat Festival or Dumpling festival, the act of dragon boat racing in rivers is reenacted in memory of **Qu Yuan**[10]. When Qu Yuan leaped into the **Miluo River**[11], in 278 BC, civilians around the area attempted to save him or to recover his body using their boats and creating noises to scare away sea creatures so that they would not attack Qu Yuan's body. **Zongzi**[12], or dumpling were also thrown into the river.

14 Now the boats are decorated to look like dragons and known as Dragon Boats. The Dragon Boat races are organized in various parts of China and are an important part of Duan Wu Jie celebration.

15 As overseas Chinese settled across the globe, this practice spread outside of China. The colorful dragon boats and the festive mood often attracted great attention. The Dragon boat celebration was appropriated and used for tourist consumption when the Hong Kong Tourism authority utilized it in their marketing campaign in the 1970s.

16 This initiative helped to popularized Dragon Boat racing around the world and transformed Dragon boat racing into a sport with a rich historical and cultural association.

While men were traditional participants in the Dragon Boat races, ladies have begun training and participating in competitions as well.

17 In 1991, the **International Dragon Boat Federation (IDBF)**[14] was founded in Hong Kong. Different member states took turns to organize an International Dragon Boat competition.

18 The spread and popularity of Dragon Boat racing created awareness of DuanWu Jie and popularized the history of Qu Yuan. Even if most people did not know of the exact historical background, most would know that it commemorated a "poet" or "Chinese minister" who committed suicide by throwing himself into a river.

19 Through this process, Qu Yuan becomes one of the most well-known Chinese historical personalities in the west and around the world.

Notes

1. Warring States Period 战国时期 The period of the Warring States (Zhanguo or Chan-Kuo) refers to the era of about 475 BCE to 221 BCE. It commenced at a time of when the numerous petty city-state kingdoms of the Spring and Autumn period had been consolidated into seven major contenders and a few minor enclaves.

2. Song Dynasty 宋朝 Song Dynasty (960–1279), Chinese dynasty that ruled the country during one of its most brilliant cultural epochs. It is commonly divided into Bei (Northern) and Nan (Southern) Song periods, as the dynasty ruled only in South China after 1127.

3. Muay Thai 泰拳 (Martial Arts [other than Judo & Karate] & Combat Sports) a martial art developed in Thailand in which blows may be struck with the fists, elbows, knees, and shins.

4. MMA 综合格斗 Mixed martial arts (MMA), hybrid combat sport incorporating techniques from boxing, wrestling, judo, jujitsu, karate, Muay Thai (Thai boxing), and other disciplines. Although it was initially decried by critics as a brutal blood sport without rules, MMA gradually shed its no-holds-barred image and emerged as one of the world's fastest-growing spectator sports in the early 21st century. MMA events are sanctioned in many countries and in all 50 U.S. states.

5. Six Noble Arts 六艺 The ancient traditional six arts can be dated back to the Zhou Dynasty, 1046 BCE. The noble class used the six arts as a standard to judge whether a son of aristocrats was fit to hold his title. The six arts included courtesy, music, archery, riding, writing and math.

6. Confucius 孔子 Confucius, original name Kongqiu, literary name Zhongni (born 551BCE, Qufu, state of Lu [now in Shandong Province, China]; died 479 BCE, Lu), China's most famous teacher, philosopher, and political theorist, whose ideas have profoundly influenced the civilizations of China and other East Asian countries.

7. Liezi 列子 (Chinese: "Master Lie") original name Lie Yukou (flourished 4th century BCE, China), one of the three primary philosophers who developed the basic tenets of Daoist philosophy and the presumed author of the Daoist work *Liezi* (also known as *Chongxu Zhide Zhenjing* ["True Classic of the Perfect Virtue of Simplicity and Emptiness"]).

8. Tang Dynasty 唐朝 Tang Dynasty (618–907), Chinese dynasty that succeeded the short-lived Sui Dynasty (581–618), developed a successful form of government and administration on the Sui model, and stimulated a cultural and artistic flowering that amounted to a golden age. The Tang Dynasty—like most—rose in duplicity and murder, and it subsided into a kind of anarchy. But at its apex, in the early 8th century, the splendor of its arts and its cultural milieu made it a model for the world.

9. Lantern Festival 元宵节 The Lantern Festival or the Spring Lantern Festival is a Chinese festival celebrated on the fifteenth day of the first month in the lunisolar Chinese calendar. Usually falling in February or early March on the Gregorian calendar, it marks the final day of the traditional Chinese New Year celebrations. As early as the Western Han Dynasty (206 BCE–25 CE), it had become a festival with great significance. During the Lantern Festival, children go out at night carrying paper lanterns and solve riddles on the lanterns.

10. Qu Yuan 屈原 Qu Yuan, one of the greatest poets of ancient China and the earliest known by name. His highly original and imaginative verse had an enormous influence over early Chinese poetry.

11. Miluo River 汨罗江 The Miluo River is located on the eastern bank of Dongting Lake, the largest tributary of the Xiang River in the northern Hunan Province. It is an important river in the Dongting Lake watershed, known as the location of the ritual suicide in 278 BCE of Qu Yuan, a poet of Chu state during the Warring States Period, in protest against the corruption of the era.

12. zongzi 粽子 Zongzi is a traditional Chinese rice dish made of glutinous rice stuffed with different fillings and wrapped in bamboo leaves (generally of the species Indocalamus tessellatus), or sometimes with reed or other large flat leaves. They are cooked by steaming or boiling. In the Western world, they are also known as rice dumplings or sticky rice dumplings.

13. Dragon Boat Festival 龙舟节或者端午节 The English language name for the

holiday is Dragon Boat Festival, used as the official English translation of the holiday by the People's Republic of China. It is also referred to in some English sources as Double Fifth Festival which alludes to the date as in the original Chinese name.

14. International Dragon Boat Federation (IDBF)国际龙舟联合会

- **Reading Comprehension**

1. **Directions**: *Discuss the following questions with your classmates.*
   1) How many players are there in each Cuju team?
   2) What is Wushu, and can you define it?
   3) What is the difference between Taolu and Sanda?
   4) Archery was one of the Six Noble Arts, and what are the other five arts?
   5) How to play the lion dance?
   6) Why do the Chinese people hold the dragon boat racing on Duanwu Jie?
2. **Directions**: *Item I is the title of each part of the text. Item II is the idea mentioned in each part of the text. Match the idea with the title.*

________Cuju	A consists of basic movements
________Wushu	B Lie Zi (a Daoist philosopher) was good at it
________Taolu	C went popular in the Song Dynasty
________Sanda	D could pray for good luck, safety, and happiness
________Chinese Archery	E to standardize the practice of traditional martial arts
________Lion Dance	F was appropriated and used for tourist consumption
________Dragon Boat	G are conducted in boxing rings

Part Three

Topic-Related Activities

1. Case Study

Sports in Some Major Western Countries

Sport in the USA

1 The United States has been a powerhouse in world sports for a long time. Americans take great pride in their sporting accomplishments, and sports is an important part of their culture. There's no doubt, United States rule in well-known sports such as basketball, baseball and their home-grown sport of American football.

2 We may consider baseball as their traditional sport for it started in the 18th century, with a semi-pro National Baseball Club in the 1860s and from that point on, baseball became

the "national pastime" of Americans. Nowadays, the most played sport in the United States is football.

3 The United States also has hosted quite a number of Olympic Games from 1904 (St. Louis, Missouri) to 2002 (Salt Lake City, Utah), and will again in 2028 in LA. They have also won more than the average Olympic medals in virtually all sports.

4 Speaking of popularity, no one ever came close from the Michael Jordan. This man popularized NBA to the world in the 1980s to 1990s. He also was the most well-rounded and marketed athlete of his generation. No wonder, every basketball player looks up to him.

5 Major/Popular Sports of the USA: football (gridiron), basketball, baseball, ice hockey, tennis, soccer, golf, Nascar, martial arts/boxing.

Sport in Russia

6 Russia's traditional popular sport is Bandy (informally called "Russian hockey"). It is considered by the country as a national sport and is one of the biggest spectator sports. Although the modern rules of the game were written in England, Russians still claim to be the inventors of this sport.

7 Among the other most played sports in Russia are basketball, ice hockey, football, rugby league, handball, weightlifting, gymnastics, figure skating, biathlon, boxing, wrestling, martial arts, volleyball, rugby union, and skiing.

8 Russian athletes have been very successful on the world stage. Up until the break up of the USSR in 1991, the Soviets were one of the world's sporting superpowers, though Russian athletes are still a force to be reckoned with.

9 Lev Ivanovich Yashin, nicknamed as "The Black Spider" was a Soviet-Russian football goalkeeper, considered by many to be the greatest goalkeeper in the history of the game. He was also vice president of the Football Federation of the Soviet Union. Andrey Sergeyevich Arshavin is a Russian professional footballer who plays for FC Zenit Saint Petersburg. He is an ex-captain of the Russian national team. Arshavin began his career at Zenit in the year 2000. He won numerous trophies with the club until his departure in 2009 including the Russian Premier League, Russian Premier League Cup, Russian Super Cup, UEFA Cup and the UEFA Super Cup.

10 Notable international sporting events recently held in Russia include the 2014 Winter Olympics and Paralympics, and the 2018 FIFA World Cup.

11 Popular sports of Russia: football (soccer), figure skating, basketball, ice hockey, tennis, handball, weightlifting, gymnastics, figure skating, biathlon, boxing, wrestling, volleyball, skiing, rugby union.

Sport in the United Kingdom

12 Commonly known as Great Britain or the UK, the United Kingdom is one of the most populated states in the world. Athletes from this region sometimes compete as the United Kingdom or Great Britain, and other times they represent their home country of England, Scotland, Wales, or Northern Ireland.

13 The United Kingdom is home to many sports like golf, cricket, rugby, boxing but none so as football. Jacques Rogge, IOC President was once quoted saying, "This great, sports-loving country is widely recognized as the birthplace of modern sport. It was here that the concepts of sportsmanship and fair play were first codified into clear rules and regulations. It was here that sport was included as an educational tool in the school curriculum."

14 UK is recognized by many governing bodies, including FIFA, as the birthplace of modern football with rules dating back as far as 1863. The UK also is the home of the most watched football league in the whole world, the Premier League.

15 David Beckham is definitely one of the most popular football players, and he has consistently ranked among the highest earners in football, and in 2013 was listed as the highest-paid player in the world, having earned over $50 million in the previous 12 months. He has been married to Victoria Beckham since 1999 and they have four children. He has been a UNICEF UK ambassador since 2005, and in 2015 he launched 7: The David Beckham UNICEF Fund.

16 Although football seems to run in every English vein, there are also a lot of sports that flourish in the UK. Rugby union is ranked as the second most popular sport in the UK. The first ever international rugby match was also between England and Scotland which took place on March 27, 1871.

17 Popular sports of the UK: football (soccer), cricket, netball, field hockey, rugby union, rugby league.

Sport in France

18 There are a lot of sports that the French love, including judo, football, tennis and rugby union. France has also hosted a lot of international sporting events like the FIFA World Cup (1938 and 1998), Rugby World Cup (2007) and the biggest cycling race, Tour de France.

19 There are also various tennis events that are held in France, among which the main one is the French Open, one of the four Grand Slam tourneys. France also is one of the biggest proponents of the revival of the Olympic Games in the end of the 19th century.

20 Football is the most popular sport in France with 18,000 registered clubs that have a total of well over 1,800,000 players in their rosters. The French national football team with

the name of "Les Bleus" is one of the most successful teams in the world with two FIFA World Cups (1998 and 2018), one FIFA World Cup second place (2006), as well as two UEFA European Championships (1984 and 2000). France has also produced many record holders such as Zinedine Zidane who was awarded the FIFA World Player of the Year three times, Michel Paltini who is a three-time recipient of the Ballon d'Or, Raymond Kopa who was the first football player to receive the Legion d'honneur, the all-time leading goalscorer of the national team Thierry Henry and the Just Fontaine who holds the record of most goals scored in a World Cup.

21 The French also love rugby union and have participated in every Rugby World Cup as well as the annual Six Nations Championships. They have won 16 Six Nations Championships that include 8 grand slam victories. They have also reached the semi-finals of the Rugby Cup 6 times as well as 3 finals. Basketball is also quite popular, and they have won the FIBA EuroBasket 2013 and have also taken two Olympic silver medals.

22 Popular sports of France: football (soccer), tennis, cycling, basketball, handball, rugby.

Sport in Australia

23 Australia has a rich history in sport on the world stage, and in many cases performs well above expectations based on its relatively small population.

24 The most popular national sport in Australia is cricket, in which Australians are very successful at. There are two major football codes Rugby League played predominantly in New South Wales and Queensland, and Aussie Rules popular in Victoria, South Australia, Tasmania and Western Australia. Rugby Union and Association Football (known mostly as soccer) is also played. The most popular female sport is netball.

25 Australians also love water sports, and Australia has been a superpower when it comes to swimming since the late 1950s. Swimmers like Dawn Fraser, Shane Gould, Kieren Perkins and Ian Thorpe have all taken in multiple gold medals since the 1956 Melbourne Olympics. Australia has hosted the Olympics twice (1956 and 2000).

26 Popular sports of Australia :AFL, cricket, Rugby League, Rugby Union, netball, football (soccer), Tennis.

Questions

1) Why has the United States been a powerhouse in the world sports for a long time?
2) Which country held the 2018 FIFA World Cup?
3) Which country is the champion of the 1998 FIFA World Cup?
4) Which country is the home to many sports?
5) What is the most popular national sport in Australia?

2. Critical Thinking & Cultural Exploration

Step One

Directions: *Ask students to discuss the most popular sports in the major eastern countries and to see if there are differences from their thoughts before.*

Step Two

Directions: *Please work in pairs and match the nation in Column A with relevant players in Column B and talk about their achievements.*

Column A		Column B
USA		Andrey Sergeyevich Arshavin
Russia		Raymond Kopa
United Kingdom		Michael Jordan
France		Dawn Fraser
Australia		David Beckham

Step Three

Directions: *Do you know about sports in other countries like Germany, Japan? And try to talk about it.*

3. Situational Conversation

Directions: *Work in pairs to talk about the most possible gold medals that a country would win in Olympic Games.*

A: The Olympic Games is coming. Which country do you think will win the first place?

B: China, the United States and Russia are the most possible ones.

A: You said it. China would win the table tennis, diving and weightlifting...

Unit Five

Body Language

Part One

Lead-in

To know what people think, pay regard to what they do, rather than what they say.

—René Descartes

The study of how body movements communicate is called kinesics. Kinesics behaviors are those visible body shifts and movements that indicate your attitude toward the other person (nodding your head when listening to your interlocutor), your emotional state (blushing if you feel a sense of shame), and your desire to control your environment (waving your hand when meeting a group of people). Many aspects of your body language will leak what you truly think about, but others can better understand this body language only by together taking all your verbal and nonverbal behaviors into considerations. That means it is advisable to understand a person's body language through studying carefully the context.

Part Two

In-Class Reading

Warm-up questions:

1. What is body language?
2. Why is body language important for communication?

Understanding Body Language

1 In our own time when most of us are increasingly **attuned** to the psychological and sociological **overtones** of human behavior, considerations of nonverbal communication or body language become more significant. Such communication has of course been practical from human beings' earliest evolution, but **systematized** awareness and observation of the phenomenon are relatively new. Recent studies of the subject, with which this article is primarily concerned, are important not only because of their **inherent** interest but also because they provide a practical means of understanding why people behave as they do. Such **inquiries** become invaluable to those engaged in professional pursuits involving human behavior: social workers, psychologists, and teachers in general and **counselors** in particular.

2 The school counselor uses the verbal interview for obtaining information that will help him or her assess the client and develop a plan of action. In the physical setting of the counseling process, the counselor is aware of appearance, **esthetic** quality, comfort and privacy or lack of privacy and comfort, and general climate. The counselor also receives other messages from the client in the form of nonverbal communication or body language. This

nonverbal communication gives **insight** into the significance of gestures that are often only vaguely understood or completely ignored. The counselor is constantly exposed to a vast field of nonverbal communication that complements, supplements, and at times **displaces** verbal exchanges. In fact, body language can actually **contradict** verbal communication. If counselors want to understand human social behavior, they will have to become fully aware of the messages being sent by body movements. The idea of nonverbal communication has **fascinated** sculptors, painters, and actors for centuries. They knew how much was conveyed in a **gesture**, a **posture**, or a look. Early in this century there was a real scientific interest in nonverbal communication, and from about 1914 to 1940 there was considerable interest in how people send messages by their facial expressions. **Anthropologists** learned that body motions are not random but learned like a language. "We respond to gestures with an **extreme** alertness and, one might almost say, in accordance with an **elaborate** code that is written nowhere, known by none, and understood by all".

3 Although anthropologists were aware of body language, they made no systematic approach to finding the key to this mysterious form of communication. During the 1950s, Ray L. Birdwhistell, Erving Goffman, Albert E. Scheflen, Edward T. Hall, and Paul Ekman attempted to **decipher** body language scientifically. In the early stages of their work their findings were met with **skepticism** and amused rejection. But attitudes have changed. The new scientific **enthusiasm** for communication research has its roots in the research done by the leaders in the field, and there is an enormous public interest in nonverbal communication.

4 Flora Davis, in her book Inside Intuition: What We Know About Non-verbal Communication, stated that communication research is the off-spring of five different disciplines: **psychology**[1], **psychiatry**[2], **anthropology**[3], **sociology**[4], and **ethology**[5]. It is a young and **contentious** science, with findings and research tactics often hotly disputed. The psychologist, for example, in looking at the whole stream of body motion, has in general picked out units of behavior to study: perhaps eye contact, smiling, touching, or some combination of these. On the other hand, the experts in kinesics (study of body motion) generally favor the systems approach. One of its basic **tenets** is the belief that communication cannot be studied a unit at a time. It is an **integrated** system and must be analyzed as a whole. Psychiatrists have long recognized that the way an individual moves his body provides clues to his character, his emotions, and his reactions to the people around him. Felix Deutsch, over a period of many years, recorded the couch postures of his patients. Then there are the sociologists, who have observed and described a kind of **subliminal etiquette** to which nearly all of us conform. For example, we all know how to avoid a head-on collision on a busy sidewalk, though we are hard put to say exactly how we do it.

5 Anthropologists have looked at the different cultural idioms in the language of the body and have discovered that an Arab, and an Englishman, a black American, and a white one, really do not move in quite the same way. **Ethologists** have made their contribution, too. In several decades of studying animals in the wild, they have turned up startling similarities between the nonverbal behavior of man and that of the other **primates**. Struck by this phenomenon, some are now turning to "human ethology," studying how people court, raise the young, dominate others or signal submission, quarrel and make up. This very physical behavior can then be compared with the way monkeys and apes handle the same relationship. What is human ethology?

6 So beyond words lies the **bedrock** on which human relationships are built-nonverbal communication. Words are beautiful, exciting, important, but we have overestimated them badly—since they are not all, or even half the message. In fact, as one scientist suggested: "Words may be what men use when all else fails."

7 According to Brill, "Non-verbal communication is the basic, **primitive** form of conveying information from one person to another. It has been estimated that in a normal communication between two people, only one-third of the meaning is transmitted on a verbal level, and nearly two-thirds on a non-verbal level".

8 A study of body language is a study of the mixture of all body movements from the very **deliberate** to the completely **unconscious**, from those that apply only in one culture to those that cut across all cultural barriers. To understand body language, kinesics experts take into consideration cultural and environmental differences. Kinesics is based on the behavioral patterns of nonverbal communication. Body movements and postural adjustments often reflect attitudes and feelings.

9 In our culture, verbal behavior is closely observed and **stereotyped**, but bodily acts are seldom noticed and have few recognized meanings. As a result, verbal behavior is carefully edited, but body movements remain free avenues of expression. Body language can include any non-reflexive or **reflexive** movement of part or all the body used by a person to communicate a message to the outside world. People are usually very open in communicating their inner thoughts and feelings nonverbally. Facial expressions such as eye contact, smiling, walking gestures, shoulder position, shaking hands, or **clenched** fists are just a few examples of such communication.

10 Nonverbal messages are conveyed through the person as well as the setting. Personal appearance—**physique**, posture, body **odor**, dress, tension, facial expressions, behavior, silence or speech, tone and quality of voice, gestures or movements, eye contact, touch, body sounds—all convey messages to the receiver as does the physical setting.

11 Our students sometimes send out messages by touching the counselor, which can mean I am lonely, I am starved for **companionship**, or simply, Help me. **Depressed** people have a tendency not to talk. They are saying, Leave me alone. We all give different signals to others. For example, lifting an eyebrow to show disbelief, rubbing the nose for puzzlement, **clasping** our arms to isolate or protect ourselves, shrugging shoulders for indifference, winking an eye for **intimacy**, tapping fingers for impatience, and slapping the forehead for forgetfulness.

(Excerpt, by Lester M. Sielski)

New Words and Expressions

attune /ə'tjuːn/ — *v.* adjust or accustom to; bring into harmony with 使协调;使调和;调音

overtone /'əʊvətəʊn/ — *n.* (usually plural) an ulterior implicit meaning or quality 暗示;弦外音;寓意

systematize /'sɪstəmətaɪz/ — *v.* arrange according to a system or reduce to a system 使系统化

inherent /ɪn'hɪərənt/ — *adj.* existing as an essential constituent or characteristic 固有的;内在的

inquiry /ɪn'kwaɪərɪ/ — *n.* a search for knowledge 调查;询问;打听;查问

counselor /'kaʊnsələ/ — *n.* someone who gives advice about problems 顾问;参事

esthetic /es'θetɪk/ — *adj.* concerning or characterized by an appreciation of beauty or good taste 审美的;美学的

insight /'ɪnsaɪt/ — *n.* clear or deep perception of a situation 洞察力;见识;深刻的理解

displace /dɪs'pleɪs/ — *v.* take the place of or have precedence over 取代;移置;替换

contradict /ˌkɒntrə'dɪkt/ — *v.* be opposite in nature or character to sth. 反驳;与……矛盾

fascinate /'fæsɪneɪt/ — *v.* charm, attract or interest greatly 使着迷,使极感兴趣

gesture /'dʒestʃə(r)/ — *n.* movement of the body or hands to show what one feels or thinks 手势; 姿势

posture /'pɒstʃə(r)/ — *n.* attitude or position of the body 姿势,姿态

anthropologist /ˌænθrə'pɒlədʒɪst/ — *n.* a social scientist who specializes in anthropology 人类学家

elaborate /ɪ'læbəreɪt/ — *adj.* very detailed and complicated; carefully prepared and finished 复杂的; 精心制作的

decipher /dɪ'saɪfə(r)/ — *v.* convert code into ordinary language 译解;辨认

skepticism /'skeptɪsɪzəm/ — *n.* doubt about the truth of something 怀疑论;怀疑态度;怀疑主义

enthusiasm /ɪnˈθjuːziæzəm/　*n.* object of admiring or interesting 巨大兴趣,热衷的事物
psychiatry /saɪˈkaɪətri/　*n.* the branch of medicine dealing with the diagnosis and treatment of mental disorders 精神病学
sociology /ˌsəʊsiˈɒlədʒi/　*n.* the study and classification of human societies 社会学
contentious /kənˈtenʃəs/　*adj.* inclined or showing an inclination to dispute or disagree, even to engage in law suits 好辩的;好争吵的;有争议的
tenet /ˈtenɪt/　*n.* a religious doctrine that is proclaimed as true without proof 教义;信条;原则;宗旨
integrate /ˈɪntɪɡreɪt/　*v.* join or cause (a member of a social group) to joint in society as a whole; join to sth. else 整合;结合
subliminal /ˌsʌbˈlɪmɪnl/　*adj.* below the threshold of conscious perception 下意识的;潜意识的
etiquette /ˈetɪket/　*n.* rules governing socially acceptable behavior 礼仪;礼节;规矩
ethologist /ɪˈθɒlədʒɪst/　*n.* a zoologist who studies the behavior of animals in their natural habitats (个体)生态学研究者, 行为研究者
primate /ˈpraɪmeɪt/　*n.* a member of the group of mammals that includes humans, monkeys, and apes 灵长目动物
bedrock /ˈbedrɒk/　*n.* solid unweathered rock lying beneath surface deposits of soil; principles from which other truths can be derived 岩床;根底;基础;基本原则
primitive /ˈprɪmətɪv/　*adj.* of or at the earliest stage of the development 原始的
deliberate /dɪˈlɪbərət/　*adj.* carefully considered 深思熟虑的;故意的
unconscious /ʌnˈkɒnʃəs/　*adj.* not conscious; lacking awareness and the capacity for sensory perception as if asleep or dead 失去知觉的;无意的
stereotype /ˈsteriətaɪp/　*v.* have, show, or encourage a fixed and usually incorrect idea of what (sb. or sth.) is like; regard as an example of a general type 对……形成模式化的看法
reflexive /rɪˈfleksɪv/　*adj.* without volition or conscious control 反射性的;反身的
clenched /klentʃ/　*v.* close or hold tightly; grasp firmly 紧握;紧咬;牢牢地抓住;确定
physique /fɪˈziːk/　*n.* constitution of the human body 体格;体形
odor /ˈəʊdə/　*n.* the sensation that results when olfactory receptors in the nose are stimulated by particular chemicals in gaseous form 气味
companionship /kəmˈpænjənʃɪp/　*n.* the state of being with someone 友谊;陪伴;交情
depress /dɪˈpres/　*v.* lower someone's spirits; make downhearted 使沮丧;压下;使萧条;降低;压抑

clasp /klɑːsp/ *v.* hold tightly or closely 扣紧
intimacy /ˈɪntɪməsi/ *n.* close or warm friendship 亲密;隐私

Notes

1. psychology 心理学 Psychology is the science of mind and behavior. Psychology includes the study of conscious and unconscious phenomena, as well as feelings and thoughts. It is an academic discipline of immense scope. Psychologists seek an understanding of the emergent properties of brains, and all the variety of phenomena linked to those emergent properties, joining this way the broader neuro-scientific group of researchers. As a social science, it aims to understand individuals and groups by establishing general principles and researching specific cases. In this field, a professional practitioner or researcher is called a psychologist and can be classified as a social, behavioral, or cognitive scientist. Psychologists attempt to understand the role of mental functions in individual and social behavior, while also exploring the physiological and biological processes that underlie cognitive functions and behaviors. Psychologists explore behavior and mental processes, including perception, cognition, attention, emotion, intelligence, subjective experiences, motivation, brain functioning, and personality. This extends to interaction between people, such as interpersonal relationships, including psychological resilience, family resilience, and other areas.

2. psychiatry 精神病学 Psychiatry is the medical specialty devoted to the diagnosis, prevention, and treatment of mental disorders. These include various maladaptations related to mood, behaviour, cognition, and perceptions. Initial psychiatric assessment of a person typically begins with a case history and mental status examination. Physical examinations and psychological tests may be conducted. On occasion, neuroimaging or other neurophysiological techniques are used. Mental disorders are often diagnosed in accordance with clinical concepts listed in diagnostic manuals such as the International Classification of Diseases (ICD), edited and used by the World Health Organization (WHO) and the widely used Diagnostic and Statistical Manual of Mental Disorders (DSM), published by the American Psychiatric Association (APA).

3. anthropology 人类学 Anthropology is the scientific study of humanity, concerned with human behavior, human biology, and societies, in both the present and past, including past human species. Social anthropology studies patterns of behaviour, while cultural anthropology studies cultural meaning, including norms and values. Linguistic anthropology studies how language influences social life. Biological or physical anthropology studies the biological development of humans. Visual anthropology, which is usually considered to be a part of social anthropology, can mean both ethnographic film (where photography, film, and

new media are used for study) as well as the study of "visuals", including art, visual images, cinema, etc. Oxford Bibliographies describe visual anthropology as "the anthropological study of the visual and the visual study of the anthropological".

4. sociology 社会学 Sociology refers to social behavior, society, patterns of social relationships, social interaction, and culture that surrounds everyday life. It is a social science that uses various methods of empirical investigation and critical analysis: to develop a body of knowledge about social order and social change. Sociology can also be defined as the general science of society. While some sociologists conduct research that may be applied directly to social policy and welfare, others focus primarily on refining the theoretical understanding of social processes. Subject matter can range from micro-level analyses of society (i. e. of individual interaction and agency) to macro-level analyses (i. e. of systems and the social structure). Traditional focuses of sociology include social stratification, social class, social mobility, religion, secularization, law, sexuality, gender, and deviance. As all spheres of human activity are affected by the interplay between social structure and individual agency, sociology has gradually expanded its focus to other subjects and institutions, such as health and the institution of medicine; economy; military; punishment and systems of control; the Internet; education; social capital; and the role of social activity in the development of scientific knowledge. The range of social scientific methods has also expanded, as social researchers draw upon a variety of qualitative and quantitative techniques. The linguistic and cultural turns of the mid-20th century, especially, have led to increasingly interpretative, hermeneutic, and philosophic approaches towards the analysis of society. Conversely, the turn of the 21st century has seen the rise of new analytically, mathematically, and computationally rigorous techniques, such as agent-based modeling and social network analysis.

5. ethology 动物行动学;人种学 Ethology is the study of animal behavior based on the systematic observation, recording, and analysis of how animals function, with special attention to physiological, ecological, and evolutionary aspects. Laboratory or field experiments designed to test a proposed explanation must be rigorous, repeatable, and show the role of natural selection. At one time, an organism's actions were classified as either instinctive or learned behavior; the former included those actions, such as common reflexes, that are not influenced by the animal's previous experience; the latter comprised those actions, such as problem solving, that are dependent on earlier experiences. Current thinking emphasizes the complex interaction of environment and genetically determined responses, especially during early development. Among the early ethologists were Herbert Spencer, Charles Darwin, G. J. Romanes, and William James. Zoologists Konrad Lorenz and Nikolaas Tinbergen are widely considered to be the founders of modern ethology. In 1973 they and zoologist Karl von Frisch

were awarded the Nobel Prize in Physiology or Medicine for their work in shaping the science of comparative animal behavior.

- **Reading Comprehension**

1. **Directions**: *Discuss the following questions with your classmates.*
   1) Who will benefit from doing the inquiries of the body language?
   2) How does the school counselor obtain information that will help him or her assess the client?
   3) What did anthropologists learn according to Sapir in 1940s?
   4) What are the five disciplines that give birth to communication research?
   5) What is human ethology?
   6) Why is non-verbal communication the basic, primitive form of conveying information?
2. **Directions**: *Read the following statements carefully, and decide whether they are true (T) or false (F) according to the text.*
   (   ) 1) To understand body language, kinesics experts take into consideration cultural and environmental differences.
   (   ) 2) Body movements and postural adjustments seldom reflect attitudes and feelings.
   (   ) 3) Verbal behavior is closely observed and stereotyped, but bodily acts are seldom noticed and have few recognized meanings.
   (   ) 4) Eye contact, smiling, walking gestures, shoulder position, shaking hands and clenched fists are not all examples of body language.
   (   ) 5) Nonverbal messages are conveyed through the person as well as the setting.
   (   ) 6) Personal appearance—physique, posture, body odor, dress, tension, facial expressions, behavior, silence or speech, tone and quality of voice, gestures or movements, eye contact, touch, body sounds—all convey messages to the receiver as does the physical setting.
3. **Directions**: *List as many as possible the examples of body language according to the text.*

• **Discussion**

1. Study examples of body language, and then work in groups to supply the verbal counterpart of their body language.
2. Spend some time in the classroom, make a list of your classmates' body language and then work in groups to tell what those actions mean.

After-Class Reading

Warm-up questions:

1. What is the most impressive example of Chinese body language?
2. What body language do you often use consciously and unconsciously?

Gestures

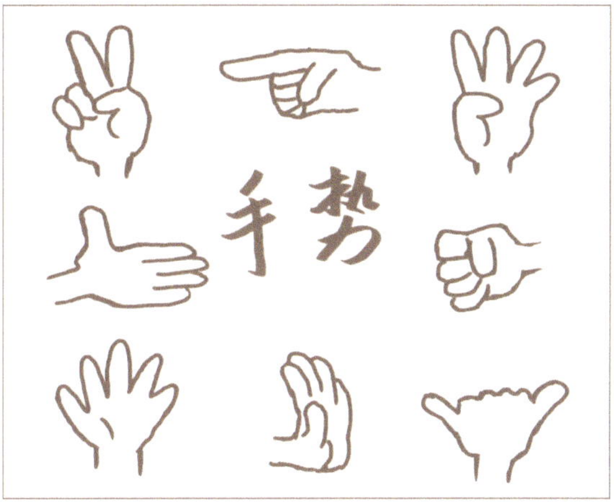

1 The body speaks through gestures. Gestures can be fitted together so that a complete picture evolves that gives the interviewer keys to the attitudes and feelings of those being observed. Gestures are grouped into a number of different clusters that indicate various dispositions and sentiments, such as

1. Openness—Men who are open or friendly frequently unbutton their coats or even take them off. A woman will have her hands down at her side.

2. Defensiveness—The very young will cross or clasp their arms when defying their parents' instructions, the very old cross their arms when they want to be heard, and others cross their arms to isolate or protect themselves.

3. Evaluation—A person who strikes a pose with hand on cheek, stroking the chin, and cocking the head slightly to one side may be said to be evaluating a situation.

4. Rejection—The most obvious gestures of the rejection group are folding the arms, moving the body away, crossing the legs and tilting the head forward, the person either peering over his or her glasses or squinting as if trying to see what is said more clearly.

5. Doubt, suspicion, puzzlement—A person rubbing or touching his or her nose lightly

with his or her index finger after being asked a question is expressing doubt or puzzlement. This gesture is usually accompanied by squirming in a chair, twisting the body into a silhouette position, or physically withdrawing.

6. Readiness—This gesture includes the posture of hands on hips, feet apart, as a running back waiting on the sidelines ready to enter the game. The person is indicating that he or she is ready and able to enter the game.

7. Reassurance—In adults, clenched hands with thumbs rubbing against each other is a common reassurance gesture. A child needing reassurance sucks his or her thumb, and a teenager worried about examinations or a date bites his or her nails.

8. Cooperation—A person sitting forward in his or her chair, feet on tiptoes, and tilting his or her head indicates that at least he or she is listening.

9. Silence—A potent form of non-verbal communication, it creates great anxiety and may be interpreted as an expression of hostility.

10. Mouth covering—The person may place his or her hand over the mouth. This gesture occurs when a speaker has been told to be quiet or when he or she has uttered a prohibited or embarrassing comment.

11. Hands outstretched, palms up—The person extends his lower arms and turns his palms out. This gesture means helplessness or resignation.

12. Eye pointing—The person will point to his or her own eye with an index finger or place a finger on the eye. This act demands attention or recognition.

13. Confidence—Confident persons have more frequent and longer lasting eye contact than those who are unsure. The confident person usually has a proud, erect stance, makes a few hand-to-face gestures when speaking, and is inclined to make gestures with his or her hands.

14. Nervousness—This is expressed by gestures such as fidgeting in a chair, jingling money in pockets, tugging at pants while sitting, biting on lip, and picking at fingernails.

15. Self-control—Holding an arm behind the back and clenching the hand tightly while the other hand grips the wrist or arm is a common gesture of self-control.

16. Boredom—A woman may indicate boredom by crossing her legs and then moving her foot in a slight kicking motion. Doodling, finger drumming, or foot tapping also indicate waning interest.

17. Acceptance—Moving closer to another person, thereby closing the gap between you, is an indicator of acceptance.

18. Honesty, credibility, sincerity—The palm is placed over the heart; frown—

disapproval; lying—person draws the index finger under the nostrils.

2 Other illustrations of meaningful gestures are

1. Fondling and touching inanimate objects gives a message that the person is lonely or is asking for companionship.
2. Lifting one eyebrow—disbelief.
3. Shrugging the shoulders—indifference.
4. Winking one eye—intimacy.
5. Tapping fingers—impatience.
6. Slapping the forehead—forgetfulness.
7. Turning up the corners of the mouth—happiness.
8. Turning down the corners of the mouth—discontent.
9. Shaking the head up and down—yes (but in India it means no).
10. Moving the head from side to side—no (but in India it means yes)

3 When two people are sitting on a couch and they cross their outside legs into each other, this gesture means that they are excluding the other people in the room. Face-to-face arrangements between two people mean that feelings or information is being exchanged. In situations in which a participant disapproves of another person but is constrained to approve, he or she will carry out kinesic actions that ordinarily serve to groom or clean himself or herself, for example, picking imaginary lint from the clothing.

4 As a person suggests a course of action he or she points a finger and drops the eyelids. This metasignal seems the equivalent of saying, if you can't see the wisdom of this course of action, then you are really naive. We cannot say that a certain gesture has one meaning all the time. Body language, just as spoken language, can be accurately understood only in the context of the entire behavior pattern of a person. Spoken language alone will not give us the full meaning of what someone is saying, but neither will body language alone.

(Excerpt, by Lester M. Sielski)

• Reading Comprehension

1. **Directions:** *Read the passage quickly and match each of the body language with its appropriate meaning.*

1) ________ Lifting one eyebrow **A.** intimacy

2) ________ Shrugging the shoulders **B.** disbelief

3) ________ Winking one eye **C.** indifference

2. **Directions**: *Complete the following table with the missing information based on the text.*

Body Language	Tapping fingers	Slapping the forehead	Turning up the corners of the mouth	Shaking the head up and down
Illustration				

Part Three

Topic-Related Activities

1. Case Study

The Influence of Appearance

As Feraro states, in the United States "people spend millions of dollars each year on running shoes, diet plans, appetite suppressants, and health spa membership to help them take off 'ugly pounds'". This notion of leanness and trimness as sign of attractiveness is not the rule in all cultures. For example, in large parts of Africa, plumpness is considered a sign of beauty, health, and wealth, and slimness is evidence of unhappiness, disease, or mistreatment at the hands of one's husband. Among Chinese, you can see another cultural standard for female attractiveness. As Wenzhong and Grove note, "Many women keep their hairstyle simple (often one or two braids) and make little attempt to draw attention to themselves through self-decoration such as colorful scarves, jewelry, or makeup."

(Excerpt, by Larry A. Samovar, Richard E. Porter, Edwin R. McDaniel)

Questions

1) What is the judgment of beauty in the United States?

2) Why is the judgment of beauty in many parts of Africa opposite to that in the United

States?

3) What is female's attractiveness in China?

4) Why does judgment of beauty differ in different regions?

2. Critical Thinking & Cultural Exploration

Step One

Directions: *Ask students to brainstorm examples and cases of body language.*

Step Two

Directions: *Please work in groups to discuss the illustrations of the body language.*

Examples for reference: fingers crossed; thumps up; thumps down; making a round ring with the hand; gazing at a person; avoiding eye contact; pointing at someone.

Step Three

Directions: *Discuss in groups why people use body language as a way of communication.*

3. Translation

Directions: *Translate the passage into English.*

汉服,全称是"汉民族传统服饰",又称汉衣冠、汉装、华服,是从黄帝即位到公元17世纪中叶,在汉族的主要居住区,以"华夏-汉"文化为背景和主导思想,以华夏礼仪文化为中心,通过自然演化而形成的具有独特汉民族风貌性格,明显区别于其他民族的传统服装和配饰体系,是中国"衣冠上国""礼仪之邦""锦绣中华"的体现,承载了汉族的染织绣(embroider)等杰出工艺和美学,传承了30多项中国非物质文化遗产以及受保护的中国工艺美术。

Unit Six

Values

Part One

Lead-in

Values are like a life compass; they represent a significant part of who we are.

—Dris Mi

Regardless of what we value or why, the importance of values cannot be ignored. They are the guideposts of our lives, and they direct us to who we want to be. By doing that, they help us become who we are and are a huge part of our makeup, ethical compass, and, ultimately, personality.

Part Two

In-Class Reading

Warm-up questions:

1. How much do you know about Western values?
2. What's the importance of understanding the values of a nation?

So you're going to visit the United States? Great! But be prepared: the values Americans live by may seem strange to you. As a result, you might find their actions confusing, even unbelievable. This is the kind of advice Dr. L. **Robert Kohls**[1] gives first-time visitors to the United States. Kohls, Director of International Programs at San Francisco State University, has developed a list of 13 commonly held values which help explain why Americans act as they do. He is careful and **cautions** visitors also, to avoid **labeling** these values positive or negative. His aim: "I simply want to help you understand the Americans with whom you will be relating—from their own value system rather than from yours." Whether one agrees with Kohls or not—or is willing to accept as **valid** any generalizations about Americans—his observations are **thought-provoking**.

Why Do Americans Act Like That?

A guide to understand the U. S. culture and its values.

L. Robert Kohls

Personal Control over The Environment/Responsibility

1 Americans do not believe in the power of fate, and they look at people who do as being backward, **primitive**, or naive. In the American context, to be "**fatalistic**" is to be superstitious, lazy, or unwilling to take **initiative**. Everyone should have control over whatever in the environment might potentially affect him or her. The problems of one's life are not seen as having resulted from bad luck as much as having come from one's laziness and unwillingness to take responsibility in pursuing a better life.

Change Seen as Natural and Positive

2 In the American mind, change is seen as **indisputably** good, leading to development, improvement, progress. Many older, more traditional cultures consider change **disruptive** and

destructive; they value stability, continuity, tradition, and a rich and ancient heritage—none of which are considered very important in the United States.

Time and Its Control

3 Time is of **utmost** importance to most Americans. It is something to be on, kept, filled, saved, used, spent, wasted, lost, gained, planned, given, even killed. Americans are more concerned with getting things accomplished on time than they are with developing interpersonal relations. Their lives seem controlled by the little machines they wear on their wrists, cutting their discussions off **abruptly** to make their next appointment on time. This philosophy has enabled Americans to be extremely productive, and productivity is highly valued in their country.

Equality[2]/Fairness

4 Equality is so cherished in the U. S. that it is seen as having a religious basis. Americans believe that all people are "created equal" and that all should have an equal opportunity to succeed. This concept of equality is strange to seven-eighths of the world which views status and authority as **desirable**, even if they happen to be near the bottom of the social order. Since Americans like to treat foreigners "just like anybody else", newcomers to the U. S. should realize that no **insult** or personal **indignity** is intended if they are treated in a less-than-**deferential** manner by waiters in restaurants, clerks in stores and hotels, taxi drivers, and other service personnel.

Individualism[3]/Independence

5 Americans view themselves as highly **individualistic** in their thoughts and actions. They resist being thought of as representatives of any **homogeneous** group. When they do join groups, they believe they are special, just a little different from other members of the same group. In the U. S., you will find people freely expressing a variety of opinions anywhere and anytime. Yet, in spite of this "independence", almost all Americans end up voting for one of their two major political parties. Individualism leads to privacy, which Americans see as desirable. The word "privacy" does not exist in many non-Western languages. If it does, it is likely to have a negative **connotation**, suggesting loneliness or forced isolation. It is not uncommon for Americans to say, and almost to believe: "If I don't have half an hour a day to myself, I go **stark-raving mad**[4]!"

Self-Help Initiative

6 Americans take credit only for what they accomplish as individuals. They get no credit for having been born into a rich family but pride themselves in having climbed the ladder of success, to whatever level, all by themselves. In an English-language dictionary, there are more than 100 **composite** words that have the word "self" as a prefix: self-aware, self-

confident, self-conscious, self-contented, self-control, self-criticism, self-deception, self-defeating, self-denial. The **equivalent** of these words cannot be found in most other languages. It is an indicator of how highly Americans regard the "**self-made**[5]" man or woman.

Competition

7 Americans believe that competition brings out the best in any individual and in any system. This value is reflected in the American economic system of "free enterprise", and it is applied in the U. S. in all areas—medicine, the arts, education, sports.

Future Orientation

8 Americans value the culture and the improvements the future will surely bring. They **devalue** the past and are, to a large extent, unconscious of the present. Even a happy present goes largely unnoticed because Americans are hopeful that the future will bring even greater happiness. Since Americans believe that humans, not fate, can and should control the environment, they are good at planning short-term projects. This ability has caused Americans to be invited to all corners of the Earth to plan, and often achieve, the miracles which their goalsetting methods can produce.

Action/Work Orientation

9 "Don't just stand there," says a typical bit of American advice, "do something!" This expression, though normally used in a crisis situation, in a sense describes most Americans' waking life, where action—any action—is seen as superior to **inaction**. Americans **routinely** schedule an extremely active day. Any relaxation must be limited in time and aimed at "recreating" so that they can work harder once their "recreation" is over. Such a "no-nonsense" attitude toward life has created a class of people known as "**workaholics**"—people addicted to, and often wholly **identified** with, their job or profession. The first question people often ask when they meet each other in the U. S. is related to work: "What do you do?" "Where do you work?" or "Who (what company) are you with?" The United States may be one of the few countries in the world where people speak about the "dignity of human labor"—meaning hard physical labor. Even corporation presidents will engage in physical labor from time to time and, in doing so, gain rather than lose respect from others.

Informality

10 Americans are even more informal and casual than their close relatives—the Western Europeans. For example, American bosses often urge their employees to call them by their first names and feel uncomfortable with the title "Mr." or "Ms.". Dress is another area where American **informality** is most noticeable, perhaps even shocking. For example, one can go to a symphony performance in any large American city and find people dressed in blue jeans.

Informality is also apparent in Americans' greetings. The more formal "How are you?" has largely been replaced with an informal "Hi". This is as likely to be used with one's superior as with one's best friend.

Directness/Openness/Honesty

11 Many other countries have developed **subtle**, sometimes highly **ritualistic**, ways of informing others of unpleasant information. Americans prefer the direct approach. They are likely to be completely honest in delivering their negative evaluations, and to consider anything other than the most direct and open approach to be "dishonest" and "insincere". Anyone in the U.S. who uses an intermediary to deliver the message will also be considered "**manipulative**" and "untrustworthy". If you come from a country where saving face is important, be assured that Americans are not trying to make you **lose face**[6] with their directness.

Practicality/Efficiency

12 Americans have a reputation for being realistic, practical, and efficient. The practical consideration is likely to be given highest priority in making any important decision. Americans pride themselves in not being very philosophically or theoretically oriented. If Americans would even admit to having a philosophy, it would probably be that of **pragmatism**[7]. Will it make money? What is the "bottom line"? What can I gain from this activity? These are the kinds of questions Americans are likely to ask, rather than: Is it aesthetically pleasing? Will it be enjoyable? Will it advance the cause of knowledge? This **pragmatic** orientation has caused Americans to contribute more inventions to the world than any other country in human history. The love of "practicality" has also caused Americans to view some professions more favorably than others. Management and economics are much more popular in the United States than philosophy or anthropology, and law and medicine more valued than the arts. Americans **belittle** "emotional" and "subjective" evaluations in favor of "rational" and "objective" assessments. Americans try to avoid being "too **sentimental**" in making their decisions. They judge every situation "on its own **merits**".

Materialism[8]/Acquisitiveness

13 Foreigners generally consider Americans much more **materialistic** than Americans are likely to consider themselves. Americans would like to think that their material objects are just the "natural benefits" that result from hard work and serious intent—a reward, they think, which all people could enjoy were they as **industrious** and hard-working as Americans. But by any standard, Americans are materialistic. They give a higher priority to obtaining, maintaining, and protecting material objects than they do in developing and enjoying relationships with people. Since Americans value newness and innovation, they sell or throw away their possessions frequently and replace them with newer ones. A car may be kept for

only two or three years, a house for five or six before buying a new one.

New Words and Expressions

caution /ˈkɔːʃn/ *v.* warn or admonish 警告；告诫

label /ˈleɪbl/ *v.* describe or classify 把……称为

valid /ˈvælɪd/ *adj.* well grounded in logic or truth or having legal force 有效的，有根据的

thought-provoking /ˈθɔːt prəvəʊkɪŋ/ *adj.* stimulating interest or thought 发人深省的；引起思考的

primitive /ˈprɪmətɪv/ *adj.* characterized by simplicity or crudity; unsophisticated 不懂世故的

fatalistic /ˌfeɪtəˈlɪstɪk/ *adj.* predetermined by fate and are therefore unalterable 宿命的

initiative /ɪˈnɪʃətɪv/ *n.* the first step or action of a matter; commencing move 主动

indisputably /ˌɪndɪˈspjuːtəbli/ *adv.* undoubtedly 毫无疑问地

disruptive /dɪsˈrʌptɪv/ *adj.* involving, causing, or tending to cause disruption 破坏的

utmost /ˈʌtməʊst/ *adj.* of the greatest possible degree or amount 最大的；极度的

abruptly /əˈbrʌptli/ *adv.* quickly and without warning 突然地；唐突地

desirable /dɪˈzaɪərəbl/ *adj.* worthy of desire or recommendation 值得拥有的，令人向往的

insult /ɪnˈsʌlt; ˈɪnsʌlt/ *n.* an offensive or contemptuous remark or action 辱骂；侮辱；冒犯

indignity /ɪnˈdɪgnəti/ *n.* injury to one's self-esteem or dignity; humiliation 侮辱

deferential /ˌdefəˈrenʃl/ *adj.* marked by or showing deference or respect; respectful 恭敬的，谦恭的

individualistic /ˌɪndɪˌvɪdʒuəˈlɪstɪk/ *adj.* concerned with the person rather than with society 个人主义的；利己主义的

homogeneous /ˌhɒməˈdʒiːniəs/ *adj.* composed of parts or elements that are all of the same kind 同种类的

connotation /ˌkɒnəˈteɪʃn/ *n.* an association or idea suggested by a word or phrase; implication 内涵，意义

composite /ˈkɒmpəzɪt/	*adj.* composed of separate parts; compound 复合的,合成的
equivalent /ɪˈkwɪvələnt/	*n.* something that is essentially equal to another 对等的事物
devalue /ˌdiːˈvæljuː/	*v.* reduce the value or worth of (something) 贬低;贬值
inaction /ɪnˈækʃn/	*n.* lack of action; idleness; inertia 不作为
routinely /ruːˈtiːnli/	*adv.* in an expected or customary manner 常规地;通常
workaholic /ˌwɜːkəˈhɒlɪk/	*n.* a person obsessively addicted to work 工作狂
identify /aɪˈdentɪfaɪ/	*v.* psychol (usually followed by with) to engage in identification 理解;认同
informality /ˌɪnfɔːˈmæləti/	*n.* the condition or quality of being informal 非正式;不拘礼节
subtle /ˈsʌtl/	*adj.* not immediately obvious or comprehensible 不易察觉的
ritualistic /ˌrɪtʃuəˈlɪstɪk/	*adj.* of, relating to, or suggestive of ritualism 仪式的;固守仪式的
manipulative /məˈnɪpjələtɪv/	*adj.* skillful in influencing or controlling others to your own advantage 操纵别人的
pragmatism /ˈprægmətɪzəm/	*n.* action or policy dictated by consideration of the immediate practical consequences rather than by theory or dogma 实用主义
pragmatic /prægˈmætɪk/	*adj.* advocating behaviour that is dictated more by practical consequences than by theory or dogma 实用主义的
belittle /bɪˈlɪtl/	*v.* consider or speak of (something) as less valuable or important than it really is 轻视;贬低
sentimental /ˌsentɪˈmentl/	*adj.* tending to indulge the emotions excessively 多愁善感的;感情用事的
merit /ˈmerɪt/	*n.* a deserving or commendable quality or act 优点
materialistic /məˌtɪəriəˈlɪstɪk/	*adj.* attaching too much importance to money and material possessions 物质至上的;金钱至上的
industrious /ɪnˈdʌstriəs/	*adj.* hard-working, diligent, or assiduous 勤奋的

Notes

1. Robert Kohls 罗伯特·科奥斯 a specialist in Intercultural Studies, Director of

International Programs at San Francisco State University

2. equality 平等　the state of being equal; As Thomas Jefferson wrote in The Declaration of Independence, "We hold these truths to be self-evident, that all men are created equal, that they are endowed by their Creator with certain unalienable rights, that among these are life, liberty, and the pursuit of happiness".

3. individualism 个人主义　belief in the primary importance of the individual and in the virtues of self-reliance and personal independence; it pertains to societies in which the ties between individuals are loose. Everyone is expected to look after himself or herself and his or her immediate family.

4. stark-raving mad 完全疯了　Totally crazy, as in the constant uncertainty over his job is making him stark raving mad. This term, meaning "completely wildly insane", is used both hyperbolically and literally. Versions of this expression appear to have sprungfrom the minds of great literary figures. Stark mad was first recorded by poet John Skelton in 1489; stark raving was first recorded by playwright John Beaumont in 1648; stark staring mad was first used by John Dryden in 1693. The current wording, stark raving mad, first appeared in Henry Fielding's *The Intriguing Chambermaid* in 1734.

5. self-made 靠自己奋斗成功的;白手起家的　owing wealth or important position to one's efforts, not to advantages given by birth, education etc.

6. lose face 丢面子　If you lose face, you do something that makes people stop admiring or respecting you. For example: He was too proud to lose face by looking nervous. You made him look bad. He lost face in front of his crew. Note: You can also say that something loses someone face. For example: The circumstances in which his most senior colleague resigned has lost him face with the Americans.

7. pragmatism 实用主义　A movement consisting of varying but associated theories, originally developed by Charles S. Peirce and William James and distinguished by the doctrine that the meaning or truth value of an idea or a proposition lies in its observable practical consequences.

8. materialism 物质主义　The doctrine that physical matter is the only reality and that everything, including thought, feeling, mind, and will, can be explained in terms of matter and physical phenomena.

• Reading Comprehension

1. **Directions**: *Discuss the following questions with your classmates.*

1) What values are Americans bestowed with?

2) What "to be fatalistic" is viewed as in the American context?

3) Why are Americans to be extremely productive?

4) How prevalent is individualism in America?

5) What are the traits of workaholics?

6) Do Americans give a higher priority to obtaining, maintaining, and protecting material objects or to developing and enjoying relationships with people?

2. **Directions:** *Read the following statements carefully, and decide whether they are true (T) or false (F) according to the text.*

( )1) Americans do believe in fate, and regard people who don't as being backward, primitive, or naive.

( )2) Many older, more traditional cultures consider change disturbing and destructive.

( )3) Americans are expected not to make their appointment punctually.

( )4) Newcomers to the U. S. should realize that no insult or personal indignity is intended if they are treated in a less than-deferential manner.

( )5) Individualism leads to privacy, which Americans see as desirable. The word privacy exists in many non-Western languages as well.

( )6) Americans appreciate the past and are conscious of the present in a large degree.

( )7) The United States may be one of the few countries in the world where people speak about the "dignity of human labor"—meaning hard physical labor.

( )8) American bosses often urge their employees to call them "Mr." or "Ms.", otherwise they might feel uncomfortable.

( )9) Anything other than the most direct and open approach is considered to be "dishonest" and "insincere" in America.

( )10) Philosophy or anthropology is much more popular in the United States than management or economics.

- **Discussion**

1. What American values do you prefer? And why?

2. Apart from the American values mentioned in the text, could you seek and list any more relevant information concerning what Americans believe in or value?

After-Class Reading

Warm-up questions:

1 What do you think are the most impressive Chinese values?

2. What philosophy do you think are Chinese values influenced by?

Chinese Values

Ⅰ. Connections

1 Possibly the most important possession to have in China is **guanxi**[1]: connections or the connectedness that helps open closed doors. While the Chinese legal system is maturing, its cultural milieu is still largely relational rather than legalistic. Most people place deeper trust in human relations than in the abstract law. Having the proper connections is essential for getting things done in China. Trying to navigate the Chinese bureaucracy without them can be excruciatingly slow, and often fruitless if you're trying to make a deal.

2 Introducers or **go-betweens**[2] can play several important roles in a business deal. Besides getting you in the door, they can also help smooth the way by acting as a back-channel for information. Additionally, they can often apply pressure through "**back scratching**"[3], calling in favors, and other "back door" methods.

Ⅱ. Reciprocal Obligation

3 Alliances and connections are often made through intentional acts as part of a strategy; **reciprocal**[4] obligation binds the parties. The concept of reciprocal obligation dictates that one must reciprocate favors, gifts, dinners, information, influence, introductions, etc. This obligation can become a valuable commodity: Depending on who the person is, just knowing that he or she "owes you one" can provide more peace of mind than a good insurance policy. Companies and government agencies can also incur obligation, and decisions may be made based on the need to fulfill outstanding obligation. When dealing with a Chinese company or agency, try to find out if it has unfulfilled obligation that could affect your proposal.

Ⅲ. Collective[5] Before Individuals

4 Compared to most Western societies, and especially the American society, Chinese are very group-oriented. Consequently, they tend to want to find protection in numbers and strive to make decisions based on a consensus. Once a consensus has been reached, however, individuals are usually expected to show loyalty to the group decision and fall in line.

5 The Chinese also like to feel connected by interdependent relationships, the sort that reciprocal obligation brings. Having an interdependent relationship with someone, however, makes you somewhat vulnerable, so being able to trust the other party becomes a critical issue. Therefore, building the right relationship, both with the right person and in the right way, is vital. Taking time to build a solid relationship before trying to do business is critical. And showing loyalty to those with whom you have a relationship is imperative.

Ⅳ. Respect for Hierarchy[6]

6 A legacy of **Confucianism**[7] is the Chinese devotion to the hierarchical system. Everyone has a social rank, and all are expected to know where they fit into the hierarchy and to behave accordingly. There are numerous ways that hierarchy is continually reaffirmed. For example, in a family of many children, younger siblings can never call their older siblings by name; rather they must address them as big brother, second big sister, third big brother, etc. Introductions in meetings, entry into a room, and seating arrangements are all determined by the hierarchy.

7 This means that it is important for you to find out where your counterparts fit into his or her hierarchy. Likewise you need to understand your position within your hierarchy and your status relative to your Chinese counterparts. If you are in a lower status in relationship to the person you are seeing, keep in mind that you will be expected to show some deference or respect to the person of higher status. If you are in a higher position than those around you, you are expected to live up to your status by being more reserved.

Ⅴ. Saving Face[8]

8 There is an Asian saying: Losing face is like dropping something down a well—the only way you can get it back is to go down after it. This means that if you cause someone to lose face, you must somehow humble yourself to retrieve it. If you do not, the only way that person can regain his or her respect is to force you down. Therefore, an incredible amount of time and effort are put into making sure no one loses face. A decision, for example, might be affected by the need to save face for an important person. Someone might stretch the truth as a face-saving measure. Disagreements are expected to be handled in private so that no one is publicly embarrassed. Even direct rejections are avoided in front of others, as a way of

protecting face. This means that if you do not have a go-between, or a close relationship with the people with whom you are working, you will have no means by which to receive and deliver the "real" truth.

Ⅵ. Protocol[9] and Ceremony

9 Embarrassment can mean a loss of face, and to avoid any loss of face, the Chinese desire the sort of predictability that an emphasis on formalities can bring. This means there is a prescribed way for doing everything. At a banquet, guests are met at the door and escorted to the banquet room or to their seats. People are then seated according to their rank. A formal banquet always begins with a toast by the host.

10 "Giving face" is also very important in China. This is a way of elevating a person in the eyes of others. Protocol rituals often exist not only to save face, but to give face to the other party. You use both hands to proffer your business card, for example, as a way of elevating the other party. Addressing others by their titles rather than by their given names shows respect and acknowledges their status within the group. During banquets, toasts are continually offered and reciprocated as a way of honoring and "giving face" to others.

Notes

1. guanxi 关系 a Chinese social concept based on the exchange of favours, in which personal relationships are considered more important than laws and written agreements

2. go-between 中间人 a person who acts as agent or intermediary for two people or groups in a transaction or dealing

3. back scratching, calling in favors, and "back door" 走关系、动用人脉、走"后门"

4. reciprocal 互惠的 done according to an arrangement by which you do something for someone who does the same thing for you

5. collective or collectivism 集体的或集体主义 the principles or system of ownership and control of the means of production and distribution by the people collectively, usually under the supervision of a government; it pertains to societies in which people from birth onwards are integrated into strong cohesive in-groups, which throughout people's lifetime continue to protect them in exchange for unquestioning loyalty.

6. hierarchy 等级制度 a system, especially in a society or an organization, in which people are organized into different levels of importance from highest to lowest

7. Confucianism 儒家 an ethical religion, rather than a religion founded on belief in god(s), which arose in the 6th century BC in China and was based on the teachings of

Confucius, who was a teacher rather than a PROPHET. The goal of Confucians is to achieve harmony with the world and nature, a gentlemanly ideal. For many centuries Confucianism was the religion of the Chinese bureaucratic class—the mandarins or literati—whose administrative posts were gained through competitive examinations in classical knowledge. Confucianism is often regarded as playing a decisive role in the legitimation of Chinese society and in providing a unified CULTURE over many centuries, overcoming even the conquest of China by 'barbarian' outsiders.

8. save face 挽回面子;保全面子;顾面子 This is a Chinese expression and refers to the covering of one's face with a fan as a sign of disgrace after revealing one's emotions. 'Face' here means the face with a calm expression on it.

9. protocol 礼仪;外交礼节 (Government, Politics & Diplomacy) the formal etiquette and code of behaviour, precedence, and procedure for state and diplomatic ceremonies

• Reading Comprehension

1. **Directions**: *Please work in pairs and match the Chinese values in Column A with relevant traits or examples in Column B.*

Column A		**Column B**
connections		When dealing with a Chinese company or agency, try to find out if it has unfulfilled obligation that could affect your proposal.
reciprocal obligation		In a family of many children, younger siblings can never call their older siblings by name.
collective before individuals		At a banquet, guests are met at the door and escorted to the banquet room or to their seats.
respect for hierarchy		Compared to most Western societies, and especially the American society, Chinese are very group-oriented.
saving face		Possibly the most important possession to have in China is guanxi.
protocol and ceremony		A decision might be affected by the need to save face for an important person.

2. **Directions**: *Read the following statements carefully, and decide whether they are true (T) or false (F) according to the text.*

( ) 1) As the Chinese legal system is maturing, its cultural milieu is still largely legalistic rather than relational.

( ) 2) The author believes that introducers or go-betweens can also help smooth the way by acting as a back-channel for information.

( ) 3) Individuals are never expected to show loyalty to the group decision and fall in line once a consensus has been reached.

( ) 4) Showing loyalty to those with whom you have a relationship is a must.

( ) 5) If you are in a lower status in relationship to the person you are seeing, you won't be expected to show some deference or respect to the person of higher status in China.

( ) 6) The author holds you must somehow humble yourself to retrieve it if you cause someone to lose face based on Chinese cultures.

( ) 7) It is suggested that you use only one of your hands to offer your business card as a way of elevating the other party in China.

( ) 8) During Chinese banquets, toasts are continually offered and reciprocated as a way of honoring and "giving face" to others.

Part Three

Topic-Related Activities

1. Case Study

An Unwanted Food Service

During a lunch buffet at a conference in China, Wu Fa, the interpreter of the conference, sat with four foreign participants. They were having a good time talking. When Wu Fa stood up for more food, she asked whether she could bring anything back for them.

Everyone thanked her and said "no". A while later, Wu Fa came back with a plate full of food, and asked whether the others would like to have something from her plate.

Again, the four others said, "No."

"Oh, please take something, I can't eat this much food myself."

The foreigners shrugged and one or two of them even frowned a little.

Questions

1) How can you explain the fact that the foreigners shrugged and one or two of them even

frowned a little in the end?

2) What do you think is the best solution to Wu Fa's dilemma?

2. Team Project

Directions: *Watch the film Pushing Hands, and try to explore the Chinese values and the American values behind it.*

3. Translation

Directions: *Translate the passage into English.*

儒家思想是中国影响最大的思想流派,也是中国古代的主流意识。自汉代以来,儒家思想就是封建统治阶级的指导思想之一。儒家思想的核心其实是一种人道主义。它提倡的自我修养,认为人是可以教化的、可完善的。儒家思想的一个宏大目标就是实现“大同社会”,在这样一个社会中,每个人都能扮演好自己的角色,并与他人维持良好的关系。

Unit Seven

Movies

Part One

Lead-in

The essence of cinema is editing. It's the combination of what can be extraordinary images of people during emotional moments, or images in a general sense, put together in a kind of alchemy.

—Francis Ford Coppola

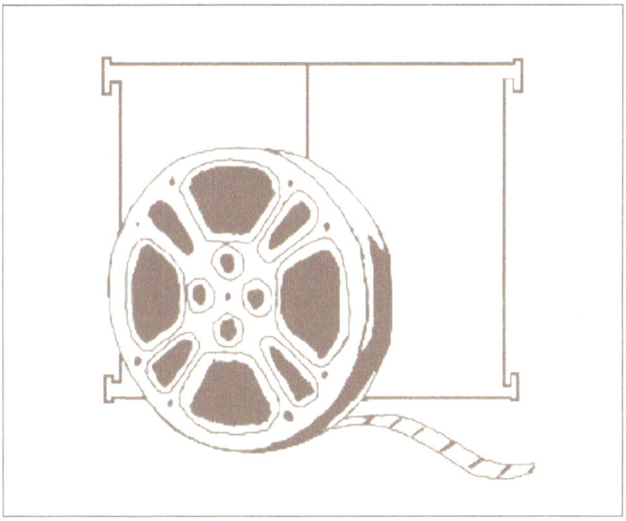

As a mainstream social ideology gradually developing in the long-term practical activities, the cultural values are not just the written signs in classic literature, but embodied in changing expressions of artistic works, penetrating through massive and complicated commercial transactions, extending into the basic necessities of common people's daily lives, and of course presented in the dazzling and colorful popular culture of movies.

Part Two

In-Class Reading

Warm-up questions:

1. Have you heard about the Academy Awards or the Oscars? Can you say something about them?

2. What's your favorite Hollywood movie star?

A History of American Movies

1 There's a saying in French that translates into English as "The more things change, the more they stay the same." That slogan provides one way of looking at history. For the history of **Hollywood**[1], it provides a good approach to summarizing its story for the twentieth century. In the early twenty-first century, much still remains of Hollywood's past. The major Hollywood companies remain in business, and all of them still are connected to the motion picture industry in some way. At the end of the first decade of the twenty-first century, Hollywood remains the dominant force in global cinema, a status it has held since the era of World War I, having been challenged seriously in that role only briefly in the 1920s and then again in the early to mid-1960s. By contrast, it is reasonable to argue exactly the opposite. Hollywood has changed enormously since its beginnings. The studios that remain are mere **shells** of what they once were. All of them are now **subsidiaries** of giant media corporations in which moviemaking is but a single, relatively small, portion of their business. These large media corporations are just as likely to be owned by financial interests from outside the United States as from within. We might **plausibly** argue that in the early twenty-first century, movie production is so far removed from Hollywood's studios of the Classic Era as to have little or no kinship with it.

2 Surely, the composition of audiences for movies has changed, and where movies are seen varies greatly from the movie theaters of the 1920s—when live musical accompaniment was the rule—to today when someone may watch a movie on a laptop computer. In the mid-twentieth century, the **abiding** question for people seriously interested in film was "What is cinema?" In the early twenty-first century, that question may have been replaced by "Where is cinema?" What for most of the twentieth century could be described sociologically as the public consumption of movies, increasingly has become a private matter. But just what may

this mean?

3 Going out to a movie theater was a public act, but the social **decorum** of movie-watching in a theater demanded there be no conversation. Watching a movie in a private space at home—with someone else or others—may facilitate more conversation and human interaction. The observation that Hollywood movies enjoyed their greatest popularity in terms of the size of movie going audiences and cultural prominence in the United States during World War II (1939 – 1945) is plausible. That observation, however, explains little in itself. The safest assertion is that Hollywood, at a period of unusual national unity and before the advent of television as a competitor, enjoyed circumstances very favorable to it. The art of movies exists always within some system of production, distribution, exhibition, and the circumstances favorable to exhibition during World War II were ideal.

4 What about the actual art and craft of making movies? Haven't the new digital technologies that have developed since the early 1990s completely taken over motion picture production? Haven't these new technologies completely changed what movies are? People who call themselves filmmakers may have never seen or touched an actual piece of **celluloid** film. The answer to these questions, again, is both yes and no. Motion picture postproduction—namely, editing and sound—has become work done by craftsmen and craftswomen with their hands on a mouse at a computer screen. Editors, who, with their assistants, used to spend time with reels of film and rewinds, now spend time **digitizing** footage and **rendering** output. Sound editors need to be expert with a program called Pro Tools. The process of capture, meaning the camerawork of actual filming, in some cases may mean working with digital cameras and tape, or solid-state tapeless formats of capture, rather than with a film camera and celluloid. Decisions about whether to shoot film, digital, hi-def, or tapeless depend on the goal for each project and its budget. Technology may influence certain artistic choices, but technology neither defines nor determines the art of film, or any of its **constituent** crafts. For editing, sound, and cinematography, the primary creative tools for filmmakers are as they've always been—the eye and the ear.

5 In the early twenty-first century, it is relatively safe to say that nearly all animation, special effects, and the like are computer generated, and that even relatively simple and straightforward feature films regularly employ **CGI**[2] for some of their scenes. The computer permits the **manipulation** of material to create illusions that are particularly convincing. Still, production designers interpret the script and bring the physical elements of a production into accord with that interpretation, and composers provide music for movies that is almost always created electronically rather than as a written score. Keeping up with changing production technologies is necessary, but the **artistry** of film remains bound to basics: textual, visual,

and auditory design. Throughout the history of the cinema, film has been about illusion. And even the creation of illusion for the viewer is less about tools and technology than it is about creative imagination. Long before computers, movies were achieving effects—both special and conventional—that is entirely convincing and believable. In a basic sense, the fundamental illusion that is most important on the screen is that of performance. The viewer has to be able to believe the character and to care about the character's role in the story that is being told on-screen. Screen talent has been sought, nurtured, and well paid throughout Hollywood's history. Who is on the screen is most important because movies depend on storytelling, and the most engaging stories are about people and the relationships between them. Storytelling in movies nearly always combines elements that **simultaneously** are literary and theatrical.

6 After any movie is made, there are many ways of interpreting it. Its meaning and value relies heavily on who sees it—when and where. The approaches to interpretation have been **formalized** in criticism, and these approaches broadly reflect and respond to changes in the **prevailing** culture. Criticism, moreover, adapts to its own culture—whether it is in popular circles or among academics. Movies are said to be about all kinds of things, but because the motion picture is a specific art, all movies are in some way or another about all other movies all the time—essentially, cinema may be regarded as a closed system. We understand it as a system that expands into spheres of culture, economics, ideologies, and social practice, but cinema may be best understood and appreciated as an artistic system unto itself.

7 Former shopkeepers, **peddlers**, and the owners and promoters of various other entertainments and amusements founded Hollywood. They wanted to do business by pleasing audiences, and they forged a cinema that for a century has made movies strongly driven by perceptions of audience taste and by the demographics of who is thought to constitute the audience. This has remained a constant of Hollywood.

8 Alongside this constant of trying to please audiences and **anticipate** shifts in taste, Hollywood learned how to **accommodate** and channel the creative talents and ambitions of filmmakers as well. Hollywood is a surprisingly **resilient** cultural system that arguably has financially rewarded the artists who work in it better than artists have ever been **remunerated** anywhere else at any time. And it has been surprisingly open in its **embrace** of talent: from the foreign immigrants who started the early studios, to talent like director **F. W. Murnau**[3] who was hired from Germany by Fox in the late 1920s to direct *Sunrise*, to the waves of talent who have come to Hollywood from Great Britain, Australia, Canada, and New Zealand, up through the Academy's selection of *Slumdog Millionaire*[4] as 2008'as Best Picture.

9 Exploring the movies of Hollywood through the **approximately** 180 films that have been selected as Best Pictures by the Academy of Motion Picture Arts and Sciences or were

voted onto either of the two lists of the greatest and most significant American movies **assembled by the American Film Institute provides us broad insights into the history of motion** pictures and their development. Accomplishment in movies is achieved through the **efficacious** practice of the various crafts. But the total art of movies exists in a financial and business system of production, **distribution**, and exhibition.

10 What may be most unusual about creativity in the movies is its **collaborative** nature. Collaboration often depends on positive interpersonal relationships among the collaborators, but it doesn't necessarily have to. In the past century, Hollywood has created an extraordinary body of work that appeals to the **aesthetic** satisfactions of **sentiment**, spectacle, and **sensation**. Hollywood craft always is accomplished and polished, but, in the long run, the crafts are practiced primarily in the service of storytelling. Truly significant movies are rarely about "cool shots", or other formal elements, that draw attention to themselves.

11 What are the most reliably effective movie stories about? The answer is that stories in movies may be about almost anything. The settings for them may be familiar or **exotic**. They may come from episodes or events that have actually happened, or they may be entirely imagined and implausible in real life. The bottom line is that the viewer needs to care about the characters no matter what situations they find themselves in. As with all generalizations, there may be exceptions. The Hollywood movies of the twentieth and early twenty-first centuries that have gained the most positive attention from other industry professionals tend to **boil down to** being about human relationships that really matter. To an exceptional degree, they are about friendship, either discovered or lost; family, discovered or lost; love, discovered or lost; or self-identity and **integrity**, discovered or lost. In being about these basics, they **transcend** the other things that they may appear to be about, such as the issues, causes, **ideologies**, and moral lessons that may be **discerned** in them thematically.

—Paul Monaco[5]

New Words and Expressions

shell /ʃel/ — *n.* an outer covering or frame work 外壳,框架

subsidiary /səbˈsɪdiəri/ — *n.* connected with sth. but less important than it, especially a company which is completely controlled by another 附属机构,子公司

plausibly /ˈplɔːzəbli/ — *adv.* easy to believe on the basis of available evidence 似真地

abiding /əˈbaɪdɪŋ/ — *adj.* lasting for a long time and not changing 永久的,持久不变的

decorum /dɪˈkɔːrəm/ — *n.* appropriateness of behavior or conduct; propriety 礼貌,

合宜

celluloid /ˈseljulɔɪd/ n. a colorless flammable material made from nitrocellulose and camphor and used to make photographic film 赛璐珞

digitize /ˈdɪdʒɪtaɪz/ v. to transcribe (data) into a digital form so that it can be directly processed by a computer 使数字化

render /ˈrendə(r)/ v. to convert (graphics) from a file into visual form, as on a video display 渲染

constituent /kənˈstɪtjuənt/ adj. constitutional in the structure of something 构成的

manipulation /məˌnɪpjuˈleɪʃn/ n. exerting shrewd or devious influence especially for one's own advantage 操纵;控制;篡改

artistry /ˈɑːtɪstri/ n. a superior skill that you can learn by study and practice and observation 艺术性;艺术才能

simultaneously /ˌsɪməlˈteɪniəsli/ adv. at the same instant 同时地

formalize /ˈfɔːməlaɪz/ v. make formal or official 使正式化

prevailing /prɪˈveɪlɪŋ/ adj. generally accepted; widespread 盛行的,广泛流传的

peddler /ˈpedlə(r)/ n. someone who travels about selling his wares (as on the streets or at carnivals) 小贩

anticipate /ænˈtɪsɪpeɪt/ v. to think, speak, or write about a matter in advance 预期;提前使用;早于……行动

accommodate /əˈkɒmədeɪt/ v. make fit for, or change to suit a new purpose 使适应

resilient /rɪˈzɪliənt/ adj. capable of returning to an original shape or position, as after having been compressed 有弹力的

remunerate /rɪˈmjuːnəreɪt/ v. make payment to; compensate 给予报酬

embrace /ɪmˈbreɪs/ n. a close affectionate and protective acceptance 拥抱

approximately /əˈprɒksɪmətli/ adv. (of quantities) imprecise but fairly close to correct 大约;近似地

assemble /əˈsembl/ v. gather or collect together into a group or into one place 集合;收集;装配

efficacious /ˌefɪˈkeɪʃəs/ adj. producing or capable of producing an intended result or having a striking effect 有效的;灵验的

distribution /ˌdɪstrɪˈbjuːʃn/ n. an act of distributing or the state of being distributed 分布;分发;分配

collaborative /kəˈlæbərətɪv/ adj. to work together, especially in a joint intellectual effort 协作的;合作的

aesthetic /iːsˈθetɪk/ adj. concerning or characterized by an appreciation of beauty

	or good taste 美学的;审美的;有美感的
sentiment /ˈsentɪmənt/	*n.* a thought, view, or attitude, especially one based mainly on emotion instead of reason 情绪;感情;观点;感伤
sensation /senˈseɪʃn/	*n.* the faculty to feel or perceive; physical sensibility 感觉
exotic /ɪɡˈzɒtɪk/	*adj.* being or from or characteristic of another place or part of the world 外来的;异国的;奇异的
integrity /ɪnˈteɡrəti/	*n.* strength and firmness of character or principle; honesty that can be trusted 正直;诚实
transcend /trænˈsend/	*v.* go or be above or beyond the limits 超越;胜过
ideology /ˌaɪdiˈɒlədʒi/	*n.* an orientation that characterizes the thinking of a group or nation 意识形态
discern /dɪˈsɜːn/	*v.* make out; discriminate; distinguish 辨别;看出;察觉

Notes

1. Hollywood 好莱坞　Hollywood is a neighborhood in the central region of Los Angeles, California. Its name has come to be a shorthand reference for the U. S. film industry and the people associated with it. Many of its studios such as Paramount Pictures, Warner Bros., and Universal Pictures were founded there and Paramount still has its studios there. Hollywood was incorporated as a municipality in 1903. It was consolidated with the city of Los Angeles in 1910, and soon thereafter a prominent film industry emerged, eventually becoming the most recognizable in the world.

2. CGI 计算机影像显示　abbreviation for (film) computer-generated image or imagery

3. F. W. Murnau 茂瑙　Friedrich Wilhelm Murnau (born Friedrich Wilhelm Plumpe; December 28, 1888 – March 11, 1931) was a German film director. He was greatly influenced by Schopenhauer, Nietzsche, Shakespeare and Ibsen plays he had seen at the age of 12, and became a friend of director Max Reinhardt. During World War I he served in the Imperial German Army, initially as an infantry company commander on the Eastern Front. Murnau later transferred to the German Army's Flying Corps, as an observer/gunner, and survived several crashes without any severe injuries. One of Murnau's acclaimed works is the film *Nosferatu* (1922), an adaptation of *Bram Stoker's Dracula*. Although not a commercial success, owing to copyright issues with Stoker's estate, the film is considered a masterpiece of German Expressionist cinema. He later directed the film *The Last Laugh* (1924), as well as a 1926 interpretation of Goethe's *Faust*. He emigrated to Hollywood in 1926, where he joined the Fox Studio and made three films: *Sunrise* (1927), *4 Devils* (1928) and *City Girl* (1930). *Sunrise* has been regarded by critics and film directors as among the best films ever made. Murnau

travelled to Bora Bora to make the film *Tabu* (1931) with documentary film pioneer Robert J. Flaherty. Flaherty left after artistic disputes with Murnau, who had to finish the movie on his own. A week before the opening of *Tabu*, Murnau died in a Santa Barbara hospital from injuries he sustained in an automobile accident that occurred along the Pacific Coast Highway near Rincon Beach, southeast of Santa Barbara. Of the 21 films Murnau directed, eight are considered to be completely lost. One reel of his feature *Marizza, genannt die Schmuggler-Madonna* survives. This leaves only 12 films surviving in their entirety.

4. *Slumdog Millionaire*《贫民窟的百万富翁》 *Slumdog Millionaire* is a 2008 British drama film that is a loose adaptation of the novel *Q&A* (2005) by Indian author Vikas Swarup, telling the story of 18-year-old Jamal Malik from the Juhu slums of Mumbai. Starring Dev Patel as Jamal, and filmed in India, the film was directed by Danny Boyle, written by Simon Beaufoy, and produced by Christian Colson, with Loveleen Tandan credited as co-director. As a contestant on the Indian version of *Who Wants to Be a Millionaire?* Jamal surprises everyone by being able to answer every question correctly. Accused of cheating, Jamal recounts his life story to the police, illustrating how he is able to answer each question correctly. After its world premiere at the Telluride Film Festival and later screenings at the Toronto International Film Festival and the London Film Festival, *Slumdog Millionaire* had a nationwide release in the United Kingdom on 9 January 2009, in India on 23 January 2009, and in the United States on 25 December 2008. Regarded as a sleeper hit, *Slumdog Millionaire* was widely acclaimed, being praised for its plot, soundtrack, direction, and performances (especially Patel's). It was nominated for ten Academy Awards in 2009 and won eight—the most for any 2008 film—including Best Picture, Best Director, and Best Adapted Screenplay. It won seven BAFTA Awards including Best Film, five Critics' Choice Awards and four Golden Globes.

5. Paul Monaco 保罗·摩纳哥 Paul Monaco has previously published five books on film and television, the most recent of these being volume 8, *The Sixties, 1960–1969*, in the History of American Cinema series (2001). He is also a co-editor on another book on historical methodology. Alongside his research and writing as a historian and a theorist, he has made more than thirty films in various genres. His work as a producer, writer, director, and editor on these films has greatly enhanced his knowledge and understanding of the medium. Paul takes great interest in teaching, especially in film education and opportunities for film-making for undergraduates. Since 1985, he has been a professor in the School of Film and Photography at Montana State University, Bozeman. Over a career spanning four decades, he also has taught film at Brandeis University, the University of Texas at Dallas, and Chapman University. Twice, Paul has been awarded Fulbright Senior Fellowships to do research and teach in Germany.

• Reading Comprehension

1. Directions: *Discuss the following questions with your classmates.*

1) What is Hollywood's status at the end of the first decade of the twenty-first century?
2) What happened to movie production in the early twenty-first century?
3) Why does the author say the public consumption of movies has increasingly become a private matter?
4) Haven't the new digital technologies that have developed since the early 1990s completely taken over motion picture production?
5) Why characters on the screen are important?
6) What is cinema according to the author?
7) Where does the total art of movies exist?
8) What are the most reliably effective movie stories about?

2. Directions: *Read the following statements carefully, and decide whether they are true(T) or false(F) according to the text.*

(　　)1) Hollywood remains the dominant force in global cinema, a status it has held since the era of World War II.

(　　)2) In the early twenty-first century, movie production still has a close relationship with Hollywood's studios of the Classic Era.

(　　)3) Hollywood movies enjoyed their greatest popularity in terms of cultural prominence in the United States during World War II.

(　　)4) Editors, who, with their assistants, used to spend time with reels of film and rewinds, now spend time digitizing footage and rendering output.

(　　)5) Decisions about whether to shoot film, digital, hi-def, or tapeless depend on the directors and editors.

(　　)6) Truly significant movies are really about "cool shots," or other formal elements, that draw attention to themselves.

3. Directions: *Choose the correct answer to each of the following questions.*

(　　)1) The circumstances favorable to exhibition during ________ were ideal.

A. World War Ⅱ　　B. World War Ⅰ

C. the early 1990s　　D. the early to mid-1960s

(　　)2) ________ has become work done by craftsmen and craftswomen with their hands on a mouse at a computer screen.

A. Cinematography　　B. Editing and sound

C. Reel of film　　D. Rewind

( )3) The process of capture, meaning the camerawork of actual filming, in some cases may mean working with ________.

A. digital cameras B. tape

C. solid-state tapeless formats of capture D. all of the above

( )4) The primary creative tools for filmmakers are ________.

A. computers B. cameras

C. the eye and the ear D. technology

( )5) The artistry of film remains bound to ________.

A. textual B. visual

C. auditory design D. all of the above

( )6) In a basic sense, the fundamental illusion that is most important on the screen is that of ________.

A. performance B. character

C. storytelling D. film star

- **Discussion**

1. What makes a film character interesting to you?

2. What factors do you think should be taken into account when casting decisions are made?

After-Class Reading

Warm-up questions:

1. What's your general impression upon Chinese movies?
2. What's your favorite Chinese movie? What does the film mean to you?

Journey to the West: Chinese Movies in the Global Market

1 Now in its seventeenth year, the Hong Kong International Film and Television Market—better known as Filmart—is among the world's largest industry trade shows. In March 2013 the forum hosted several seminars by industry executives, convened to debate the expansion of Chinese-language cinemas throughout Asia and across foreign markets. What follows is a report on two roundtables, respectively entitled "The Selling and Branding of Chinese-language Films Internationally" (held on 18 March 2013) and "Challenges, Opportunities and Partnership for Asia's Film Industry" (held on 20 March 2013). *China Daily*'s Alexander Wan presented recent statistics confirming Hollywood's global hegemony: in

2012, Hollywood productions dominated the global box-office, while North America remained the world's largest movie going market, generating US $ 10.8 billion in theatrical revenue. In the same period, China surpassed Japan as the world's second-largest cinema market, registering US $ 2.69 billion in box-office earnings. Wan noted that in 2012 China'a Mainland continued its pattern of 30% annual growth in box-office revenue. China's staggering growth rate is set to continue, the executives agreed, as the Mainland builds and opens four new theatre screens every day.

2 Several of the year's Chinese-produced films, such as *Cold War* (2012) and *CZ12* (2012), proved highly profitable domestically, while local comedy *Lost in Thailand* (2012) became one of the most earning Chinese films. However, foreign imports—chiefly from Hollywood—claimed over 50% of China's gross ticket revenue for 2012, reinforcing America's grip on Southeast Asian markets. Against this background the panelists pursued a cluster of inquiries: how to sustain industry growth in China and throughout Asia? What are the opportunities for Chinese movies within the global marketplace? What obstacles hinder the growth of Chinese cinemas, and how to surmount them? Though optimistic for Chinese cinema's prospects, the panelists remained pragmatic about the challenges at hand.

3 Despite Hollywood's primacy, a potentially vast market for Asian films exists within Asia—so argued Wilfred Wong, chairman of the Hong Kong International Film Festival Society. Fifty percent of Asia's population is under age thirty, Wong pointed out, furnishing a large consumer demographic for mass movies. As the disposable income of Asia's youth culture increases, the youth market for Asian films will continue to expand. Further, Wong claimed, the Asian audience does not inevitably favor Hollywood imports. *Lost in Thailand* and *Titanic 3D* (2012) may have amassed comparable grosses in the Mainland (US $ 159 million and US $ 150 million respectively), but the surcharges for 3D screenings greatly contributed to Titanic's grosses; in terms of total admissions, *Lost in Thailand* (a 2D film screened at regular ticket prices) far outstripped those of its Hollywood rival. Chinese audiences respond to movies that mirror their cultural experience, Wong asserted. A locally-produced film always has the added advantage of being close to the culture and taste of the local population.

4 William Pfeiffer, CEO of Dragongate Entertainment, argued that China's continuing growth will yield positive long-term effects. As the emergence of new screens produces greater theatrical returns, most of the profits will be channeled into film production, enabling filmmakers to ramp up production values and overall quality. Consequently, Chinese films will become more attractive in overseas territories, which in turn will increase international revenue and help to attract foreign investment. In addition, Pfeiffer noted, Chinese film studios can

exploit new revenue sources, such as legitimate online video for feature film distribution. Above all, the future is in partnerships. Coproductions between Chinese and Western firms yield clear advantages for the Mainland's film industry, engendering an exchange of craft knowledge and skills, attracting greater investment, and ensuring strong distribution capability overseas. Effective overseas distribution in turn provides the film widespread exposure, and fosters global recognition of Chinese movies.

5 A more general set of problems assails the Chinese film industry, the panelists argued. The domestic industry has grown too localized, ignoring international tastes. Here again *Lost in Thailand* might serve as an example. Though massively profitable at home, the low-budget comedy took only US $29,143 on its opening weekend in the US. For Pfeiffer, Mainland directors lack the "international perspective" of director **Ang Lee**[1], whose *Life of Pi* (2012) and *Crouching Tiger, Hidden Dragon* (2000) successfully mesh Hollywood-style storytelling with Asian subject matter. In Wilfred Wong's view, the global success of *Life of Pi* points to deeper deficiencies within Asia's film industries. "Why did the investment for *Life of Pi* and *Slumdog Millionaire* (2008) come from Hollywood and not Asia? Why is Asia not investing in these films?" Asian investors balk at film production, Wong concluded, because China lacks an industrial system comparable to Hollywood. Wang pointed out that Hollywood studios often spend US $50 – 70 million on worldwide distribution per theatrical film—a sum greater than the entire production cost of a typical Chinese movie. No matter the virtues of a given Chinese film, its capacity for global success cannot match that of even a mediocre Hollywood blockbuster, owing to the massive marketing resources that US studios pour into their productions. For this reason, Wang averred, China's distribution infrastructure needs to be rapidly and aggressively developed.

6 No less urgent is the need to cultivate fresh talent. Defending the global visibility of Chinese cinema, Wilfred Wong invoked China's world-renowned auteurs, but the directors he mentioned—**Chen Kaige**[2], **Zhang Yimou**[3], **Tsui Hark**[4], **Ann Hui**[5]—exposed the industry's reliance on veteran filmmakers. Most recently, moreover, China's highest-grossing domestic movies trade on the popularity of long-established stars: **Jackie Chan**[6] (*CZ12*), **Stephen Chow**[7] (*Journey to the West: Conquering the Demons* [2013]), and **Aaron Kwok**[8] and **Andy Lau**[9] (*Cold War*). These films attest to the enduring popularity of their star players, but they also remind us of the dearth of international marquee talent in China. Chinese stars possess huge name recognition in Asia, but few of them achieve an international profile. A film industry with global ambitions, the panelists warned, cannot rival Hollywood without fresh marquee attractions; the industry must find systematic ways to develop young actors with

international crossover potential.

7 Future growth depends on a constellation of factors. Espousing major industrial renovation, Fred Wang argued that China must challenge Hollywood hegemony by emulating its business strategies. Wilfred Wong pinpointed distribution networks and market research as key areas of reform. Asian territories must relax import quotas, Wong urged, thereby lubricating distribution in pan-Asian markets. William Pfeiffer similarly promoted strategic convergence among Asian film industries.

8 If, as seems likely, China's growth rate continues to escalate, then future box-office hegemony seems skewed toward China. Nevertheless, for US as well as Chinese firms, as Wilfred Wong maintained, "there is no lack of opportunities"—but there is also no clear certainty as to the most fertile business strategy to adopt. Sino-US cooperations remain an attractive prospect, as Hollywood profits from examples such as *Iron Man 3* (2013), a summer behemoth. To be sure, as the two Filmart panels indicated, China-US partnerships present challenges as well as opportunities for both parties. Covetous of the Mainland market, Hollywood pursues coproductions so as to increase its market share in the territory. While the Hollywood firm receives a greater percentage of box-office revenue, the movie itself, by virtue of its coproduction status, skirts the quota restriction on US imports. For China, by contrast, making inroads into North America and Europe would seem to be the key challenge. In **Patrick Frater's**[10] view, the Chinese government ought to better support international sales—for instance, by introducing export incentives. And yet **Lim Teck's**[11] earlier remark raises its head again here: if the domestic market is booming, who cares about the rest of the world?

—Gary Bettinson[12]

Notes

1. Ang Lee 李安 Ang Lee (born 23 October 1954) is a Chinese American film director, producer, and screenwriter. Born in the Pingtung County of southern Taiwan, Lee was educated in Taiwan and later in the United States. During his filmmaking career he has received international critical and popular acclaim and a range of accolades. Lee's early successes include *Pushing Hands* (1991), *The Wedding Banquet* (1993), and *Eat Drink Man Woman* (1994), which explore the relationships and conflicts between tradition and modernity, Eastern and Western; the three films are informally known as the "Father Knows Best" trilogy. The films are critically successful both in his native Taiwan and internationally.

His first entirely English-language film was *Sense and Sensibility* (1995), for which he received critical praise and a number of accolades. He went on to direct films in a broad range of genres, including the drama *The Ice Storm* (1997); *Ride with the Devil* (1999); the martial arts drama *Crouching Tiger, Hidden Dragon* (2000); the superhero blockbuster *Hulk* (2003); the romantic drama *Brokeback Mountain* (2005); the erotic espionage period film *Lust, Caution* (2007); and the magic realist survival drama *Life of Pi* (2012). Many of Lee's works are known for their emotional charge and exploration of repressed, hidden emotions.

Lee has been nominated for nine Academy Awards, of which he has won three: Best Foreign Language Film for *Crouching Tiger, Hidden Dragon* and Best Director for *Brokeback Mountain* and *Life of Pi*, becoming the first non-white director to win the latter. For *The Wedding Banquet* and *Sense and Sensibility*, Lee won the Golden Bear at the Berlin International Film Festival; for *Brokeback Mountain* and *Lust, Caution*, he won the Golden Lion at the Venice Film Festival. Lee is one of four directors to win the Golden Lion twice and the sole filmmaker to have been awarded the Golden Bear twice. Lee has also been awarded Directors Guild of America, Golden Globe and British Academy Film Awards.

2. Chen Kaige 陈凯歌　Chen Kaige (born 12 August 1952) is a Chinese film director and a leading figure of the fifth generation of Chinese cinema. His films are known for their visual flair and epic storytelling. Chen won the Palme d'Or at 1993 Cannes Film Festival and the International Federation of Film Critics (FIPRESCI) Award in 1993.

3. Zhang Yimou 张艺谋　Zhang Yimou (born 14 November 1951) is a Chinese film director, producer, writer and actor, and former cinematographer. He is one of the fifth generation of Chinese filmmakers, having made his directorial debut in 1987 with *Red Sorghum*. Zhang has won numerous awards and recognitions, with three Academy Awards nominations for Best Foreign Language Film for *Ju Dou* in 1990, *Raise the Red Lantern* in 1991, and *Hero* in 2003, a Silver Lion and two Golden Lion prizes at the Venice Film Festival, Grand Jury Prize at the Cannes Film Festival, the Golden Bear and the Silver Bear Grand Jury Prize at the Berlin International Film Festival. In 1993, he was a member of the jury at the 43rd Berlin International Film Festival. Zhang directed the opening and closing ceremonies of the 2008 Beijing Summer Olympic Games, which received considerable international acclaim. One of Zhang's recurrent themes is the resilience of Chinese people in the face of hardship and adversity, a theme which has been explored in such films as *To Live* (1994) and *Not One Less* (1999). His films are particularly noted for their rich use of color, as can be seen in some of his early films, like *Raise the Red Lantern*, and in his martial arts films like *Hero* and *House of Flying Daggers*. His highest budgeted film to date is the 2016

monster film *The Great Wall*, set in Imperial China and starring Matt Damon.

4. Tsui Hark 徐克 Tsui Hark (born 15 February 1950), born Tsui Man-kong, is a Hong Kong film director, producer and screenwriter. Tsui has directed several influential Hong Kong films such as *Zu Warriors from the Magic Mountain* (1983), the *Once Upon a Time in China* film series (1991—1997) and *The Blade* (1995). Tsui also has been a prolific writer and (a very hands-on) producer. His productions include *A Better Tomorrow* (1986), *A Chinese Ghost Story* (1987), *The Killer* (1989), *The Legend of the Swordsman* (1992), *The Wicked City* (1992), *Iron Monkey* (1993) and *Black Mask* (1996). He is viewed as a major figure in the Golden Age of Hong Kong cinema and is regarded by critics as "one of the masters of Asian cinematography". In the late 1990s, Tsui had a short-lived career in the United States, directing the Jean-Claude Van Damme-led films *Double Team* (1997) and *Knock Off* (1998). Both films were commercially unsuccessful and critically panned. Tsui himself was unsatisfied with his lack of creative control and returned to Hong Kong to continue his career. He has since found new commercial and critical success with blockbusters such as the *Detective Dee* film series (2010 – present), *Flying Swords of Dragon Gate* (2011), and *The Taking of Tiger Mountain* (2014).

5. Ann Hui 许鞍华 Ann Hui (born 23 May 1947) is a Hong Kong film director, producer, screenwriter and actress who is one of the most critically acclaimed Hong Kong New Wave filmmakers. She is known for her films about social issues in Hong Kong. Her film works cover different categories, including: literary adaptation, martial arts masterpieces, semi-autobiographical works, female issues, social phenomena, political changes, and also thrillers. She served as the president of the Hong Kong Film Director's Guild from 2004 to 2006. Hui has won numerous awards for her films. She won Golden Horse Awards (GHA) for Best Director three times (1999, 2011, 2014); Best Film at the Asia Pacific Film Festival; and Best Director at the Hong Kong Film Awards six times (1983, 1996, 2009, 2012, 2015, 2018). Only two films have achieved a Grand Slam (winning best picture, best director, best screenplay, best actor, and best actress) at the Hong Kong Film Awards: they are *Summer Snow* and *A Simple Life*, both of which were directed by Ann Hui. She was honored for her lifetime accomplishments at the 2012 Asian Film Awards. In 2017, the Academy of Motion Picture Arts and Sciences (AMPAS) invited Hui to become a member.

6. Jackie Chan 成龙 Chan Kong-sang (born 7 April 1954), known professionally as Jackie Chan, is a Hong Kong martial artist, actor, stuntman, filmmaker, action choreographer, and singer. He is known in the cinematic world for his slapstick acrobatic fighting style, comic timing, use of improvised weapons, and innovative stunts, which he

typically performs himself. He has trained in Wushu or Kung Fu and Hapkido, and has been acting since the 1960s, appearing in more than 150 films. Chan is one of the most recognizable and influential cinematic personalities in the world, gaining a widespread following in both the Eastern and Western hemispheres, and has received stars on the Hong Kong Avenue of Stars and the Hollywood Walk of Fame. He has been referenced in various pop songs, cartoons, and video games. He is an operatically trained vocalist and is also a Cantopop and Mandopop star, having released a number of albums and sung many of the theme songs for the films in which he has starred. He is also a globally known philanthropist and has been named as one of the top 10 most charitable celebrities by *Forbes* magazine. In 2015, *Forbes* estimated his net worth to be $350 million, and as of 2016, he was the second-highest-paid actor in the world.

7. Stephen Chow 周星驰 Stephen Chow (born 22 June 1962) is a Hong Kong filmmaker, actor, and producer. Chow began his career as an extra for Rediffusion Television. He later joined TVB in 1981. Chow made his film debut in the 1988 film *Final Justice*, which won him the Golden Horse Award for Best Supporting Actor at the 25th Golden Globe Awards. The following decade, he appeared in more than 40 films. *Fight Back to School* (1991) became Hong Kong's top-grossing film of all time. In 1994, he began directing films, starting with *From Beijing with Love*. In the latter half of the 1990s, China began to warm to his films and he became the Stephen Chow Phenomenon. In 2013, his film *Journey to the West: Conquering the Demons* became the highest-grossing Chinese film of all time. In 2016, his film *The Mermaid* broke numerous box office records, and became the highest-grossing film of all time in China. It has now grossed over US $553.81 million worldwide and until the release of *Wolf Warrior 2*, it was the highest-grossing movie of all time in China. Chow became the ninth-top-grossing Hollywood Director in 2016.

8. Aaron Kwok 郭富城 Aron Kwok (born 26 October 1965) is a Hong Kong singer, dancer and actor. Active since the 1980s, Kwok is one of the "Four Heavenly Kings" of Hong Kong. Kwok's onstage dancing is influenced by Michael Jackson. While most of his songs are in the dance-pop genre, he has experimented with rock and roll, ballad, rock, R&B, electronic and traditional Chinese music.

9. Andy Lau 刘德华 Andy Lau (born 27 September 1961), is a Hong Kong actor, singer-songwriter and film producer. He has been one of Hong Kong's most commercially successful film actors since the mid-1980s, performing in more than 160 films while maintaining a successful singing career at the same time. In the 1990s, Lau was branded by the media as one of the "Four Heavenly Kings" of Cantopop and was named as "Fourth Tiger"

among the "Five Tiger Generals" of TVB during the 1980s. Lau was entered into the Guinness World Records for the "Most Awards Won by a Cantopop Male Artist". By April 2000, he had already won an unprecedented total of 292 awards. Lau also holds numerous film acting awards, having won the Hong Kong Film Award for Best Actor three times and the Golden Horse Award for Best Leading Actor twice. In 2005, Lau received the "No. 1 Box Office Actor 1985 - 2005" award of Hong Kong, yielding a box office total of HK $1,733,275,816 for shooting 108 films in the past 20 years, and in 2007, he received the "Nielsen Box Office Star of Asia" award by the Nielsen Company (ACNielsen). On 25 June 2018, Lau was invited to be a member of the Academy of Motion Picture Arts and Sciences.

10. Patrick Frater 帕特里克·弗雷特 Patrick Frater has been an international film critic and analyst for over 20 years. His articles have appeared in leading newspapers such as *Variety*, *Screen International* and *The Hollywood Reporter*. In 2010, Frater co-founded *Asian Film Business*, a regional film trade publication, and F Media, a film consultancy. Frater lives in Hong Kong and is a frequent presenter and speaker at conferences, forums and radio events in the Asia Pacific region.

11 Lim Teck 林·特克 Lim Teck is the CEO of Clover Films, a Singaporean film producer and distributor.

12. Gary Bettinson 加里·贝廷森 Gary Bettinson is Senior Lecturer in Film Studies at Lancaster University, UK and author of The Sensuous Cinema of Wong Kar-wai: Film Poetics and the Aesthetic of Disturbance (Hong Kong University Press), and chief editor of Asian Cinema journal.

• Reading Comprehension

1. **Directions**: *Read the following statements carefully, and decide whether they are true (T) or false(F) according to the text.*

( )1) China surpassed Japan as the world's first-largest cinema market in 2012.

( )2) Though optimistic for Chinese cinema's prospects, the panelists remained pragmatic about the challenges at hand.

( )3) William Pfeiffer argued that China's continuing growth will yield negative long-term effects.

( )4) Effective overseas distribution in turn provides the film with widespread exposure, and fosters global recognition of Chinese movies.

( )5) Chinese stars possess huge name recognition in Asia, and many of them achieve an international profile according to the author.

(　　)6) Wilfred Wong points out that the Chinese film industry needs to cultivate fresh talent.

2. **Directions**: *Please work in pairs and match the film in Column A with its translation in Column B.*

Column A		ColumnB
Cold War		《泰坦尼克号》
CZ12		《泰囧》
Lost in Thailand		《贫民窟的百万富翁》
Titanic		《西游·降魔篇》
Crouching Tiger, Hidden Dragon		《钢铁侠 3》
Life of Pi		《十二生肖》
Slumdog Millionaire		《寒战》
Journey to the West: Conquering the Demons		《卧虎藏龙》
Iron Man 3		《少年派的奇幻漂流》

Part Three

Topic-Related Activities

1. Case Study

The film *The Gua Sha Treatment*, directed by Zheng Xiaolong, tells a compelling story of the culture clash between East and West. It is a story about cultural conflicts experienced by a Chinese family in the USA. It is a moving portrayal of the enormous gulfs between cultures and their possible repercussions.

After years of hard work, Xu Datong, a Chinese immigrant to the US, has finally achieved success as an outstanding video game designer. With his promising career and loving family, he feels he has become a true American. Datong's father comes over from China to visit his family in St. Louis. While there, the grandfather uses a traditional Chinese medical technique, called guasha, to treat Datong's son, Dennis. Unexpectedly, an American doctor thinks the bruises on Dennis' back left by the guasha treatment are signs of child abuse. The family goes through hell when the child is taken away by the child protection agency. Meanwhile, the grandfather leaves America because he finds that the living environment is really not suitable for him, as he feels that a simple, harmless treatment like guasha which is so common in China is treated as child abuse in America. Furthermore, he cannot converse in English. Later, an American friend of Datong tries guasha and proves that the treatment leaves painful-looking marks that are not actually painful or harmful at all. Finally, the child is able to return home and the family is reunited. The film was screened at the 2001 Cannes Film Festival.

Questions

1) What is the cultural conflict reflected in the film?

2) What is the reason for the clash?

2. Critical Thinking & Cultural Exploration

Step One

Directions: *Work in groups and act out a typical scene of the movie and ask students to guess what movie it is.*

Step Two

Directions: *Choose one of the students from each group as the judge and comment on the performance of each group based on the criteria offered by the teacher. The group which has got most points will be awarded the best group of the performance.*

Suggested criteria:

1) Content: healthy, positive, energetic and connected with the theme firmly; innovative idea and with reasonable structure. (2 points)

2) Performance: natural, committed and full of emotion. (2 points)

3) Script: artistic and affective. (2 points)

4) English pronunciation: standard and clear. (2 point)

5) Costume and prop: satisfy the demand of scene and the plot. (1 point)

6) Timing control: within 12 – 15 minutes, point deduction will be added for the overtime or the lack of time. (1 point)

Step Three

Directions: *After all the groups complete their task, all the students are required to choose their favorite actor or actress, and the student who receives the most votes will be the winner of the award.*

Step Four

Directions: *Winners may have one minute to deliver an acceptance speech.*

3. Writing

Directions: *Write a movie review according to the following structure.*

Ⅰ. Synopsis or summary of the plot;

Ⅱ. Main characters;

Ⅲ. Conclusion: What message is being told? What was the director's purpose or intention or the theme of the film? Compare with other realities you know (your country, historical fact or event, other film from the same director or genre...) What's your opinion?

Unit Eight

Colours

Part One

Lead-in

The best colour in the whole world, is the one that looks good, on you!
最适合你的颜色,才是世界上最美的颜色。

By the fountain's brink.
What is red? A poppy's red
In its barley bed.
What is blue? The sky is blue
Where the clouds float thro.
What is white? A swan is white
Sailing in the light.
What is yellow? Pears are yellow,
Rich and ripe and mellow.
What is green? The grass is green,
With small flowers between.
What is violet? Clouds are violet
In the summer twilight.
What is orange? Why, an orange,
Just an orange!

Colors by C. G. Rossetti

Part Two

In-Class Reading

Warm-up questions:

1. What is your favourite colour? And why?
2. How much do you know about colour symbolism?

Culture and Context of Colours

Black

1 Black is a **neutral**, **authoritative** colour that can **evoke** both positive and negative emotions. It can create the feeling of sophistication and emptiness at the same time: it can represent power and dignity as well as pessimism and sadness. In colour psychology, black represents protection from the outside world, and the concealing of emotions. Black is also a classic neutral colour that people often wear to feel slimmer or to fit right in. It is the colour of **mourning** in the West. The custom of wearing black, non-decorative clothing for days of mourning goes back all the way to the Roman Empire.

2 Black has mysterious effect on people—some people may feel **intimidated** by a person wearing black in either formal or casual occasions. It is often associated with **seduction** and **intrigue**. It also has a **submissive** quality to it, like a priest wearing black in order to feel faithful and submissive to God. In Western cultures, black is represented as a colour of power, danger, death and **rebellion** while in Eastern cultures black is seen more as a symbol of wealth, elegance and prosperity.

White

3 White is a crisp, neutral colour that encourages us to think more purely and clearly. It is associated with cleanliness, **decluttering** and organizing. In colour psychology, it is known as a colour of fresh starts and new creations, acting as a blank **canvas**. Many people associate the colour white with innocence youth, recalling a time when they were naive and protected by their families. On the negative side, white can have a cold, **isolated** feeling, as demonstrated in many medical offices and hospitals.

4 Since white is a combination of all colours, it is considered an **equalizer**, often associated with fairness and neutrality. Western cultures **perceive** white to be representative of purity and peace whereas Eastern cultures believe it represents death, mourning and sadness,

especially in China, India and Africa. Even though the colour white may convey feelings of isolation and coldness, it's overall a clean, pure colour that can brighten up a space and make way for the future.

Red

5 Red is a **vibrant**, stimulating colour associated with our basic **instincts** and senses. While it represents love, passion and beauty in some cultures, it can also represent anger, **aggression** and war. Red's **visual** energy promotes a need for action and assertiveness, mainly because it excites our emotions. Physiologically, it activates the body and senses which can result in increased blood pressure and heart rate if largely exposed to it.

6 Restaurants often use red because of its ability to stimulate one's appetite. While Western cultures see red as a representation of love, warning and anger, Eastern cultures view red as the colour of prosperity, beauty and good fortune, especially China. American cultures perceive blue as a colour of sacrifice and mourning. In general, Western cultures interpret blue as colour of peace and trust, while Eastern cultures view it as a colour of **immortality** and **virtue**.

Orange

7 Orange is a warm, **inviting** colour that combines the physical energy of red with the bright happiness of yellow. It represents adventure and risk-taking and like red. It evokes confidence and enthusiasm. This is why most sportsmen and thrill-seekers prefer orange **apparel** and **accessories** for their professions and hobbies. Orange is also associated with **spontaneity** and encourages social communication, interaction, friendship and communities.

8 Orange has a **rejuvenating** effect on people as it has a balanced **vitality** to it. In Eastern cultures, orange is representative of happiness and **spirituality**, whereas in Western cultures, it represents affordability and optimism. More specifically, orange is often used for safety devices in the United States. The Occupational Safety and Health **Administration**[1] (OSHA) requires some construction equipment to be manufactured in orange.

Yellow

9 Yellow is a warm, bright colour that stimulates the mind and encourages communication. It is known psychologically as the happiest colour in the **spectrum**. It is said that it helps people to focus, aiding with decision-making and with **clarity** of ideas. Its close relation to the sun makes yellow the best colour for representing **enlightenment**, happiness and optimism.

10 Yellow can have a creative effect on some but generates anxiety in others. While being mentally activating, yellow can also **unearth** a great amount of confidence in someone. Some cultures find yellow to have a negative meaning, like the Greek and the French, who perceive

it to be related to sadness, envy and jealousy, respectively. In general, yellow is perceived to represent happiness, **cowardice** and caution in the Western culture, whereas it is perceived as **sacred** and **imperial** in most Eastern cultures.

Green

11 Green is a cool, **soothing** colour that provides emotional and mental balance. It is known to help people relax both mentally and physically, as it is a soothing colour that can help with depression and anxiety. It is an emotionally positive colour that is abundantly present on earth in nature. As a combination of yellow and blue, green provides the mental sharpness of yellow, along with the soothing calmness of blue.

12 Most Western cultures see green as the colour of luck and nature, while most Eastern cultures see green as a sign of regeneration, hope and **fertility**. The Japanese culture regards green as the colour of **eternal** life.

Blue

13 Blue is a cool, calming colour that is connected with trust across cultures as it is perceived as a reliable and responsible colour that **exudes** confidence and trustworthiness. Most hues of blue evoke a sense of physical and mental relaxation, providing inner peace, **tranquility** and calmness. Since blue is a safe colour, it is connected with devotion and religious studies, as well as with authority. In fact, most banks, corporations and brands use the colour blue to evoke a feeling of reassurance and reliability to the customers. On the negative side, blue can also be perceived as predictable, boring and **conservative**.

14 Blue has a stress-reducing effect on people mainly because it tends to be orderly and sincere. It is a neutral colour that doesn't like to draw attention, and that may be why it's the most dominant "favourite colour" in the world.

15 **Iran**[2] perceives several hues of blue to **signify** paradise, while **Central American**[3] cultures perceive blue as a colour of sacrifice and mourning. In general, Western cultures interpret blue as a colour of peace and trust, while Eastern cultures view it as a colour of immortality and virtue.

Purple

16 Purple is a cool, uplifting colour with a sense of spirituality. It can calm the mind and nerves, as well as encourage creativity. From a psychological perspective, purple provides a link between thought and activity, offering a sense of mental balance. As a combination of red and blue, it carries the stimulation of red and the calmness and **integrity** of blue. Too much purple, however, can **aggravate** depression in some people. Purple's connection to spirituality also makes it related to the imagination and dreams. It is known as an **introspective** colour that promotes enlightenment. Its close relation and history to royalty and the nobility make

purple also a colour of luxury and wealth with **regal**, **extravagant** qualities to it.

17 Western cultures believe purple is a colour of royalty and spirituality, while most Eastern cultures think purple is a colour of sorrow, wealth and mourning. In Iran, purple is a colour of the future, while some **Latin American**[4] countries perceive it as the colour of death and mourning.

Silver

18 Silver is a cool, **metallic** colour that is associated with the moon and the **feminine** energy. Its **illuminative** quality implies that silver is a cleansing colour that provides calmness and helps release mental and physical stress. Silver has a reflective effect on people and is believed to draw negative energy out of the body and replace it with positive energy. Its metallic refinement makes it a livelier, sophisticated version of grey, conveying elegant neutrality.

19 Eastern cultures, like the Japanese and **Muslims**[5], perceive silver to represent intelligence and peace, respectively. In the Western world, Native Americans believe silver to be a colour of agreement and **truce**. In the contemporary world, silver is very **versatile**; being applied to both high-tech electronics and elegant fashion **garments**. It is also associated with wealth and prosperity, and more specifically to the professional and corporate arena.

Gold

20 Gold is a warm, metallic colour that represents wealth and **prestige** in both Western and Eastern cultures and in almost every country today. Gold relates to **masculinity** and brings to mind the brightness and energy of sun, illuminating and radiating energy.

21 This colour is connected to yellow and brown, becoming a **hybrid** of brightness and stability. Gold has traditionally been associated with the riches of royalty around the world, which makes it closely related to prosperity.

22 Although gold has bright, cheerful quality to it, it can also be perceived as traditional and not as modern as silver. It is connected to all that is successful, **triumphant** and extravagant.

Liliana Becerra[6]

New Words and Expressions

neutral /ˈnjuːtrəl/	*adj.* (of a colour) dull, but harmonizing with most other colours 中性的
authoritative /ɔːˈθɒrətətɪv/	*adj.* possessing or supported by authority 权威的
evoke /ɪˈvəʊk/	*v.* call or summon up (a memory, feeling, etc.), especially from the past 引起,唤起

mourning /ˈmɔːnɪŋ/ *n.* the act or feelings of one who mourns; grief 哀痛；哀悼

intimidated /ɪnˈtɪmɪdeɪtɪd/ *adj.* prevented or discouraged from acting because of fear 害怕的；受到恐吓的

seduction /sɪˈdʌkʃn/ *n.* the act of seducing or the state of being seduced 诱惑

intrigue /ɪnˈtriːɡ/ *n.* the act or an instance of secret plotting, etc. 阴谋；诡计

submissive /səbˈmɪsɪv/ *adj.* inclined or willing to submit 顺从的

rebellion /rɪˈbeljən/ *n.* defiance toward an authority or established convention 叛乱；反抗

declutter /diːˈklʌtə(r)/ *v.* simplify or get rid of mess, disorder, complications, etc. 清理

canvas /ˈkænvəs/ *n.* a piece of canvas or a similar material on which a painting is done, usually in oils 画布

isolated /ˈaɪsəleɪtɪd/ *adj.* being or feeling set or kept apart from others 孤立的；孤独的

equalizer /ˈiːkwəlaɪzə(r)/ *n.* a person or thing that equalizes 平等之人或物

perceive /pəˈsiːv/ *v.* become aware of (something) through the senses, especially the sight; recognize or observe 感知

vibrant /ˈvaɪbrənt/ *adj.* giving an impression of vigour and activity 充满生机的，生气勃勃的

instinct /ˈɪnstɪŋkt/ *n.* innate aspect of behavior 本能，直觉

aggression /əˈɡreʃn/ *n.* any offensive activity, practice, etc. 攻击性，侵略

visual /ˈvɪʒuəl/ *adj.* of, relating to, done by, or used in seeing 视觉的

immortality /ˌɪmɔːˈtæləti/ *n.* endless life or existence 不朽

virtue /ˈvɜːtʃuː/ *n.* the quality or practice of moral excellence or righteousness 美德

inviting /ɪnˈvaɪtɪŋ/ *adj.* tempting; alluring; attractive 诱人的

apparel /əˈpærəl/ *n.* (Clothing & Fashion) something that covers or adorns, especially outer garments or clothing 服装

accessory /əkˈsesəri/ *n.* (often plural) a small accompanying item of dress, especially of women's dress 配饰

spontaneity /ˌspɒntəˈneɪəti/ *n.* (often plural) the exhibiting of actions, impulses, or behaviour that are stimulated by internal preprocess 自发行为；自然举动

rejuvenate /rɪˈdʒuːvəneɪt/ *v.* make (someone or something) look or feel younger, fresher, or more lively 使看起来年轻，使感觉更年轻；使

	恢复青春活力
vitality /vaɪˈtæləti/	*n.* physical or intellectual vigor; energy or liveliness 活力
spirituality /ˌspɪrɪtʃuˈæləti/	*n.* the state, quality, or fact of being spiritual 灵性
spectrum /ˈspektrəm/	*n.* (General Physics) the distribution of colours produced when white light is dispersed by a prism or diffraction grating 光谱
clarity /ˈklærəti/	*n.* clearness, as of expression 明晰；清楚
enlightenment /ɪnˈlaɪtnmənt/	*n.* the act of enlightening or the state of being enlightened 启蒙
unearth /ʌnˈɜːθ/	*v.* reveal or discover 发掘;发现
cowardice /ˈkaʊədɪs/	*n.* lack of courage in facing danger, pain, or difficulty 胆小；怯懦
sacred /ˈseɪkrɪd/	*adj.* worthy of or regarded with reverence, awe, or respect 神圣的
imperial /ɪmˈpɪəriəl/	*adj.* of or relating to a specified empire 帝国的;至高无上的
soothe/suːð/	*v.* gently calm(a person or their feelings)安慰(人,感情);使平静
fertility /fəˈtɪləti/	*n.* the ability to produce offspring 生育力
eternal /ɪˈtɜːnl/	*adj.* without beginning or end; lasting for ever 永恒的;不朽的
exude /ɪgˈzjuːd/	*v.* make apparent by mood or behavior 显露,洋溢
tranquility /træŋˈkwɪləti/	*n.* a state of peace and quiet 宁静;平静
conservative /kənˈsɜːvətɪv/	*adj.* traditional or restrained in style 保守的
signify /ˈsɪgnɪfaɪ/	*v.* convey or express a meaning 表示;意味
integrity /ɪnˈtegrəti/	*n.* adherence to moral principles; honesty 正直;诚实
aggravate /ˈægrəveɪt/	*v.* make worse 加重;使恶化
introspective /ˌɪntrəˈspektɪv/	*adj.* given to examining own sensory and perceptual experiences 反省的；内省的
regal /ˈriːgl/	*adj.* belonging to or befitting a supreme ruler 帝王的;王室的
extravagant /ɪkˈstrævəgənt/	*adj.* recklessly wasteful 奢侈的;浪费的
metallic /məˈtælɪk/	*adj.* of, concerned with, or consisting of metal 金属的
feminine /ˈfemənɪn/	*adj.* suitable to or characteristic of a woman 女性的
illuminative /ɪˈljuːmɪneɪtɪv/	*adj.* of, causing, or capable of causing illumination 反

	光的
truce /truːs/	*n.* a state of peace agreed to between opponents so they can discuss peace terms 停战;休战
versatile /ˈvɜːsətaɪl/	*adj.* used for many different purposes 用途广泛的
garment /ˈɡɑːmənt/	*n.* a piece of clothing 衣服
prestige /preˈstiːʒ/	*n.* a high standing achieved through success or influence or wealth, etc. 威望,声望
masculinity /ˌmæskjəˈlɪnəti/	*n.* qualities, especially sexual qualities, which are considered to be typical of men 阳刚之气
hybrid /ˈhaɪbrɪd/	*n.* a mixture of other things 混合物
triumphant /traɪˈʌmfənt/	*adj.* experiencing or displaying triumph 胜利的

Notes

1. The Occupational Safety and Health Administration (OSHA) 美国劳工部职业安全卫生管理局　With the Occupational Safety and Health Act of 1970, Congress created the Occupational Safety and Health Administration (OSHA) to ensure safe and healthful working conditions for workers by setting and enforcing standards and by providing training, outreach, education and assistance.

2. Iran 伊朗　a republic in SW Asia, between the Caspian Sea and the Persian Gulf: a monarchy until an Islamic revolution in 1979 headed by the Ayatollah Khomeini when the Shah was obliged to leave the country; consisted chiefly of a high central desert plateau almost completely surrounded by mountains, a semitropical fertile region along the Caspian coast, and a hot and dry area beside the Persian Gulf; oil is the most important export; official language: Persian (Iranian or Farsi); official religion: Muslim majority; currency: rial; capital: Tehran

3. Central America 中美洲　a region of southern North America extending from the southern border of Mexico to the northern border of Colombia; it separates the Caribbean Sea from the Pacific Ocean and is linked to South America by the Isthmus of Panama. It consists of Guatemala, Belize, Honduras, El Salvador, Nicaragua, Costa Rica and Panama.

4. Latin America 拉丁美洲　those areas of America whose official languages are Spanish and Portuguese, derived from Latin: South America, Central America, Mexico, and certain islands in the Caribbean

5. Muslims 穆斯林　people who follow or practice Islam, a monotheistic Abrahamic religion; the derivation of "Muslim" is from an Arabic word meaning "submitter (to God)". Muslims consider the Quran, their holy book, to be the verbatim word of God as revealed to the Islamic prophet and messenger Muhammad. The majority of Muslims also follow the

teachings and practices of Muhammad as recorded in traditional accounts.

The beliefs of Muslims include: that God is eternal, transcendent and absolutely one; that God is incomparable, self-sustaining and neither begets nor was begotten; that Islam is the complete and universal version of a primordial faith that has been revealed before through many prophets including Abraham, Ishmael, Isaac, Moses, and Jesus; that these previous messages and revelations have been partially changed or corrupted over time and that the Quran is the final unaltered revelation from God. As of 2015, 1.8 billion or about 24.1% of the world population are Muslims.

6. Liliana Becerra 莉莉安娜. 贝塞拉 an independent design strategist, professor, writer and curator based in Los Angeles, CA, United States; Through her studio, Becerra and her team of global experts advise Fortune 500 companies and brands on the recognition of global insights, trends and their articulation into strategic design opportunities. She is also faculty member of the Product Design Department at the Art Center College of Design in California, where she teaches design research, design insights and colour, material and finish design.

- **Reading Comprehension**

1. **Directions**: *Discuss the following questions with your classmates.*

   1) Why is blue warmly welcome by most banks, corporations and brands?
   2) Why do most sportsmen and thrill-seekers prefer orange apparel and accessories for their professions and hobbies?
   3) How is white interpreted in colour psychology?
   4) How do Western cultures and Eastern cultures view purple?
   5) Why do restaurants tend to prefer red?
   6) How is yellow conveyed in the Greek and the French cultures?
   7) What does black symbolize in Western cultures and Eastern cultures?
   8) Which color has the soothing function?

2. **Directions**: *Read the following statements carefully, and decide whether they are true (T) or false (F) according to the text.*

   (　　)1) Black has a submissive quality to it, like a priest wearing black in order to feel faithful and submissive to God.

   (　　)2) Silver is a warm, metallic colour that represents wealth and prestige in both Western and Eastern cultures and in almost every country today.

   (　　)3) In Iran, purple is a colour of the future.

   (　　)4) North American cultures perceive blue as a colour of sacrifice and mourning.

   (　　)5) The Western cultures regard green as the colour of eternal life.

(　　)6) Yellow is perceived as sacred and imperial in most Eastern cultures.

(　　)7) The Occupational Safety and Health Administration (OSHA) requires some construction equipment to be manufactured in red.

(　　)8) Eastern cultures view red as the colour of prosperity, beauty and good fortune, especially China.

- **Discussion**

1. Why is yellow preferential among Chinese emperors?

2. Could you share more relevant information concerning colours from any reliable sources?

After-Class Reading

Warm-up questions:

1. Have you encountered any embarrassing situations caused by colour misunderstanding?
2. What do you know about the Five Elements Theory?

Color Symbolism in Chinese Culture: What Do Traditional Chinese Colors Mean?

1 One doesn't need to be a designer to have a special relationship with colors. Everyone has a favorite and in many cases, their culture also plays a significant role when it comes to associating symbolic or hidden meanings with different colors. The same is true in Chinese culture. A country with a rich heritage, China uses colors symbolically within every ritual, ceremony, festival and, lately, even in business. In fact, compared to the West, China has a

surprisingly different and more powerful color symbolism.

2 Let us study what different colors mean in Chinese culture.

Color Symbolism in Chinese Culture

3 Just as **the Five Elements**[1] Theory (of Metal, Fire, Water, Wood and Air) plays an important role in influencing many of the Chinese beliefs and customs, the color theory is also based on the five elements. Hence five of the most popular colors in China also correspond to these five elements namely:

4 **Red—Fire**: Red is an auspicious as well as a popular color in Chinese culture. It symbolizes luck, happiness and joy. It also represents summer season and the southern direction. It is the color worn by brides, since it is believed to be an auspicious color for warding off evil. Red also represents vitality, celebration and fertility in traditional Chinese color symbolism. Today, Westerners take red to be a representation of China's revolution or political system. However, this is definitely not the case since ancient Chinese roots certainly did not factor in the revolution for it. If you are doing business in China, make use of bit of red in marketing, but not too much.

5 **Yellow—Earth**: Yellow is an imperial color representing power, royalty and prosperity in traditional Chinese color symbolism. It mainly represents late summer and central direction. Today, yellow is symbolic of pornography in publications in China. So, do be careful when using yellow, particularly for **brand marketing**[2].

6 **Black—Water**: As surprising as this might seem, Water element is not represented by blue, but with black. Black color in Chinese culture is associated with destruction, evil, profundity, disasters, cruelty, sadness and suffering. It is bad fortune and must not be worn on auspicious occasions like weddings. The Chinese word for black is "hei" which itself stands for bad luck, irregularity, illegality, etc. Avoid using black in your brand marketing.

7 **White—Metal**: White stands for the metal element and also symbolizes purity in Chinese culture. However, in some instances, it is associated with death and is the color worn at funerals. Today, white is a popular color in cars in China and (along with black) is used widely for making consumer goods such as watches, cell phones, clothes, etc. Be judicious in using white in marketing and avoid wrapping presents in white paper when gifting them to someone.

8 **Blue—Wood**: Blue represents the Wood element and also symbolizes spring, immortality and advancement. Blue can be used quite liberally in case of marketing product or service.

Other Traditional Chinese Colors and What They Represent

9 **Gold**—Like in Western culture, gold also symbolizes wealth and riches in China. One

can easily use it and related colors in their marketing materials (though too much of it could make things a bit gaudy and even cheap-looking).

10 **Green**—There is not much difference between Western **symbolism**[3] associated with green and that of it in Chinese traditions. The important differences include: Green stands for wealth, harmony, growth, eco friendliness in the West, whereas it stands for clean, and contamination free in China. Green is also used to describe organic things. For example, green milk means organic or toxin free milk and green vegetables mean ones without pesticides. "A man said to wear a green hat" means he has an unfaithful wife. Thus, green should be used carefully as it could symbolize something totally different.

11 **Purple**—In the Western culture, purple symbolizes royalty while in Chinese symbolism it stands for divinity and immortality. In modern times, purple is being used to represent love or romance in China just as red color does in the West. Younger consumers are highly attracted to purple when it is used in brands and for marketing.

12 **Multiple Colors or Rainbow Colors**—The Chinese rarely use multiple colors since the rainbow seen in the sky was taken as a sign that the emperor would die soon.

As is evident, China is a vast country with multitude of facets. While one must certainly use freedom and creativity in their use of colors especially when marketing in this country; one should also be extra careful in order to avoid pitfalls posed by the use of certain colors with negative connotations.

Jacob Olesen[4]

Notes

1. the five elements 五行 metal, wood, water, fire and earth, held by the ancients to compose the physical universe and later used in traditional Chinese medicine to explain various physiological and pathological phenomena

2. Brand marketing 品牌营销 an important marketing strategy; through marketing, it enables customers to recognize the brand and products of the enterprise, which can greatly improve the brand awareness of the enterprise. At the same time, it improves the customer's concern and demand for products, so as to achieve good and sustainable profit growth for the enterprise.

3. Symbolism 象征主义 originated in France as an intellectual alternative to the straight visual work of the Impressionists; there were two main strands those, e. g. Redon, influenced by literature, and those, e. g. van Gogh, who explored the symbolic use of color and line to express emotion.

4. Jacob Olesen 雅各布·奥利森 the founder of Color Meanings, a website about color

symbolism and design; he is a world-renowned color expert and a recognized leader in understanding how colors affect human emotion and behavior.

- **Reading Comprehension**

1. **Directions**: *Please work in pairs and fill in the blanks.*

Color	Symbolism in Chinese Culture
Red	
Yellow	
Black	
White	
Blue	
Gold	
Green	
Purple	

2. **Directions**: *Read the following statements carefully, and decide whether they are true (T) or false (F) according to the text.*

(   ) 1) Red is an auspicious as well as a popular color in Chinese culture.

(   ) 2) Be free to use yellow, particularly for Chinese brand marketing.

(   ) 3) The author believes that black is allowed to be worn on auspicious occasions like weddings.

(   ) 4) White is associated with death and is the color worn at funerals in China.

(   ) 5) Gold can be used at one's will for it symbolizes wealth and riches both in Western culture and in China.

(   ) 6) "A man said to wear a green hat" means he has a faithful wife.

(   ) 7) In modern times, red is being used to represent love or romance in China just as purple color does in the West.

(   ) 8) The Chinese scarcely use multiple colors since the rainbow seen in the sky was taken as a sign that the emperor would die soon.

Part Three

Topic-Related Activities

1. Case Study

Jim, an American-born Chinese, was invited to a beach party. It was hot, so he decided to wear a sun helmet. Before he left, his father, who grew up in China and moved to America when he was a college student, warned him not to pick out a green hat to the party attended by the Chinese. Jim took his father's warning lightly. When he arrived on the scene, most of the Chinese of his father's age laughed. He and his counterparts were totally confused.

Questions

1) How can you explain the fact that most of the Chinese of his father's age laughed at the sight of Jim in a green hat?

2) What's the symbolism of the color green in Western cultures and Eastern cultures?

2. Team Project

Directions: *Watch the film **Green Hat**, and try to explore the Chinese values behind it.*

3. Translation

Directions: *Translate the passage into English.*

在中国文化中,红色通常象征着好运、长寿和幸福。在春节和其他喜庆场合,红色到处可见。人们把现金作为礼物送给家人或亲密朋友时,通常放在红信封里。红色在中国流行的另一个原因是人们把它与中国革命和共产党相联系。然而,红色并不总是代表好运与快乐。因为从前死者的名字常用红色书写,用红墨水写中国人名被看成是一种冒犯行为。

Unit Nine

Festivals

Part One

Lead-in

Festivals promote diversity; they bring neighbors into dialogue; they increase creativity; they offer opportunities for civic pride; they improve our general psychological well-being.

—David Binder

Festivals are special days that come around periodically to celebrate special events or commemorate important figures. They carry a nation's historical memories, cultural creations and social mechanisms. Festivals are not only the sources of cultural and artistic traditions, but also main carriers epitomizing, displaying and inheriting culture. It revives and explains the past; shapes and maintains the present; and inspires and helps mold the future.

Part Two

In-Class Reading

Warm-up questions:

1. What is the difference between Chinese and Western festivals in origin?

2. Why the Christmas season is inextricably connected to the red-and-green color combination?

Christmas in Western Countries

1 Christmas is celebrated on December 25 and is both a sacred religious holiday and a worldwide cultural and commercial phenomenon. For two **millennia**, people around the world have been observing it with traditions and practices that are both religious and **secular** in nature. Christians celebrate Christmas Day as the anniversary of the birth of Jesus of Nazareth, a spiritual leader whose teachings form the basis of their religion. Popular customs include exchanging gifts, decorating Christmas trees, attending church, sharing meals with family and friends and, of course, waiting for Santa Claus to arrive. December 25—Christmas Day—has been a **federal** holiday in the United States since 1870.

A Brief History of Christmas

2 Christmas is a festival of light in two senses: as the church **feast** of the **Nativity** of Christ—the **transcendent** light of the world entering it as a lowly human being, and as the **pagan** celebration of the winter **solstice**—when sunlight starts growing back in strength just after having reached its lowest ebb. The two meanings of Christmas are intertwined in the host of seasonal **observances** that have developed around it in the many cultures of the Christian world, as varied as the local backgrounds out of which they grew, yet united by certain **recurrent** themes from ancient nature religions as well as from **theology**.

3 The middle of winter has long been a time of celebration around the world. Centuries before the arrival of the man called Jesus, early Europeans celebrated light and birth in the darkest days of winter. Many people **rejoiced** during the winter solstice, when the worst of the winter was behind them and they could **look forward to** longer days and extended hours of sunlight. In Scandinavia, the Norse celebrated Yule from December 21, the winter solstice, through January. In **recognition** of the return of the sun, fathers and sons would bring home large logs, which they would set on fire. The people would feast until the log burned out,

which could take as many as 12 days. The Norse believed that each spark from the fire represented a new pig or calf that would be born during the coming year.

4 The end of December was a perfect time for celebration in most areas of Europe. At that time of year, most cattle were **slaughtered** so they would not have to be fed during the winter. For many, it was the only time of year when they had a supply of fresh meat. In addition, most wine and beer made during the year was finally **fermented** and ready for drinking. In Germany, people honored the pagan god Oden during the mid-winter holiday. Germans were terrified of Oden, as they believed he made **nocturnal** flights through the sky to observe his people, and then decide who would prosper or perish. Because of his presence, many people chose to stay inside.

Christmas Meals

5 As for the special Christmas meals, their main course depends on local custom. For Estonians, it was long vital to have blood-pudding heated with lard on Christmas Eve, or major trouble might ensue over the coming year. Their Finnish cousins however used to have rice **porridge** (still favored in Denmark) and stockfish after coming back from the outdoor **sauna** that night, but now they mostly have cold cuts. Pork was the favorite dish in Europe from Greece to Germany, as well as in Canada, whose **tourtière** meat pies **stands out** in the midst of English-speaking North America with its Christmas turkeys. Yet pork was originally preferred in England too, where Christmas turkeys appeared in 1542, after the species was introduced from America; but they only became popular at the turn of the next century—partly in imitation of King James I, who did not like pork. In France, customs vary: if Parisians have oysters, caviar and foie gras, turkeys are also eaten in Burgundy, and geese are preferred in Alsace—as they are in Denmark, along with ducks. Among traditional desserts are fruitcakes, because they are a promise of plenty in the New Year. This also goes for Britain's plum pudding, eaten at lunch on Christmas day.

6 In Poland, the Christmas meal takes place long before midnight mass, at the end of a day of fasting that can only be broken when the first star appears. On a pattern also found in Southern Europe (though the symbolic number there may also be thirteen or seven), but mostly, through much of Eastern Europe, the Polish dinner consists of twelve traditional dishes, supposed to stand for the Twelve Apostles. It starts with the solemn breaking of a Christmas loaf, said to **evoke** the Last Supper, which the father passes to all family members standing around the table (one place being left empty for Christ), so each of them can make three wishes.

Christmas in the UK

7 In Britain, Christmas Day is normally spent at home, with the family, and it is

regarded as a celebration of the family and its **continuity**. The present-day Christmas festivities see the celebrators **adorning** their homes with Christmas trees, lights, **tinsel**, **wreaths** and other decorative items. Shops start selling Christmas decorations from mid-November to enthusiastic Christmas shoppers who prefer to have one-upmanship over their friends and neighbors. In England as well as in other nations of the UK, the beautiful Christmas trees are an essential part of traditional Christmas decorations. In England, decorating Christmas trees has been widely popular since around the 1850s when **Prince Albert**[1] had a Christmas tree set up in Windsor Castle for his wife **Queen Victoria**[2] and their children.

8 Some houses are decorated with evergreens (plants which do not lose their leaves in winter); a wreath of **holly** on the front door and **garlands** of holly, **ivy** and **fir** indoors. Bunches of **mistletoe** are often hung above doorways. Presents are bought and wrapped, and traditionally placed under the Christmas tree on Christmas Eve. Christmas is both a secular and a religious holiday, and many families like to attend a midnight service at church on Christmas Eve, or celebrate Christmas in church on Christmas morning.

9 The traditional Christmas dinner in England is a mouth-watering affair with the main dish being roasted turkey with vegetables and sauces. The dessert is usually a rich, fruity Christmas pudding with brandy sauce. For kids, Christmas is the time to have fun with family and friends and receive gifts from Father Christmas, who is pictured as an old man with red clothes and a long white beard. Father Christmas is said to leave presents for children in their stockings (or pillowcases) that they hang at the end of their beds on Christmas Eve.

10 The festive spirit can be **discerned** all over Britain with most public places such as department stores, gift shops, town halls and restaurants decorated beautifully with electric lights and **festoons** for the occasion. Churches and **cathedrals** all over the country hold masses, with many people attending the Midnight Mass on Christmas Eve or a service on Christmas morning. In London and the provinces, a number of theatres traditionally organize for kids a special Christmas **pantomime** based on some popular children's stories such as ***Little Red Riding Hood***[3] and ***Aladdin***[4], with a deliberately made subtle connection to the festival.

11 In England, the day after Christmas is called **Boxing Day**[5]. It is named so because it was the day when the rich people gave presents to servants, tradesmen and poor people, which could be money or food. They would put them in a small box, which was smashed open when it was full. The Boxing Day is still celebrated and is a bank holiday in all of the four nations of the UK. If it happens to fall on a weekend, a special bank holiday is declared on Monday.

Christmas in the USA

12 The United States of America has many different traditions and ways that people celebrate Christmas, because of its multi-cultural nature. Many customs are similar to ones in the UK, France, Italy, The Netherlands, Poland and Mexico. The traditional meal for Western European families is turkey or ham with cranberry sauce. Families from Eastern European origins favor turkey with **trimmings**, cabbage dishes, and soups.

13 Some Americans use pop-corn threaded on string to help decorate their Christmas tree. Making gingerbread houses is also popular to make and eat at Christmas! **Eggnog** is a traditional Christmas drink in the USA. Many Americans, especially Christians will go to Church to celebrate the birth of Jesus at Christmas. Many churches have special Christmas carol services and events where the story of Christmas is told. In New England (the American States of Massachusetts, Connecticut, Rhode Island, Vermont, New Hampshire and Maine), there are shops called "Christmas Shops" that only sell Christmas decorations and toys all the year round! Americans also send out Christmas cards, like carol singing and there's the unusual custom of the Christmas **pickle**! People in America like to decorate the outside of their houses with lights and sometimes even statues of Santa Claus, Snowmen and Reindeer. Some cookies and a glass of milk are often left out as a snack for Santa on Christmas Eve!

14 Towns and cities often decorate the streets with lights to celebrate Christmas. Perhaps the most famous Christmas street lights in the USA are at the Rockefeller Center in New York where there is a huge Christmas tree with a public ice-skating rink in front of it over Christmas and the New Year. Customs such as Mumming take place in some communities. On New Year's Day in Philadelphia there is a Mummer's Day **parade** which lasts over six hours! Clubs called "New Years Associations" perform in amazing costumes which take months to make. There are four categories (Comics, Fancies, String Bands, and Fancy Brigades) which are judged. In the Southwest, there are some special customs which have some similarities to those in parts of Mexico. These include "**luminarias**" or "**farolitos**" which are paper sacks partly filled with sand and then have a candle put in them. They are lit on Christmas Eve and are put the edges of paths. They represent "lighting the way" for somewhere for Mary and Joseph to stay.

15 Today in the West, not many people consider the religious meaning to Christmas. Most people in the UK or the US will not go to a religious church meeting, even at Christmas. It has become a busy race to spend money on presents, and get ready for the Day.

New Words and Expressions

millennia /mɪˈleniə/ *n.* a span of 1,000 years 千禧年(millennium 的复数)

secular /ˈsekjələ(r)/ *adj.* of or relating to the doctrine that rejects religion and religious considerations; characteristic of or devoted to the temporal world as opposed to the spiritual world 世俗的;现世的;不朽的;非宗教的

federal /ˈfedərəl/ *adj.* national; especially in reference to the government of the United States as distinct from that of its member units 联邦制的;联邦政府的;同盟的

feast /fiːst/ *n.* a ceremonial dinner party for many people 宴会;酒席;节会

nativity /nəˈtɪvəti/ *n.* the event of being born 出生;诞生

transcendent /trænˈsendənt/ *adj.* exceeding or surpassing usual limits especially in excellence; beyond and outside the ordinary range of human experience or understanding 卓越的;超然的

pagan /ˈpeɪɡən/ *adj.* not acknowledging the God of Christianity and Judaism and Islam 异教的;异教徒的;无宗教信仰的

solstice /ˈsɒlstɪs/ *n.* either of the two times of the year when the sun is at its greatest distance from the celestial equator 至;至点;至日

observance /əbˈzɜːvəns/ *n.* the act of observing; taking a patient look; a formal event performed on a special occasion 遵守;仪式;纪念

recurrent /rɪˈkʌrənt/ *adj.* recurring again and again 再发生的;周期性的;循环的

theology /θiˈɒlədʒi/ *n.* the rational and systematic study of religion and its influences and of the nature of religious truth 神学

rejoice /rɪˈdʒɔɪs/ *vi.* & *vt.* feel great joy; show signs of great happiness 欣喜; 高兴; 快乐

recognition /ˌrekəɡˈnɪʃn/ *n.* recognizing or being recognized 认识; 认出; 承认

slaughter /ˈslɔːtə(r)/ *v.* kill cruelly 屠杀,杀戮; 屠宰

ferment /ˈfəment/ *v.* go sour or spoil(使)发酵

nocturnal /nɒkˈtɜːnl/ *adj.* belonging to or active during the night 在夜间的;(指生物)夜间活动的

porridge /ˈpɒrɪdʒ/ *n.* soft food made by boiling oatmeal or other meal or legumes in water or milk until thick 粥;麦片粥

sauna /ˈsɔːnə/ *n.* a Finnish steam bath; steam is produced by pouring water over heated rocks 桑拿浴

tourtière /tuːrtɪˈɛə/ *n.* (French) a meat pie that is usually eaten at Christmas in Quebec(加拿大)肉馅饼

evoke /ɪˈvəʊk/ *v.* bring to mind; summon up; produce or cause a response, reaction, etc. 产生; 引起; 唤起

continuity /ˌkɒntɪˈnjuːəti/ *n.* continuance; continuation 连续(性),持续(性)

adorn /ə'dɔːn/ — *v.* make something or somebody look more attractive by decorating it or them with something 装饰；装扮

tinsel /'tɪnsl/ — *n.* a thread with glittering metal foil attached 闪亮的金属片；俗丽的东西

wreath /riːθ/ — *n.* a circle of leaves or flowers placed on the head or round the neck of somebody to honor them 花冠，花环

holly /'hɒli/ — *n.* any tree or shrub of the genus Ilex having red berries and shiny evergreen leaves with prickly edges 冬青树

garland /'gɑːlənd/ — *n.* flower arrangement consisting of a circular band of foliage or flowers for ornamental purposes 花环

ivy /'aɪvi/ — *n.* climbing plant with dark, shiny leaves 常春藤

fir /fɜː(r)/ — *n.* nonresinous wood of a fir tree 枞树；冷杉；枞木

mistletoe /'mɪsltəʊ/ — *n.* parasitic shrub having branching greenish stems with leathery leaves and waxy white glutinous berries; the traditional mistletoe of Christmas 槲寄生（一种常用作圣诞节室内悬挂的植物）

discern /dɪ'sɜːn/ — *vt. & vi.* see clearly (with the eyes or with the mind); see with an effort ;make out; discriminate; distinguish 看见；辨明

festoon /fe'stuːn/ — *n.* flower chains suspended in curves between points as a decoration 花彩

cathedral /kə'θiːdrəl/ — *n.* main church of a district under the care of a bishop 总教堂，大教堂

pantomime /'pæntəmaɪm/ — *n.* a performance using gestures and body movements without words 哑剧；童话剧

trimming /'trɪmɪŋ/ — *n.* the accessories that normally accompany (something or some activity) 添头；辅料

eggnog /'egnɒg/ — *n.* a punch made of sweetened milk or cream mixed with eggs and usually alcoholic liquor 蛋奶酒

pickle /'pɪkl/ — *n.* vegetables (especially cucumbers) preserved in brine or vinegar 腌汁；泡菜

parade /pə'reɪd/ — *n.* a public procession 游行

luminaria /ljuːmɪ'neərɪə/ — *n.* a Mexican Christmas lantern consisting of a lighted candle set in sand inside a paper bag（墨西哥的）传统圣诞灯（一种棕色纸灯；内燃蜡烛）

farolito /færə'liːtəʊ/ — *n.* a paper lantern used by Hispanic people in Christmas processions 沙袋灯（拉丁美洲人在圣诞节游行时使用的一种纸

	灯)
look forward to	to wait or hope for, especially with pleasure 展望,期待(后接动词的 ing 形式)
stand out	be highly noticeable; distinguish oneself 突出;脱颖而出

Notes

1. Prince Albert 阿尔伯特亲王　Prince Albert of Saxe-Coburg and Gotha (26 August 1819 - 14 December 1861) was the husband of Queen Victoria of the United Kingdom of Great Britain and Ireland. Albert was born in the Saxon duchy of Saxe-Coburg-Saalfeld to a family connected to many of Europe's ruling monarchs. At the age of twenty, he married his cousin, Victoria; they had nine children. Initially he felt constrained by his role of prince consort, which did not afford him power or responsibilities. He gradually developed a reputation for supporting public causes, such as educational reform and the abolition of slavery worldwide, and was entrusted with running the Queen's household, office and estates. He was heavily involved with the organization of the Great Exhibition of 1851, which was a resounding success. Victoria came to depend more and more on Albert's support and guidance. He aided the development of Britain's constitutional monarchy by persuading his wife to be less partisan in her dealings with Parliament—although he actively disagreed with the interventionist foreign policy pursued during Lord Palmerstone's tenure as Foreign Secretary. Albert died at the relatively young age of 42. Victoria was so devastated at the loss of her husband that she entered into a deep state of mourning and wore black for the rest of her life. On her death in 1901, their eldest son succeeded as Edward VII, the first British monarch of the House of Saxe-Coburg and Gotha, named after the ducal house to which Albert belonged.

2. Queen Victoria 维多利亚女王　Victoria (24 May 1819-1822 January 1901) was Queen of the United Kingdom of Great Britain and Ireland from 20 June 1837 until her death. Known as the Victorian era, her reign of 63 years and seven months was longer than that of any of her predecessors. It was a period of industrial, political, scientific, and military change within the United Kingdom, and was marked by a great expansion of the British Empire. In 1876, Parliament voted her the additional title of Empress of India. Victoria was the daughter of Prince Edward, Duke of Kent and Strathearn (the fourth son of King George III), and Princess Victoria of Saxe-Coburg-Saalfeld. After both the Duke and his father died in 1820, she was raised under close supervision by her mother and her comptroller, John Conroy. She inherited the throne aged 18 after her father's three elder brothers died without surviving legitimate issue. Though a constitutional monarch, privately, Victoria attempted to influence government policy and ministerial appointments; publicly, she became a national icon who was

identified with strict standards of personal morality. Victoria married her first cousin Prince Albert of Saxe-Coburg and Gotha in 1840. Their children married into royal and noble families across the continent, earning Victoria the sobriquet "the grandmother of Europe" and spreading haemophilia in European royalty. After Albert's death in 1861, Victoria plunged into deep mourning and avoided public appearances. As a result of her seclusion, republicanism in the United Kingdom temporarily gained strength, but in the latter half of her reign, her popularity recovered. Her Golden and Diamond Jubilees were times of public celebration. She died on the Isle of Wight in 1901. The last British monarch of the House of Hanover, she was succeeded by her son Edward VII of the House of Saxe-Coburg and Gotha.

3. *Little Red Riding Hood*《小红帽》 *Little Red Riding Hood* is a European fairy tale about a young girl and a big bad wolf. Its origins can be traced back to the 10th century to several European folk tales, including one from Italy called *The False Grandmother*. The two best known versions were written by Charles Perrault and the Brothers Grimm. The story has been changed considerably in various retellings and subjected to numerous modern adaptations and readings. Other names for the story are: *Little Red Cap* or simply *Red Riding Hood*.

4. *Aladdin*《阿拉丁》 *Aladdin* is a folk tale most probably of Middle-Eastern origin. Despite not being part of the original Persian/Arabic text of *The Book of One Thousand and One Nights* (*The Arabian Nights*), it is one of the best-known tales associated with that collection. It was actually added by the Frenchman Antoine Galland, who acquired the tale from Maronite Christian storyteller Hanna Diyab.

5. Boxing Day 节礼日 Boxing Day is a holiday celebrated the day after Christmas Day, occurring on the second day of Christmastide. Though it originated as a holiday to give gifts to the poor, today Boxing Day is primarily known as a shopping holiday. It originated in the United Kingdom and is celebrated in a number of countries that previously formed part of the British Empire. Boxing Day is on 26 December, although the attached bank holiday or public holiday may take place either on that day or one or two days later (if necessary to ensure it falls on a weekday). Boxing day is also concurrent with the Christian holiday Saint Stephen's Day.

• Reading Comprehension

1. **Directions**: *Discuss the following questions with your classmates.*

1) What is the religious origin of Christmas?
2) What are the popular customs of Christmas?
3) What are the major Christmas decorative items?
4) What is the traditional Christmas dinner in England?
5) Where do children find their Christmas gifts?

6) What is the special Christmas pantomime for children?

7) What is the origin of Boxing Day?

8) What special activities are held in the US?

2. **Directions**: *Read the following statements carefully, and decide whether they are true(T) or false(F) according to the text.*

(   )1) Christmas Day is celebrated as a major festival and public holiday in countries around the world, including many whose populations are mostly Christian.

(   )2) Christmas is the period of highest annual church attendance.

(   )3) Green is the first color associated with Christmas.

(   )4) A special Christmas meal is traditionally an important part of the holiday's celebration, and the food in every country is the same.

(   )5) The popularity of decorating Christmas trees had something to do with Prince Albert.

(   )6) There are shops called "Christmas Shops" that only sell Christmas decorations and toys on Christmas.

3. **Directions**: *Fill in the form based on the information of Christmas meals provided in the text.*

Nation	Food
Estonia	
Finland	
Greece/Germany	
Canada	
England	
France	
Denmark	
America	

- **Discussion**

1. How do Westerners celebrate Christmas? Work in groups and tell each other the typical customs of Christmas.

2. Why do you think Christmas is so popular around the world nowadays? Work with your partners and talk about the possible reasons.

After-Class Reading

Warm-up questions:

1. What are the differences between Chinese and Western festivals in origin?
2. Which Chinese festival do you like best? Why?

Chinese Festivals

1 Traditional festivals, which serve as an illustration of the vitality of traditional culture and an important carrier of national culture, bear collective national emotions and cultural memory, and result from the accumulation of spiritual and material cultures in past generations. The traditional festival culture is therefore one of the richest expressions of the national culture, concerning nearly all aspects of social life. Various elements of the national culture, including patterns of thought and behavior, are embodied in these festivals.

2 Traditional Chinese festival culture includes not only material elements such as food, clothes, housing, and transportation, but also elements of social structure and institution. In addition, it contains elements of national history, beliefs and religions, customs and rituals, social entertainments, ethics and morality, and aesthetic psychology, and therefore it can reveal the in-depth contents and essence of the national culture. Compared with Western festivals, traditional Chinese festivals, especially those of the Han nationality, are by and large agriculture-oriented and secular.

3 Traditional Western festivals, which focus on religion, highlight the relationship between man and God, whereas traditional Chinese festivals put more emphasis on the heavens and reflect an agricultural relationship between man and the heavens. Most traditional Western festivals have a religious origin. For example, Christmas, the biggest festival in Christian countries, is a festival to celebrate the birthday of Jesus Christ. Easter is a festival in memory of the resurrection of Jesus. Festival activities in the West are closely related to religious faiths, and most Western festivals involve certain religious rituals.

4 On the other hand, traditional Chinese festivals, especially those of the Han nationality, are not religion-oriented but agriculture-oriented. The origins and evolution of traditional Chinese festivals are related to agricultural production in ancient times. Not only are the festival customs rich in obvious agricultural characteristics, but the festivals themselves are indicative of the life patterns of the agricultural society.

5 Traditional Chinese festivals fall in certain seasons of the year. Ancient Chinese people observed and classified climatic changes in nature and put the climate characteristics

for each season in a certain order. Such observations and classifications of climate and nature were conducted for the purpose of farming because they are useful for guiding agricultural activities. Thus, the ancient Chinese calendar is also known as the "Agricultural Calendar". In this calendar, a year is divided into twelve months, **twenty-four solar terms**[1], seventy-two pentads, and 365 days. The twenty-four solar terms refer to certain climatic changes in nature that are significant for farming. Among these solar terms, several appeared quite early since they signify the most obvious climatic changes in nature: four "beginnings" (beginning of spring, beginning of summer, beginning of autumn, and beginning of winter), two "equinoxes" (spring equinox and autumn equinox), and two "solstices" (summer solstice and winter solstice). For traditional seasonal festivals, celebration activities were intimately related to these solar terms. For instance, the Summer Solstice Festival and the Winter Solstice Festival were the most important seasonal holidays in ancient times. It is recorded in *Rites of Zhou* that people sang and danced on the summer solstice and the winter solstice to offer sacrifices to heaven, earth, mountains, and rivers, and such ceremonies were conducted to enable people to guard against evils and disasters. These seasonal festivals became formal national holidays in the Han Dynasty, when the emperor led the whole country in conducting sacrificial rites. Such rites continued to be conducted through the late Qing Dynasty. Other solar terms appeared gradually based on the needs of agricultural activities and changes in nature, and later seasonal festivals such as the Dragon Boat Festival (Double Fifth Festival), the Magpie Festival (Double Seventh Festival), the Mid-Autumn Festival (the fifteenth of the eighth lunar month), and the Double Ninth Festival came into being. These were apparently seasonal, although they are not solar terms.

6 Traditional Chinese festivals were developed according to the farming cycle—sowing in spring, weeding in summer, harvesting in autumn, and storing in winter. The Spring Festival, the Clear and Bright Festival, the Dragon Boat Festival, and the Mid-Autumn Festival were typical festivals for winter, spring, summer, and autumn respectively. The most important festival of the year, the Spring Festival, is set at the end of one year and the beginning of the next in the Xia Calendar. It symbolizes cycles, germination, and the fresh appearance of nature. Therefore, nearly all cultural forms of the Spring Festival reflect an agricultural origin. People consume foods made of agricultural products, enjoy the relaxed, leisurely winter time, and make sacrifices to pray for favorable weather and a good harvest in the coming year. Traditional Chinese festivals are closely related to the twenty-four solar terms, and the Clear and Bright Festival falls on the same day of the solar term with the same name. The magnificence of traditional festivals and customs is based on seasonal changes and the farming cycle.

7 The four major traditional Chinese festivals are the Spring Festival, the Clear and Bright (Qingming) Festival, the Dragon Boat (Duanwu) Festival, and the Mid-Autumn Festival. In recent years, China has been carrying out its Intangible Cultural Heritage Protection Project, and these four major festivals have been declared national holidays. It can be said that they are the most important traditional festivals in the history of China.

Spring Festival

8 The Spring Festival is the grandest, warmest, and most important traditional festival and is unique to the Chinese people. The custom of celebrating the Spring Festival has been observed since the Western Han Dynasty. The Spring Festival normally refers to New Year's Eve and the first day of the first lunar month. However, the festival season lasts from the eighth day of the twelfth lunar month (called the Laba Day) until the fifteenth day of the first lunar month (the Lantern Festival), with New Year's Eve and the lunar New Year as the climax of the celebration. The folk custom of the Spring Festival was ratified by the State Council as the state's First Batch of Intangible Cultural Heritages on May 20, 2006. The Spring Festival is popularly known as "passing the year" (guonian). It seems that the customs of guonian originate from the heaven-worshiping activity of praying for a bumper harvest for the coming year by the ancestors of the Chinese people.

9 During the traditional holidays of the Spring Festival, various celebration activities are carried out by the Han people and most minorities. These activities focus on offering sacrifices to gods, Buddha, and ancestors, doing general sweeping and cleaning of the house, welcoming and meeting the new year and good fortune, and praying for a good harvest in the new year. Some of the folk customs that are still observed in China are briefly discussed below.

10 As the Chinese saying goes, "On the twenty-fourth of the twelfth lunar month, one should dust the house." Since "dust" in Chinese is homophonous with "old" (both characters are pronounced *chen* in Chinese pinyin), dusting the house during this time symbolizes "getting rid of the old and arranging for the new" in order to get rid of all bad luck. The spring couplets is a literary form unique to the Chinese language. It comprises two parallel lines of exactly the same number of Chinese characters, with the matching words in each line in the same part of speech. It normally uses concise and exquisite words to express good wishes. Besides **Spring Festival couplets**[2], people also put up a character fu of different sizes on the door, on the walls, or in other locations in the house as a wish for a bright future. Sometimes the character is placed upside down, literally meaning *fudao* in Chinese, which is homophonous with "fortune comes". Legend says that the monster Nian is afraid of the noise of fireworks, so the ancestors of the Chinese people drove off the monster with fireworks. Later, setting off

fireworks was gradually endowed with new connotations of doing away with misfortune and poverty, and having a colorful and prosperous life in the coming year. On New Year's Eve, people may stay up all night to see out the old year and welcome in the new year, which is called *shousui*, literally "guarding the year." At this time people send each other gifts (known as *kuisui*), invite each other for drinks and foods (known as *biesui*), send everyone, old and young, good wishes (known as *fensui*), and they stay up all night to wait for daybreak (known as *shousui*). All family members get together, have a sumptuous family reunion dinner, light candles or oil lamps, sit around the stove chatting, and wait for the coming of the new year. This custom signifies driving off all evil and welcoming an auspicious new year.

11 Nearly all families make New Year cakes using glutinous rice flour. These cakes are called *niangao*, homophonous with "the year is higher". They are square-shaped, in yellow or white, symbolizing gold and silver respectively and embodying wealth in the coming year. Eating *jiaozi* is a custom observed by people in the north for the Spring Festival. During the time for family reunions, people traveling or residing in other places try their best to come back home no matter how far away they are, and the whole family gathers together to have *jiaozi* around the table. In Chinese, *jiaozi* symbolizes getting together or a family reunion, and since *jiaozi* is shaped like the silver ingot used as money in feudal China, having jiaozi during the Spring Festival also symbolizes letting riches and treasures come into the house. "Worshiping the year" refers to wishing a Happy New Year to family members, relatives, and friends. When youngsters wish good health, safety, and longevity to an elder, that person will present them with a red packet containing money. This is called "lucky money". It is believed that the young can live happily and smoothly in the coming year if they have received such lucky money on New Year's Day.

Qingming Festival

12 Qingming Festival, or the Clear and Bright Festival falls on the fifth day of the twenty-four solar terms (around April 5). At this time of year, the scenery becomes bright, and everything in nature appears clear. The temperature rises, and there is an increase in rainfall, which provides good conditions for cultivating crops. Thus, Qingming is a solar term closely related to farming. However, the Qingming Festival is not exactly the same as the solar term with the same name. As a solar term, it reflects the changes in nature and symbolizes changes in the season. As a festival, it also signifies certain customs and cultural meanings.

14 The Qingming Festival is said to originate from the ceremony of offering sacrifices to dead kings, princes, generals, and ministers at their tombs. Later the ceremony was imitated and carried out by the common people, and gradually it grew into a fixed custom of the Chinese nation. Nowadays the Qingming Festival is not only a day for people to hold memorial

ceremonies for their ancestors, but it is also a bond to link people of the same clan and a ritual in spring to go out hiking and to get close to nature. The customs of the Qingming Festival are rich and colorful. In the progress of its development, the Qingming Festival has taken in the customs of the **Cold Food Festival**[3] and the Double Third Festival. The major customs and activities for the Qingming Festival include eating cold food, sweeping the grave, wearing willow twigs, going hiking, and flying kites.

Duanwu Festival

15 The Dragon Boat Festival falls on the fifth day of the fifth lunar month. It has over twenty different names, including the Duanwu Festival, the Double Fifth Festival, the Summer Festival, the May Day Festival, and the *Zongzi* Festival.

16 Major customs and habits of the Duanwu Festival include eating *zongzi*, dragon-boat racing, taking a bath in hot water with herbs, putting up bundles of calamus and wormwood, drinking medicinal liquor, making herbal tea, wearing jewels, and gathering herbal medications. *Zongzi* is pyramid-shaped and is made of glutinous rice wrapped in bamboo or reed leaves. It is said that after Qu Yuan drowned himself in the river, people missed him very much and threw *zongzi* into the river as a sacrifice to him. Another saying goes that people threw *zongzi* into the river to feed the dragon so that it would not damage Qu Yuan's body. According to literature, dragon-boat racing is a collective paddling race commemorating Qu Yuan. As a traditional aquatic activity, it has been popular among the Chinese people for two thousand years, and it is mostly held during the Dragon Boat Festival. Dragon boats differ from one another in size, ranging normally from 20 meters to 30 meters long. Each boat holds about thirty sailors. All the racing boats start at the same time from the start line, and those who cover the designated length of waterway the fastest win the game. The herbs used in the bath were initially fragrant plants of the composite family. Later fragrant calamus and wormwood were also simmered in the water. This custom still survives in some places, and it is said that such a bath helps cure skin diseases and can ward off evil. On the Duanwu Festival, bundles of calamus and wormwood are hung on the door. Calamus leaves are swordlike, and they are called by necromancers "water swords" that can destroy all evils. Wormwood is a kind of herbal medicine symbolizing the invitation of all good fortune and hanging wormwood on the door helps keep the family healthy. The custom of drinking medicinal liquor, including realgar wine, is widespread. In order to prevent epidemic diseases and ward off poisonous creatures and worms, people spray wine and water in the garden. It is said that medicinal herbs gathered on this day are capable of getting rid of poisonous gases. Since the leaves and stems of herbs are at their best around this time of year and thus have the greatest medicinal effect, gathering medicinal herbs at this time has gradually become a custom.

The Mid-Autumn Festival

17 The Mid-Autumn Festival falls on the fifteenth day of the eighth lunar month. Autumn in China lasts roughly from the seventh lunar month to the ninth lunar month with the eighth month in the middle. Furthermore, the fifteenth day is also in the middle of the eighth month. Consequently, this day is called the Mid-Autumn.

18 The importance of the Mid-Autumn Festival is second only to the Spring Festival. The moon on this night is especially bright and clear since the autumn sky is high and the air is brisk. The full moon is linked to the reunion of family members, and thus the day is also called the Moon Festival or the Reunion Festival.

19 As for the origin of the Mid-Autumn Festival, there are roughly three versions. One says that the festival originates from the worship of the moon in ancient times; another says that it originates from the custom of looking for one's spouse by singing and dancing under the moon; still another says that it results from the custom of offering sacrifices to the god of earth in response to the god's blessings after the year's harvest. There are many beautiful stories about the Mid-Autumn, among which the most well-known is *Goddess Chang'e's Flight to the Moon*. It is said that Hou Yi, the great archer who shot down nine suns out of ten in the sky, married Chang'e. He received from Lady Queen Mother a packet of elixir which could make people immortal and enable people to fly up to heaven. Chang'e swallowed the elixir of immortality and immediately flew to the Palace of the Moon and became a fairy. When the common people found out that Chang'e had become a fairy and had gone to the moon, they set tables under the moon, offered sacrifices to her, and prayed for her blessings.

20 With its vast territory, China boasts various customs in different places, and there are a variety of customs for the Mid-Autumn Festival, many of which are rich in regional characteristics. Prevalent customs for this day include admiring and worshiping the moon and eating moon cakes. Appreciation of the moon is a cheerful aesthetic entertainment, especially for those in literary circles. Numerous poets, such as Bai Juyi, Liu Yuxi, and Su Shi, wrote masterpieces on the full moon of Mid-Autumn. Another important custom for this festival is eating moon cakes. The moon cake was first used as a sacrifice to the god of the moon in ancient times, but it gradually developed into a required gift on the festival day to signify family reunion. Thus, people customarily eat moon cakes to symbolize "reunion".

21 In addition to the four major festivals, there are some other important traditional festivals worth mentioning here: the Lantern Festival, the Magpie Festival, and the Double Ninth Festival. It's obvious that Chinese traditional festivals are rooted in the historical culture of our Chinese civilization and the habits and customs of our ancestors, which have profound cultural significance.

Notes

1. twenty-four solar terms 二十四节气 A solar term is any of twenty-four (24) periods in traditional Chinese lunisolar calendars that matches a particular astronomical event or signifies some natural phenomenon. The points are spaced 15° apart along the ecliptic and are used by lunisolar calendars to stay synchronized with the seasons, which is crucial for agrarian societies. The solar terms are also used to calculate intercalary months in East Asian calendars; which month is repeated depends on the position of the sun at the time. According to the *Book of Documents*, the first determined term was the Winter Solstice, also named dongzhi by Zhou Gong, while he was trying to locate the geological center of his kingdom, by measuring the length of the sun's shadow on an ancient timekeeper instrument named Tu Gui. Then four terms of seasons were set, which were soon evolved as eight terms; until 104 B. C. in the book *Taichu Calendar*, the entire twenty-four solar terms were officially included in the Chinese calendar. In 2016, the 24 solar terms were listed as UNESCO's Intangible Cultural Heritage.

2. Spring Festival couplets 春联 Spring Festival couplets, *chunlian* in Chinese, is also known as spring couplets or Chinese New Year couplets. It is the most common and important custom when celebrating Chinese New Year. This tradition is widely kept both in modern cities and rural areas of China. With black or golden characters written on red paper, Spring Festival couplets are composed of a pair of poetry lines vertically pasted on both sides of the front door and a four-character horizontal scroll affixed above the doorframe. Pasting couplets expresses people's delight in the festival and wishes for a better life in the coming year. The first line (upper scroll) and the second line (lower scroll) have parallel structures and antithetical meanings. The two lines should have an equal number of characters, while their meaning must be related and antithetical. There must be a one-to-one correspondence between the two lines. The tone pattern is emphasized but rhythm is not important. The horizontal scroll is a four-character phrase, which sums up the two lines' meaning.

3. Cold Food Festival 寒食节 The Cold Food Festival is a traditional Chinese holiday celebrated for three consecutive days starting the day before the Qingming Festival in the Chinese calendar, which falls on the 105th day after dongzhi. It is celebrated in China as well as the nearby nations of Korea and Vietnam. At this time of year, the sky becomes clearer and buds sprout in the field. Farmers sow various seeds and supply water to their rice paddies.

This custom is said to have something to do with Jie Zitui, a virtuous official of Kingdom Jin during the Spring and Autumn Period (770–476 B. C.). According to tradition, Chong'er, Prince of Jin, was once in exile to flee from a national calamity. When he was nearly starved to death, Jie Zitui, one of his followers, cut a piece of meat from his leg, roasted it, and sent it to Chong'er. Later Chong'er was able to come back to Jin and claim the throne as Jin Wengong (Duke Wen of Jin). He granted titles and territory to all the subjects that followed him while he was in exile, but unfortunately he forgot Jie Zitui out of negligence. Jie Zitui hid in Mount Mian (now in the southeast of Jiexiu County, Shanxi Province) with his mother. Later Duke Wen was reminded of Jie and sent for him. Jie refused to come out of the mountain and would not receive Duke Wen's reward. In order to drive Jie out of the mountain, Duke Wen had no choice but to set fire to Mount Mian from three sides. The fire lasted for three whole days and the mountain was turned into scorched earth, but Jie did not come out. Only after the fire was extinguished did people find Jie's body hugging a willow tree with his mother on his back. Duke Wen was regretful, and he ordered that, in order to commemorate Jie Zitui, people should not use fire and thus could only eat cold food on the day when Jie was burned. Hence there is the Cold Food Festival, which happens to be one day before the Qingming Festival, and the two festivals are always celebrated together.

- **Reading Comprehension**

1. Directions: *Match the Chinese names of the 24 solar terms in the left column with their English translations in the right column and talk about their meanings.*

	Chinese	English
	立春	A. Spring Equinox
	雨水	B. Pure Brightness
	惊蛰	C. White Dew
	春分	D. Beginning of Summer
	清明	E. Lesser Heat
	谷雨	F. Grain Rain
	立夏	G. Beginning of Autumn
	小满	H. Lesser Fullness of Grain
	芒种	I. Summer Solstice
	夏至	J. Rain Water
	小暑	K. Beginning of Spring
	大暑	L. Beginning of Winter
	立秋	M. Greater Heat
	处暑	N. Grain in Beard

	Chinese	English
	白露	O. Cold Dew
	秋分	P. Waking of Insects
	寒露	Q. Autumn Equinox
	霜降	R. Frost's Descent
	立冬	S. End of Heat
	小雪	T. Lesser Cold
	大雪	U. Lesser Snow
	冬至	V. Greater Snow
	小寒	W. Winter Solstice
	大寒	X. Greater Cold

2. **Directions**: *Choose the best answer from the four choices.*

( )1) How many festivals are mainly introduced in the passage?

A. Six. B. Four. C. Seven. D. Eight.

( )2) Which festival is one of the 24 seasonal division points in China, falling on April 4–6 each year?

A. Qingming Festival. B. Summer Solstice Festival.

C. Winter Solstice Festival. D. Dragon Boat Festival.

( )3) What is the essential food of the Dragon Boat Festival?

A. Zongzi. B. Niangao. C. Jiaozi. D. Tangyuan.

( )4) Which festival is Chinese Valentine's Day?

A. Double Ninth Festival. B. Double Seventh Festival.

C. Mid-autumn Festival. D. Winter Solstice Festival.

( )5) Most traditional Chinese festivals are said to have originated in the ________.

A. Pre-Qin Period. B. Han Dynasty.

C. Tang Dynasty. D. Shang Dynasty.

( )6) The major customs and activities for the Qingming Festival include ________.

A. eating cold food and going hiking B. sweeping the grave and flying kites

C. wearing willow twigs D. all of the above

Part Three

Topic-Related Activities

1. Case Study

I have an American friend. I have invited him several times, and at long last he invited me to his home one day. He told me to get there at 3 p. m. I thought we could chat and have a meal together. I gave him a Chinese calendar, a woman's scarf and a bottle of Chinese white wine. He only took out a dish of nuts, a plate of bread and a bottle of wine. After two hours' chat, I found there was no hint of a meal and said good-bye to him. He only gave me a box of chocolate as a present for the New Year. After I got home, I found the box already been opened. I was very surprised.

Question: What surprised me?

2. Critical Thinking & Cultural Exploration

Step One

Directions: *Ask students to list some famous Chinese festivals and Western festivals and their ways of celebration.*

Step Two

Directions: *Valentine's Day is recognized as a significant cultural and religious celebration of romance and romantic love in many countries in the world. Please compare it with the Double Seventh Festival in China from the perspectives of popularity, origin and customs.*

Step Three

Directions: *A handwritten letter or card of thanks is one of the most meaningful ways to express gratitude. Write your own thank-you message to whoever has recently helped you.*

Letter of Thanks—states in the first sentence why you are expressing thanks. The rest includes details about the situation. Tell how useful or appropriate it is, how you plan to use it, where you have placed it (home, office, wardrobe) or how it enhances your life. Be specific about what pleased you. A letter of thanks ends by re-expressing your appreciation. Thank-you letters should remain friendly in tone and common courtesy is welcomed by the reader.

Be clear and attentive to your audience.

Sign the letter in handwriting.

Example:

For a gift

Dear Mrs. Beck,

How did you ever find those wonderful glasses? They are perfect, and Jim and I want to thank you a thousand times!

The presents will be shown on the day of the wedding, but do come over Thursday morning if you can for a cup of coffee and an earlier view.

Thank you again, and with love from us both.

Mary

For hospitality

Dear Mr. Zhang,

Please accept my thanks for the very pleasant time I spent on Tuesday evening at your office.

I very much appreciated your hospitality and also thoroughly enjoyed the three very interesting and colorful films which were shown to us.

Yours faithfully,

Susan

3. Translation

Directions: *Translate the passage into English.*

重阳节,由于它是在中国农历九月初九这一天,所以又被称为重九节,至今有约两千年的历史。在中国古代,重阳节是一个重要的节日,这一天要举行各种庆祝活动,如:登高、赏菊(chrysanthemum)、插茱萸(cornel)、吃重阳糕等。登高是重阳节的主要习俗。古人认为,在这一天登高可以避祸免灾。近年来,这个古老的节日被赋予新的含义,逐渐成为开展各种敬老活动、一年一度的"老年节"。

Unit Ten

Wedding

Part One

Lead-in

Marriage is an institution in which a man loses his bachelor's degree and the woman gets her master's.

—Socrates

In ancient times, the marriage of a man and a woman meant two families, tribes or political groups joined forces to fight against their enemy, or simply to reproduce. And they should hold a ceremony to celebrate it and invite guests to join. Traditionally we call this ceremony a wedding. Nowadays the marriage of two people may bear the meaning of ancient times but mostly for love. Still they are supposed to hold a ceremony, the wedding.

Part Two

In-Class Reading

Warm-up questions:

1. Do you know some wedding customs?
2. Have you ever been to a wedding? What's that wedding like?

Everything You Need to Know About Princess Diana's Wedding

1 From the **sapphire** engagement ring to the **intricate** wedding gown, here are all the **glamorous** details.

2 This season of *The Crown* will include a much-anticipated royal event: **Prince Charles**[1] and **Princess Diana's**[2] wedding. While it's unclear exactly how the show will handle the momentous day, Emma Corrin, who plays Princess Diana, will definitely wear a recreation of that famous dress.

3 Indeed, this season takes on the beginning of Prince Charles and Princess Diana's relationship. The couple met when Diana was only a teenager and Charles was dating her older sister. Several years later, after only 12 dates, the couple got engaged and were married within six months, on July 29, 1981 at **St. Paul's Cathedral**[3]. The wedding was broadcast on television and seen by around 750 million people around the world.

4 An international event, it is remembered as one of the most famous weddings in royal history, even after Princess Diana and Prince Charles' divorce in 1992. Keep reading for a look back at some of the most interesting moments from the couple's real-life big day.

The Night Before

5 While the big day is traditionally considered an important **occasion** for the bride, in this case, the groom was just as nervous about the upcoming wedding. In fact, Prince Charles reportedly cried the night before the wedding because he was still **torn over** his feelings for former girlfriend Camilla Parker-Bowles, according to *Prince Charles: The Passions and Paradoxes of an Improbable Life*. Several years after Diana's death, Prince Charles would later marry Parker-Bowles on April 8, 2005.

The Venue

6 Princess Diana's wedding to Prince Charles took place at St. Paul's Cathedral in London. Lady Diana left **Clarence House**[4] and was transported to the main venue in a Glass

Coach with her father, Earl Spencer. One of few royal weddings not to take place at the royal church at **Westminster Abbey**[5], Princess Diana's royal union was unique from the dress to the venue itself. The last royal wedding to be held at St. Paul's Cathedral was 480 years before that of Princess Diana and Prince Charles, between Prince Arthur, eldest son of **King Henry VII**[6], and Princess Catherine on November 14, 1501.

The Guest List

7 The streets of London were flooded with around 600, 000 people trying to **catch a glimpse of** Prince Charles and the **bride-to-be** on their special day. The ceremony itself was seen by a crowd of 3,500 people, including important guests like the groom's parents (Prince Philip and **Queen Elizabeth** Ⅱ[7]) and the bride's parents (Earl and Countess Spencer). Other notable guests included the groom's brothers (Prince Andrew and Prince Edward), as well as Princess Anne, Princess Margaret, Princess Alice, and the Duke and Duchess of Kent.

The Dress

8 Princess Diana's dress was an **extravagant** and much-anticipated sight to see. Covered in 10,000 pearls and complete with a 25-foot train—the longest in royal history—Diana's gown was designed by husband-and-wife design team **David and Elizabeth Emanuel**[8]. The intricate ivory **taffeta** gown was paired with a 153-yard veil, an 18th-century era heirloom tiara, and silk shoes embroidered with 542 **sequins** and 132 matching pearls.

The Vows

9 While most royal couples like to keep the wedding ceremony as traditional as possible, Diana wasn't opposed to making a few changes when it came to her **vows**. In fact, she was the first royal to **omit** the word "obey" from her wedding vows, according to a 1981 article by *The New York Times*. Following his mother's lead, Prince William and Duchess Kate did the same at their wedding in 2011. Princess Diana also **showcased** her nerves on the big day when she mixed up Prince Charles' full name during their vows, referring to him as Philip Charles Arthur George, while Charles is his actual first name, according to the BBC.

The Ring

10 Much like her dress, Princess Diana's ring has been the focus of designers and brides-to-be for many years. A 12-carat sapphire stone surrounded by 14 **solitaire** diamonds set in a white gold band, the ring is estimated to have cost around $40,000 at the time. One of the few royal wedding rings to not be custom-made, Diana chose the ring from the **Garrard jewelry**[9] collection catalogue, and some believe it was because it reminded her of her mother's wedding ring. The intricate sapphire ring has since been **passed down** to Duchess Kate of Cambridge after Prince William used it to **propose** in 2010.

The Cakes

11 With several thousand guests in attendance, it was only **appropriate** to have more than one cake at the reception. While there were 27 wedding cakes at the celebration following Princess Diana and Prince Charles' wedding, the official cake was provided by David Avery, the head baker at the Royal Naval cooking school. A multi-tiered fruit cake, the **pastry** was divided into small silver presentation boxes as **souvenirs** for guests. According to the *Tampa Bay Times*, in 2014, a Florida man paid $1,375 at an auction to purchase a now nearly 37-year-old slice of the cake.

New Words and Expressions

sapphire /ˈsæfaɪər/	*n.* a precious stone, usually bright blue, that is often used in jewellery 蓝宝石
intricate /ˈɪntrɪkət/	*adj.* having a lot of small parts or details that are arranged in a complicated way and are therefore sometimes difficult to understand, solve, or produce 错综复杂的;复杂精细的;难理解的;难解决的
glamorous /ˈglæmərəs/	*adj.* attractive in an exciting and special way 有魅力的;令人向往的;富于刺激的;独特的
occasion /əˈkeɪʒən/	*n.* a particular time, especially when something happens or has happened (尤指某事发生的)时刻,时候
bride-to-be	*n.* a woman who is going to be married soon 准新娘
extravagant /ɪkˈstrævəgənt/	*adj.* spending too much money, or using too much of something 奢侈的,铺张的;浪费的
taffeta /ˈtæfətə/	*n.* a stiff, shiny cloth made from silk or artificial material, used especially for dresses to be worn at special events(丝绸或尼龙制成的)塔夫绸
sequin /ˈsiːkwɪn/	*n.* a small, shiny metal or plastic disc sewn onto clothes for

	decoration(服装上作装饰用的)闪光亮片
vow /vaʊ/	*v.* to make a determined decision or promise to do something 发誓,立誓
	n. a serious promise or decision 誓言;誓约
omit /əʊˈmɪt/	*v.* to fail to include or do something 疏忽,遗漏;删节,排除
showcase /ˈʃəʊkeɪs/	*v.* to show the best qualities or parts of something 展示……的优点;充分展示
solitaire /ˌsɒlɪˈteər/	*n.* a single jewel (= precious stone) that is part of a piece of jewellery, especially a ring, or the ring itself(尤指戒指上的)独粒宝石
propose /prəˈpəʊz/	*v.* to offer or suggest a possible plan or action for other people to consider; to ask someone to marry you 提议;提出; 求婚
appropriate /əˈprəʊpriət/	*adj.* suitable or right for a particular situation 适当的,恰当的;合适的
pastry /ˈpeɪstri/	*n.* a food made from a mixture of flour, fat, and water, rolled flat and either wrapped around or put over or under other foods, and then baked 油酥糕点;油酥点心
souvenir /ˌsuːvəˈnɪər/	*n.* something you buy or keep to help you remember a holiday or special event 纪念品;纪念物
tear over	to pull or be pulled apart, or to pull pieces off 撕碎
catch a glimpse of	spot, notice, spy, catch sight of 瞥见;看一眼
pass down	to teach or give something to someone who will be alive after you have died 传承

Notes

1. Prince Charles 查尔斯王子 Charles Philip Arthur George, Prince of Wales and Earl of Chester, Duke of Cornwall, Duke of Rothesay, Earl of Carrick and Baron Renfrew, Lord of the Isles, and Prince and Great Steward of Scotland (born on November 14, 1948, Buckingham Palace, London, England), is the heir apparent to the British throne as the eldest son of Queen Elizabeth II and Prince Philip, Duke of Edinburgh.

2. Princess Diana 戴安娜王妃 Diana(born on July 1, 1961, Sandringham, Norfolk, England; died on Aug. 31, 1997, Paris, France), former consort (1981–1996) of Charles, Prince of Wales, Daughter of Viscount Althorp (later Earl Spencer); she was a kindergarten teacher at the time of her engagement to Charles, whom she married on July 29, 1981, in a globally televised ceremony. They had two sons, Princes William (1982) and Henry (1984).

3. St. Paul's Cathedral 圣保罗大教堂　Saint Paul's Cathedral is a cathedral of the Anglican bishop. It is located within the central City of London, atop Ludgate Hill and northeast of Blackfriars.

4. Clarence House 克拉伦斯宫　Clarence House, which stands beside St. Jame's Palace, was built between 1825 and 1827 to the designs of John Nash for Prince William Henry, Duke of Clarence.

5. Westminster Abbey 威斯敏斯特大教堂　London church that is the site of coronations and other ceremonies of national significance. It stands just west of the Houses of Parliament in the Greater London borough of Westminster. Situated on the grounds of a former Benedictine monastery, it was refounded as the Collegiate Church of St. Peter in Westminster by Queen Elizabeth I in 1560. In 1987 Westminster Abbey, St. Margaret's Church, and the Houses of Parliament were collectively designated a UNESCO World Heritage site.

6. King Henry VII 国王亨利七世　King Henry Ⅶ, also called (1457 – 1485) Henry Tudor, Earl of Richmond (born on January 28, 1457, Pembroke Castle, Pembrokeshire, Wales; died April 21, 1509, Richmond, Surrey, England), King of England (1485 – 1509), who succeeded in ending the Wars of the Roses between the houses of Lancaster and York and founded the Tudor dynasty. Henry, son of Edmund Tudor, Earl of Richmond, and Margaret Beaufort, was born nearly three months after his father's death.

7. Queen Elizabeth Ⅱ 伊丽莎白二世　Elizabeth Ⅱ, in full Elizabeth Alexandra Mary, officially Elizabeth Ⅱ, by the Grace of God, of the United Kingdom of Great Britain and Northern Ireland and of her other realms and territories Queen, Head of the Commonwealth, Defender of the Faith (born on April 21, 1926, London, England), Queen of the United Kingdom of Great Britain and Northern Ireland from February 6, 1952. In 2015 she surpassed Victoria to become the longest-reigning monarch in British history. Elizabeth was the elder daughter of Prince Albert, Duke of York, and his wife, Lady Elizabeth Bowes-Lyon.

8. David and Elizabeth Emanuel 大卫和伊丽莎白 · 伊曼纽尔　British designers. David was born in Bridgend, Wales on November 17, 1952 while Elizabeth Weiner was born in London, England on July 5, 1953. The couple started a dressmaking shop in London in 1977 and in 1979 decided to close their ready-to-wear business and concentrate instead on made-to-order business. Their designs are worn by royalty such as Prince Charles of Wales and Lady Diana Spencer and Her Royal Highness the Duchess of Kent.

9. Garrard jewelry 杰拉德珠宝(曾被维多利亚女王指定为“王冠珠宝商”)　Every Garrard design is handcrafted in the studio, from jewellery suites to tiaras, headdresses to brooches. Design, craftsmanship and the most beautiful of natural materials combine to capture a spirit that is uniquely British.

• Reading Comprehension

1. **Directions**: *Discuss the following questions with your classmates.*

1) When did Prince Charles met Diana according to the text? Where did Prince Charles and Diana get married? And when did they get divorced?

2) What happened to Prince Charles the night before?

3) Where do the royal weddings usually take place?

4) How many people were there trying to catch a glimpse of Prince Charles and the bride-to-be on their special day?

5) What's the difference between Princess Diana's vows and previous ones?

6) Why did Princess Diana choose the ring from the Garrard jewelry collection catalogue?

2. **Directions**: *Read the following statements carefully, and decide whether they are true(T) or false(F) according to the text.*

( )1) Princess Diana, whose real name is Emma Corrin will definitely wear a recreation of that famous dress on her wedding.

( )2) Prince Charles had dated with Princess Diana's eldest sister.

( )3) Diana left a Glass Coach and was transported to the main venue in Clarence House with her father, Earl Spencer.

( )4) Prince Andrew and Prince Edward are Prince Charles' brothers.

( )5) Prince Charles's real full name is Philip Charles Arthur George.

( )6) Princess's wedding ring has been passed down to Duchess Kate of Cambridge after Prince William used it to propose in 2010.

3. **Critical thinking**

1) Was one wedding cake enough for so many guests on the wedding, and how did they solve the problem?

2) Are there wedding vows, wedding rings and wedding cakes in a traditional Chinese wedding?

After-Class Reading

Warm-up questions:

1. What is the most impressive characteristic of Chinese wedding in your mind?
2. Which kind of wedding do you like best? Why?

Traditional Chinese Wedding Customs

1. The Proper Procedures: Three Letters and Six Etiquette[1]

1 This is the elaborate process on the groom's parents' part to look for the right kind of bride for their family. Rich families will look for a bride who can take care of household finances and most importantly, give birth to sons to inherit the wealth of the family. Poor families will look for a bride who can work hard in the fields and give birth to sons to help out on the farm.

2 In the old days, marriages were arranged so it's quite normal for the parents to dominate the bride-seeking process. Girls from rich family will be sought out by other rich families and poor girls will probably marry into poor families. Hence the Chinese saying: **Bamboo door is to bamboo door as wooden door is to wooden door**[2].

3 There are some circumstances where the marriage has been arranged when both the bride and the groom were very young or not even born. In the former case, a young girl may be bought by the rich family as a servant girl to serve the rich boy. When the boy grew up, she may become either his wife or one of his concubines. In the latter case, two pregnant mothers will make the promise that when the babies are born, if they were both boys or both girls, they would become brothers or sisters and if one baby was a boy and the other a girl, they would get married. Hence the saying: **pointing to the bosom as a marriage promise**[3]. However, a lot of times when the boy grew up, his family may have fallen from prestige and sometimes the girl's family may refuse to let them get married. There are numerous folktales about tragedies that stem from arranged marriage. However, there are also many happy endings to arranged marriage. All we can say is that it was the fact of life at that time.

1a. Three Letters

4 In the old days, all communication was through formal letters. Therefore, the letters play an important role in the events.

Request Letter[4]

5 This letter confirms the formal arrangement of a marriage. It is sent by the groom's family to the bride's family. This letter is normally presented with the initial gifts for the bride's

family.

Gift Letter[4]

6 This letter accompanies the formal gifts for the bride's family. It is actually a gift list that records the description and quantity of the gifts.

Wedding Letter[4]

7 This letter is presented to the bride's family on the day of the wedding. It confirms the act of bringing the bride into the groom's family.

1b. Six Etiquette

8 The Chinese word for etiquette can mean both customs and gifts. The following customs are known as the Six Etiquette.

Request for Marrying the Bride[5]

9 After the groom's family has spotted a young girl whom the groom wants to marry, the family will hire a spokeswoman who will communicate their wish to the potential bride's family. (In the old days, it was popular to hire elderly ladies as midwives or spokeswomen for the groom.) This lady will persuade the potential bride's family to accept the offer from the groom's family. Both sides will negotiate certain terms. If successful, both families will proceed to the next step.

Request for Bride and Groom's Birthdates[5]

10 This is the second step in arranging a marriage. Upon successful completion of the previous step, the groom's family will request for the bride's "Eight Letters" through the spokeswoman. In Chinese calendar, there are 22 "letters" that we use to represent date. Ten are known as "Tiangan" and twelve are "Dizhi". Two letters are used to represent each of the following: year, month, day and time. Altogether, eight letters will accurately represent the bride's birthdate.

Birthdates Matching[5]

11 After obtaining the "Eight Letters" of the groom and potential bride, a fortune telling master will be hired to determine whether the two match each other. If there is nothing wrong with the bride's birthdate, the groom's family will proceed to the next step. Otherwise, there will be no further contact between the families and the groom's family may look for another suitable bride.

Presenting Betrothal Gifts[5]

12 If the potential bride's birthdate is acceptable, the groom's family will request the spokeswoman to send some initial gifts accompanied by the gift letter.

13 The groom's family will pick a "good day" and send the bride's family the following bridal gifts: gifts, cash, cakes and food and sacrifices for worshiping the ancestors. This act

confirms the marriage agreement between the two families.

Wedding Date Fixing[5]

14 The fortune telling master will select a "good day" according to the bride's and groom's and their family's birthdates.

Wedding Day[5]

15 On the big day, both the bride and the groom's house will be decorated in red. The groom's family will send out a procession of servants, musicians and a carriage which is carried by four servants to the bride's family to bring the bride back. The bride will then be brought back to the groom's house and the two will perform the marriage ceremony witnessed by all the relatives and friends.

16 The bride and groom will worship the heavens and the earth, the groom's ancestors and they will also serve tea to all their superiors in the family. After that, the superiors will give them red packages with monetary gifts and wish them well. The groom's family will then throw a huge feast (if they can afford it) for the friends and relatives to celebrate the wedding. All along, the spokeswoman will oversee the whole process and keep toasting the couple.

17 After the meal, the newly wed couple will return to the bridal room and some naughty friends may tag-along and play tricks on the groom. When all is done, the couple will drink and toast and the spokeswoman will offer sweets and fruits to the couple to wish them long life and lots of kids. Then, the couple will finally be left with themselves, and the groom can take off the red cloth that covers the bride's face.

2. Preparation for the Wedding

2a. Setting up the Bridal Bed

18 After the groom's family has selected a "good day" as the wedding day, a man who's considered to have had good fortune all through his life will be hired to move the bridal bed to the right place. Then a lady who's considered to have had good fortune (with a healthy and living husband and sons) will make the bed and place certain good fortune food and fruits on the bed. Then the bed will be left untouched until the day of the wedding.

2b. The Bride's Gifts for the Groom

19 The bride's gifts for the groom will either arrive a couple of days before the wedding day or if she's a relatively long-distance bride, she'll bring along the gifts with her maids as she arrives at the groom's home on the wedding day.

20 The bride's gifts usually consist of valuable jewelry and precious stones, kitchen utensils, proper bridal linen such as sheets, pillow covers and clothes. In some areas, the bride's family is expected to furnish the bridal except for the bridal bed. There's a saying that if the bride supplies the bridal bed, then the family is practically giving the bride away for free.

2c. Combing Hair

21 The night before the wedding, both the bride and the groom need to find a "good fortune" woman and man to comb their hair in her/his home respectively. Both the bride and the groom need to take a shower before the event, put on some fresh new underwear and incense needs to be burnt. The bride also needs to sit next to a window where the moon can be seen. Their hair needs to be combed four times and each has a special meaning:

The first combing symbolizes: from beginning till the end;

The second combing symbolizes: harmony from now till old age;

The third combing symbolizes: sons and grandsons all over the place;

The fourth combing summaries good wealth and a long-lasting marriage.

22 The whole action also symbolizes the adulthood of the couple. If either has been married before, then the combing event can be skipped for that person.

3. Wedding Day Activities

3a. Wedding Day: Welcoming the Bride

23 On the day of the wedding, the groom will send a carriage over to the bride's family to bring the bride home. The carriage is decorated in red and is carried by four servants. Musicians will accompany the procession and they will play wedding music all the way. A lot of gifts are also brought to the bride's family at the same time.

24 At the bride's home, the bride will put on her bright red wedding gown and the bride's parents will give her jewelry to wear.

3b. Bride Leaving Home

25 As the groom's procession arrives, the groom's spokeswoman will enter the bride's house and carry the bride on her back. The bride cannot touch the ground with her feet until she arrives at the groom's house. In some regions, the bride's relatives will throw rice into the air, hoping that the chickens around will eat the rice instead of pecking at the bride. Sometimes, a red umbrella is used to shield the bride as the opening of the umbrella will symbolize her bringing many descendants to the groom's family. As the bride leaves the house, her parents and her relatives will bid her farewell as she rides the carriage and leaves home. Wealthy brides often have servant girls who will follow her to the groom's family and continue to serve her. These maids are known as ones who "accompany the marriage".

3c. Bride Arriving at the Groom's Home

26 After the bride arrives at the groom's house, the couple will again worship the ancestors and worship the heavens and earth. Then they will serve tea to the groom's family according to their seniority and the relatives will give them red packets or bridal jewelry in return.

3d. The Wedding Banquet

27 To celebrate the marriage, the groom's family will throw a wedding feast as large as they can afford. In the old days, some villagers may use up to seven continuous days to entertain the relatives during a wedding. Every night, delicious food is being served to all the guests.

4. Post Wedding Activities

The Bride Returning Home after 3 Days

28 Three days after the wedding, the bride is expected to return to her family. The bride will bring along roasted pigs and gifts for the family. In some regions, the groom is required to accompany her while the groom is not required to do so in some others. Nonetheless, this is probably the last chance the bride gets to see her parents, for the long distance and inconvenient transportation. And to show their great respect for the bride's parents, the new couple will bring along a lot of gifts for the family and she may even stay for a couple of days or even more.

29 As a tradition, the bride's family will also return part of the gifts to the groom's family as a courtesy. Some regional customs require that the family should return the head and tail of the roasted pig to the groom's family, symbolizing the good beginning and end of the wedding.

Notes

1. Three Letters and Six Etiquette 三书六礼 Traditional proper procedures of Chinese wedding customs. Three Letters are request letter, gift letter and wedding letter. Six Etiquette is request for marrying the bride, request for bride's and groom's birthdates, birthdates matching, presenting betrothal gifts, wedding date fixing and wedding day.

2. Bamboo door is to bamboo door as wooden door is to wooden door 门当户对 In the old days, marriages were arranged so it's quite normal for the parents to dominate the bride-seeking process. Girls from rich family will be sought out by other rich families and poor girls will probably marry into poor families.

3. pointing to the bosom as a marriage promise 指腹为婚 There are some circumstances where the marriage has been arranged when both the bride and the groom were very young or not even born. Two pregnant mothers and their families will make the promise that when the babies are born, if they were both boys or both girls, they would become brothers or sisters and if one baby was a boy and the other a girl, they would get married.

4. request letter, gift letter and wedding letter 聘书、礼书和迎书

5. request for marrying the bride 纳彩、问名、纳吉、纳征、请期和迎亲 request for bride's and groom's birthdates, birthdates matching, presenting betrothal gifts, wedding date fixing and wedding day

• Reading Comprehension

1. **Directions**: *Read the passage quickly and match each of the activities with the Three Letters and Six Etiquette it belongs to.*

________The houses will be decorated in red.

________To determine whether the two match each other.

________To confirm the formal arrangement of a marriage.

________The fortune telling master will select a "good day".

________To confirm the marriage agreement between the two families.

________To negotiate certain terms.

________To confirm the act of bringing the bride into the groom's family.

________To request for the bride's "Eight Letters".

________To send the formal gifts to the Bride's family.

A. Gift Letter

B. Request for Marrying the Bride

C. Presenting Betrothal Gifts

D. Request for Bride and Groom's Birthdates

E. Wedding Day

F. Wedding Letter

G. Birthdates Matching

H. Wedding Date Fixing

I. Request Letter

2. **Directions**: *Fill the blanks according to the passage.*

After the groom's family has ________ a "good day" as the wedding day, a man who's considered to have had ________ all through his life will be hired to move the ________ to the right place. Then a lady who's considered to have had good fortune (with a healthy and living husband and sons) will make the bed and place certain good fortune food and fruits on the bed. Then the bed will be left ________ until the day of the wedding.

The night before the wedding, both the bride and the groom need to find a "good fortune" woman and man to comb their hair in her/his home ________. Both the bride and the groom need to ________ before the event, put on some fresh new underwear and incense needs to be burnt. The bride also needs to sit next to a window where the moon can be seen. Their hair needs to be combed four times and each has a ________.

________ after the wedding, the bride is expected to return to her family. The bride will bring along ________ for the family. In some regions, the groom is required to accompany her while the groom is not required to do so in some others. Nonetheless, this is probably the last chance the bride gets to see her parents for the long distance and inconvenient transportant. And to show their great respect for the bride's parents, the new couple will bring along a lot of gifts for the family and she may even stay for ________ days or even more.

Part Three

Topic-Related Activities

1. Case Study

American Wedding Customs

1 Customs and superstitions surrounding weddings, those that have survived countless generations up to the modern day, and a few for after the wedding.

2 Wedding days are often considered the most important day of many people's lives. For this reason alone, throughout the past and into modern days, numerous customs and superstitions have developed around the wedding event, in hopes of creating "The Perfect Day!"

3 A very common custom still honored today is in reference to a time-old saying, "Something old, something new, something borrowed, something blue, and a silver sixpence inside your shoe." So old is this that tracing it back to its origination is nearly impossible. Some contribute it to Victorian times; others say it is even older than that.

4 The "old" is believed to be the friends and family attending the wedding. The "new" is represented by the couple themselves, as a "new" union.

5 The "borrowed" is something from the families that is to be returned, such as the bride's wedding dress, or the veil, borrowed from her own mother.

6 Something "blue" is often interpreted to represent the bride's virginity, as in the opposite of red, which throughout time has come to represent a woman of many men.

7 Modern-day brides often wear a bit of blue material tucked out of sight. The sixpence can be any form of money, tucked into the bride's shoe, this to bring wealth, both in monetary means and love, to the union.

8 The veil and the bridesmaids were originated not as decorations or to allow your friends to share in your happy day, but to help confuse the evil spirits that were believed to be lurking about on this holy day.

9 The veil, by hiding the face, particularly the eyes, confused the evil spirits. Bridesmaids would surround the bride, thus confusing the evil spirits as to who was the actual

bride.

10 In a similar belief, the best man is supposed to protect the groom from the day the wedding is first set in motion, until he is rightfully married to his impending bride.

11 Weddings have historically taken place in higher numbers during the month of June than any other month of the year. This ties into the old belief that it was lucky to be married on the day of the full moon.

A wedding on the June day of a full moon was considered to be the most prosperous and long-lasting union of all.

12 These go together with the belief that a wedding on a bright, sunny day, which June is well known for, foretold good luck for the bride and groom, compared to being married on a rainy day, which foretold bad luck and a short marriage.

13 The world over, people throw rice at weddings. Why? It shows that the guests wish fertility, prosperity, and long-lasting happiness for the newly married couple.

14 Colors have long played a part in the planning of weddings. While many believe that the white of the wedding dress signified that the bride is a virgin, this is not actually true in all societies. An old saying sums up the colors in a wedding very well:

Marry in white, you will do all right,
Marry in blue, your man will be true,
Marry in brown, you will live in town,
Marry in green, you should be ashamed to be seen,
Marry in red, wish yourself dead,
Marry in black, better turn back,
Marry in yellow, not marrying the right fellow,
Marry in gray, sadness will come your way.

15 The day of the week that the wedding is to take place is also steeped in custom, hence the saying:

Marry on Monday for wealth,
Tuesday for health,
Wednesday the very best day of all,
Thursday you will soon be counting your losses,
Friday your crosses,
And if married on Saturday, you will have no luck at all!

16 One tradition that has been around so long is whether or not it is good luck for the bride to make her own wedding dress. Some people believe it is lucky; others feel it is very unlucky for the bride to even help with the making of the dress.

17 Throwing of the bride's bouquet is good luck for the bride and foretells the next of her friends to be married. Whoever catches the bouquet should take a small sliver of the wedding cake home with her and place it beneath her pillow just as she goes to sleep that night. She will dream of her future husband on that single night.

18 Many superstitions also exist for right after the wedding to start the marriage off right. The new couple should borrow a coffeepot for the first three months, then purchase one together.

19 A new broom and frying pan is needed to start the couple off on a road to happiness, never start off a marriage with these two items old, or already used.

20 The bride should cook her new husband and herself their first meal; it should not be eaten at a restaurant or an in-law's house. Never sell the wedding dress. It can be borrowed out, or even given away, but never let money be received for the dress or the marriage will come to a quick end.

21 Keep in mind these are all just customs and superstitions. Marriage is a union between two people who love each other! (But it never hurts to add a little luck in whatever way you can!)

Questions

1) What are the differences between Chinese and American wedding customs? Can you give any examples?

2) Do you think the customs are somewhat superstitious? And why?

3) What's your opinion about the wedding customs?

4) Which wedding custom do you like, the Chinese or the American?

2. Writing

Directions: *You might have attended a wedding or learned of something about wedding. Write a composition to describe the wedding ceremony according to your knowledge.*

3. Translation

Directions: *Translate the passage into English.*

婚姻是人生的一件大事,俗话说“男大当婚,女大当嫁”。婚礼,在中国原为“昏礼”,属于汉族文化精粹之一,是华夏文化的重要组成部分。古人认为黄昏是吉时,所以会在黄昏行娶妻之礼。在中国传统婚俗中,婚礼分为婚前礼、正婚礼和婚后礼三个阶段,均源自周代“六礼”(即纳彩、问名、纳吉、纳征、请期、迎亲)。

Unit Eleven

Coffee and Tea

Part One

Lead-in

Coffee—the favorite drink of the civilized world. Coffee and tea is a blend of the West and the East.

—Thomas Jefferson

I do not think that, considered from the point of view of human culture and happiness, there have been more significant inventions in the history of mankind, more vitally important and more directly contributing to our enjoyment of leisure, friendship, sociability and conversation, than the invention of smoking, drinking and tea.

Lin Yutang

Part Two

In-Class Reading

Warm-up questions:

1. Do you prefer to sip a cup of coffee in your leisurely time? Why or why not?
2. How much do you know about the history of coffee?

The History of Coffee

1 No one knows exactly how or when coffee was discovered, though there are many legends about its origin.

An Ethiopian Legend

2 Coffee grown worldwide can **trace** its **heritage** back centuries to the ancient coffee forests on the **Ethiopian Plateau**[1]. There, legend says the goat **herder** Kaldi first discovered the potential of these beloved beans.

3 The story goes that Kaldi discovered coffee after he noticed that after eating the berries from a certain tree, his goats became so energetic that they did not want to sleep at night.

4 Kaldi reported his findings to the **abbot** of the local **monastery**, who made a drink with the berries and found that it kept him **alert** through the long hours of evening prayer. The abbot shared his discovery with the other monks at the monastery, and knowledge of the energizing berries began to spread.

5 As word moved east and coffee reached the **Arabian Peninsula**[2], it began a journey which would bring these beans across the globe.

The Arabian Peninsula

6 Coffee cultivation and trade began on the Arabian Peninsula. By the 15th century, coffee was being grown in the Yemeni district of Arabia and by the 16th century it was known in Persia, Egypt, Syria, and Turkey.

7 Coffee was not only enjoyed in homes, but also in many public coffee houses—called qahveh khaneh—which began to appear in cities across the Near East. The popularity of the coffee houses was **unequaled** and people **frequented** them for all kinds of social activity.

8 Not only did the **patrons** drink coffee and engage in conversation, but they also listened to music, watched performers, played chess and kept current on the news. Coffee houses quickly became such an important center for the exchange of information that they were

often referred to as "Schools of the Wise."

9 With thousands of **pilgrims** visiting the **holy** city of **Mecca**[3] each year from all over the world, knowledge of this "wine of Araby" began to spread.

Coffee Comes to Europe

10 European travelers to the Near East brought back stories of an unusual dark black **beverage**. By the 17th century, coffee had made its way to Europe and was becoming popular across the continent.

11 Some people reacted to this new beverage with suspicion or fear, calling it the "bitter invention of **Satan**[4]". The local clergy **condemned** coffee when it came to Venice in 1615. The controversy was so great that **Pope Clement VIII**[5] was asked to **intervene**. He decided to taste the beverage for himself before making a decision, and found the drink so satisfying that he gave it **papal** approval.

12 Despite such **controversy**, coffee houses were quickly becoming centers of social activity and communication in the major cities of England, Austria, France, Germany and Holland. In England "penny universities" **sprang up**, so called because for the price of a penny one could purchase a cup of coffee and engage in stimulating conversation.

13 Coffee began to replace the common breakfast drink beverages of the time—beer and wine. Those who drank coffee instead of alcohol began the day alert and energized, and not surprisingly, the quality of their work was greatly improved. (We like to think of this a **precursor** to the modern office coffee service.)

14 By the mid-17th century, there were over 300 coffee houses in London, many of which attracted like-minded patrons, including merchants, shippers, **brokers** and artists.

15 Many businesses grew out of these specialized coffee houses. **Lloyd's of London**[6], for example, came into existence at the Edward Lloyd's Coffee House.

The New World

16 In the mid-1600's, coffee was brought to New Amsterdam, later called New York by the British.

17 Though coffee houses rapidly began to appear, tea continued to be the favored drink in the New World until 1773, when the **colonists revolted against** a heavy tax on tea imposed by King George III. The revolt, known as the **Boston Tea Party**[7], would forever change the American drinking preference to coffee.

Plantations Around the World

18 As demand for the beverage continued to spread, there was fierce competition to cultivate coffee outside of Arabia.

19 The Dutch finally got **seedlings** in the latter half of the 17th century. Their first

attempts to plant them in India failed, but they were successful with their efforts in Batavia, on the island of Java in what is now Indonesia.

20 The plants **thrived** and soon the Dutch had a productive and growing trade in coffee. They then expanded the cultivation of coffee trees to the islands of Sumatra and Celebes.

Coming to the Americas

21 In 1714, the Mayor of Amsterdam presented a gift of a young coffee plant to **King Louis XIV**[8] of France. The King ordered it to be planted in the Royal Botanical Garden in Paris. In 1723, a young naval officer, **Gabriel de Clieu**[9] obtained a seedling from the King's plant. Despite a challenging voyage—complete with **horrendous** weather, a **saboteur** who tried to destroy the seedling, and a **pirate** attack—he managed to transport it safely to **Martinique**[10].

22 Once planted, the seedling not only thrived, but it's **credited** with the spread of over 18 million coffee trees on the island of Martinique in the next 50 years. Even more incredible is that this seedling was the parent of all coffee trees throughout the Caribbean, South and Central America.

23 The famed Brazilian coffee owes its existence to Francisco de Mello Palheta, who was sent by the emperor to French Guiana to get coffee seedlings. The French were not willing to share, but the French Governor's wife, **captivated** by his good looks, gave him a large **bouquet** of flowers before he left— buried inside were enough coffee seeds to begin what is today a billion-dollar industry.

24 Missionaries and travelers, traders and colonists continued to carry coffee seeds to new lands, and coffee trees were planted worldwide. Plantations were established in magnificent **tropical** forests and on rugged mountain highlands. Some crops flourished, while others were short-lived. New nations were established on coffee economies. Fortunes were made and lost. By the end of the 18th century, coffee had become one of the world's most profitable export crops. After **crude** oil, coffee is the most sought **commodity** in the world.

New Words and Expressions

trace /treɪs/	*v.* to follow, discover, or ascertain the course or development of (something) 追溯
heritage /ˈherɪtɪdʒ/	*n.* practices that are handed down from the past by tradition 遗产；传统
herder /ˈhɜːdə(r)/	*n.* someone who drives a herd 牧人
abbot /ˈæbət/	*n.* the superior of an abbey of monks 男修道院院长
monastery /ˈmɒnəstri/	*n.* the residence of a religious community 修道院

alert /ə'lɜːt/ *adj.* very attentive or observant 警觉的;机敏的

unequaled /ʌn'iːkwəld/ *adj.* radically distinctive and without equal 无与伦比的

frequent /'friːkwənt; fri'kwent/ *v.* be a regular or frequent visitor to a certain place 常到,常去

patron /'peɪtrən/ *n.* a regular customer 常客

pilgrim /'pɪlgrɪm/ *n.* someone who journeys to a sacred place as an act of religious devotion 朝圣者

holy /'həʊli/ *adj.* belonging to or derived from or associated with a divine power 神圣的

beverage /'bevərɪdʒ/ *n.* any drink, usually other than water 饮料

condemn/kən'dem/ *v.* express strong disapproval of 谴责,严厉指责

intervene /ˌɪntə'viːn/ *v.* get involved, so as to alter or hinder an action, or through force or threat of force 干预,干涉

papal /'peɪpl/ *adj.* of or relating to the pope 教皇的

controversy /'kɒntrəvɜːsi/ *n.* a contentious speech act; a dispute where there is strong disagreement 争论,争议

precursor /pri'kɜːsə(r)/ *n.* a person or thing that precedes and shows or announces someone or something to come 先驱

broker /'brəʊkə(r)/ *n.* a businessman who buys or sells for another in exchange for a commission 经纪人

colonist /'kɒlənɪst/ *n.* a person who settles in a new colony or moves into a new country 殖民者

seedling/'siːdlɪŋ/ *n.* a young plant that has been grown from a seed 幼苗

thrive /θraɪv/ *v.* to grow strongly and vigorously 茁壮成长

horrendous /hə'rendəs/ *adj.* causing fear or dread or terror 可怕的;惊人的

saboteur /ˌsæbə'tɜː(r)/ *n.* someone who commits sabotage or deliberately causes wrecks 破坏分子

pirate /'paɪrət/ *n.* someone who robs at sea or plunders the land from the sea without having a commission from any sovereign nation 海盗

credit /'kredɪt/ *v.* (followed by with) to ascribe (to); give credit (for) 归功于

captivate /'kæptɪveɪt/ *v.* attract; cause to be enamored 迷住,使……着迷

bouquet /bu'keɪ/ *n.* a bunch of flowers which is attractively arranged 花束

tropical /'trɒpɪkl/ *adj.* situated in, used in, characteristic of, or relating to the tropics 热带的

crude /kruːd/ *adj.* not refined or processed 未加工的

commodity /kə'mɒdəti/ *n.* articles of commerce 商品
spring up come into existence; take on form or shape 出现;涌现
revolt against rise up in rebellion against 反抗

Notes

1. Ethiopian Plateau 埃塞俄比亚高原 highlands covering much of Ethiopia and central Eritrea, Africa

2. Arabian Peninsula 阿拉伯半岛 a peninsula between the Red Sea and the Persian Gulf; strategically important for its oil resources

3. Mecca 麦加(沙特阿拉伯城市) a city of western Saudi Arabia near the coast of the Red Sea; the birthplace of Muhammad, and the holiest city of Islam and a pilgrimage site for devout Muslims

4. Satan 撒旦 the chief evil spirit and adversary of God and humanity; the devil

5. Pope Clement VIII 教皇克莱门特八世 Pope Clement VIII, born in Fano, Italy to a prominent Florentine family, initially came to prominence as a canon lawyer before being made a Cardinal-Priest in 1585. In 1592 he was elected Pope and took the name of Clement.

Coffee aficionados often claim that the spread of its popularity among Catholics is due to Pope Clement VIII's influence. He was pressed by his advisers to denounce coffee. However, upon tasting coffee, Pope Clement VIII declared: "Why, this Satan's drink is so delicious that it would be a pity to let the infidels have exclusive use of it." Clement allegedly blessed the bean because it appeared better for the people than alcoholic beverages. The year often cited is 1600. It is not clear whether this is a true story, but it may have been found amusing at the time.

6. Lloyd's of London 伦敦劳埃德公司 Lloyd's of London, generally known simply as Lloyd's, is an insurance and reinsurance market located in London, England. Unlike most of its competitors in the industry, it is not an insurance company; rather, Lloyd's is a corporate body governed by the Lloyd's Act 1871 and subsequent Acts of Parliament. It operates as a partially-mutualised marketplace within which multiple financial backers, grouped in syndicates, come together to pool and spread risk.

The market began in Lloyd's Coffee House, owned by Edward Lloyd, some time in 1686 on Tower Street in the City of London. This establishment was a popular place for sailors, merchants, and ship-owners, and Lloyd catered to them with reliable shipping news. The coffee house soon became recognised as an ideal place for obtaining marine insurance.

7. Boston Tea Party 波士顿倾茶事件 The Boston Tea Party was a political protest by the Sons of Liberty in Boston, a city in the British colony of Massachusetts, against the tax

policy of the British government and the East India Company that controlled all the tea imported into the colonies. On December 16, 1773, after officials in Boston refused to return three shiploads of taxed tea to Britain, a group of colonists boarded the ships and destroyed the tea by throwing it into Boston Harbor. The incident remains an iconic event of American history.

8. Louis XIV 路易十四 King of France (1643 - 1715). His reign, the longest in French history, was characterized by a magnificent court, the expansion of French influence in Europe, and the establishment of overseas colonies. Louis waged three major wars and revoked (1685) the Edict of Nantes, causing thousands of Huguenots to leave France.

9. Gabriel de Clieu 加布里埃尔·德·克留 Francois D'ceus de Clieu (c. 1687 - 1729 November 1774) was a French naval officer and the governor of Guadeloupe from 1737 to 1752 and the founder of Pointe-à-Pitre. He was awarded the rank of commander of the Royal and Military Order of Saint Louis.

De Clieu is celebrated for his claim to have introduced coffee to the French colonies of the Western Hemisphere in the 1720s and his support for its cultivation.

10. Martinique 马提尼克(拉丁美洲向风群岛中部法属岛屿,首府法兰西堡) an island in the eastern Caribbean in the Windward Islands; administered as an overseas region of France

- **Reading Comprehension**

1. **Directions**: *Discuss the following questions with your classmates.*

   1) According to the Ethiopian legend, how did the goat herder Kaldi discover coffee?
   2) What did patrons do in coffee houses across the Near East?
   3) How did some people react to the unusual dark black beverage when it was brought back to Europe?
   4) Why were coffee houses called "penny universities" in England?
   5) What incident that happened in the New World would forever change the American drinking preference to coffee?
   6) How did Gabriel de Clieu manage to transport the young coffee plant safely to Martinique during his challenging voyage?

2. **Directions**: *Choose the best answer for each blank.*

   (　　) 1) Legend says the goat herder ________ first discovered the potential of these beloved beans.

   A. Gabriel de Clieu　　B. Kaldi

   C. Francisco de Mello Palheta

( ) 2) Coffee houses quickly became such an important center for the exchange of information that they were often referred to as "________".

A. Schools of the Talented

B. Schools of the Sophisticated

C. Schools of the Wise

( ) 3) ________ decided to taste the beverage for himself before making a decision, and found the drink so satisfying that he gave it papal approval.

A. King George Ⅲ B. Pope Clement Ⅷ

C. King Louis ⅪⅤ

( ) 4) Some people reacted to this new beverage with suspicion or fear, calling it the "________" when coffee had made its way to Europe and was becoming popular across the continent.

A. bitter invention of Satan B. wine of Araby

C. Schools of the Wise

( ) 5) Coffee began to replace the common breakfast drink beverages of the time—________.

A. beer and tea B. wine and tea C. beer and wine

( ) 6) In the mid-1600's, coffee was brought to New Amsterdam, later called ________ by the British.

A. Yemeni B. New York C. Mecca

( ) 7) The famed Brazilian coffee owes its existence to ________, who was sent by the emperor to French Guiana to get coffee seedlings.

A. Kaldi B. Francisco de Mello Palheta

C. Gabriel de Clieu

( ) 8) With thousands of pilgrims visiting the holy city of ________ each year from all over the world, knowledge of this "wise of Araby" began to spread.

A. Yemeni B. New York C. Mecca

- **Discussion**

1. What is the Ethiopian legend concerning how coffee was discovered?
2. How was coffee brought to nearly every place across the world?

After-Class Reading

Warm-up questions:

1. How much do you know about the history of tea culture in China?
2. What can sipping a cup of tea bring to you?

Chinese Tea

1 Tea is a simple beverage, and one that has long been central to the lives of millions of people, originally in the East, and now virtually worldwide. It is said to aid meditation and self-reflection and to induce tranquility, even perhaps inspiring imagination.

Six Types of Tea

2 There are six major types of tea in China—green tea, black tea, Oolong tea, dark tea, white tea, and reprocessed tea, distinguished mainly by different methods of production. Folklore relates each type of tea to certain human characteristics.

3 Thus it is said that green tea, simple and light, stands for the scholasticism of south China; black tea, mild and reserved, is regarded as rather ladylike; Oolong tea, warm and persistent, resembles the perseverance of philosophers; dark tea, with its lingering aftertaste, symbolizes the wisdom of the elderly, and so on and so forth.

History of Tea Culture

4 China, the homeland of tea, is a leading producer and consumer, and the discovery and usage of tea have a history of four or five thousand years. Tea developed from the earliest fresh-boiled tea taken as a kind of soup, to later dried-and-preserved tea, and from simple green tea to the blending of six major kinds of tea.

5 Drinking tea first started to become popular in the Tang (618 –907) and Song (960 – 1279) Dynasties, and has continued into contemporary times. The flavor of tea, which may be drunk weak or strong, contains both bitter and sweet elements.

6 The origin of tea is lost among history and legend. What can be roughly confirmed is that tea originated in the southwest of China. In Yunnan, and elsewhere, there are still some wild tea trees that are over 1,000 years old.

Who Discovered Chinese Tea?

7 It is said that the first person to discover the effects of tea was Sheng Nong—the father of agriculture and herbal medicine in China.

8 In time immemorial, people knew very little about plants. In order to find out which plants could be eaten safely, Shen Nong tasted various kinds of plants to test them as food or medicine. After he had eaten the plants, Shen Nong observed their reactions in his stomach—he is reputed to have had a "transparent stomach"!

How Did the Ancient Chinese Drink Tea?

9 By the Zhou Dynasty (1046-256 BC), the function of tea to refresh the body and clear the mind had gradually replaced its function as medicine. People started drying the leaves to preserve tea. When they made tea, they put the leaves into a pot and made a kind of thick soup.

10 In the Han Dynasties (206 BC-AD 220), both the collecting and processing of wild tea leaves were improved. Tea became a tasty drink and was very popular amongst the nobility.

11 In the Wei Period (220 - 265) and Jin Dynasties (265 - 420), tea came to be the drink of banquets and lubricated philosophical and metaphysical discussions. Tea's "freshness and purity" came to be referred to as the "violence and intoxication" of wine.

The Relationship between Tea and Wine

12 In fact, the relationship between tea and wine has always been subtle. Wine drinking is appropriate for a joyous occasion; while tea drinking is best suited to tranquility. These two drinks differ in many aspects, but they are also the best partners because tea can counter the effects of drunkenness.

13 In later times, the opposing aspects of tea and wine were reflected in a dialogue between them in a book called *On Tea and Wine*.

Development of Chinese Tea

14 It is often said that "tea started in the Tang Dynasty and flourished in the Song Dynasty". In the Tang Dynasty a method called "green steaming" was invented, the aim of which was to rid tea leaves of their "grassy" flavor.

15 After steaming, the tea leaves were ground, made into cakes, and then dried and sealed for storage.

Before Tang Dynasty

16 Before the Tang, tea was known by many names, one of these being a Chinese character meaning "bitter".

17 It was also in the Tang Dynasty that teahouses in their true sense came into being, and

in some big cities, there were also tea shops, which stored large amounts of tea leaves and prepared tea for their customers. Poems and articles dedicated to tea also appeared, and poets such as **Lu Tong**[1] and **Bai Juyi**[2] all wrote about tea.

Tang Dynasty

18 Furthermore, the Tang Dynasty also saw the first definitive publication about tea—*The Classic of Tea*, which was the first of its kind in the world.

19 This book which contained a comprehensive summary of all aspects of the culture of tea including medicinal uses, picking, tea making, cooking, and utensils was then a complete synthesis of knowledge about tea. Its author, **Lu Yu**[3], was consequently dubbed the "Sage of Tea" by later generations.

20 During this period, tea became the most popular commodity in foreign trade, and Japanese Buddhists brought tea leaves back from China to Japan. For the sake of easier transportation, tea leaves were made into bricks, from which convenient pieces could be broken off to prepare tea.

Song Dynasty

21 The Song Dynasty was a golden age for tea, and the teahouse played a prominent role. The calligrapher **Cai Xiang**[4] wrote *Record of Tea* and *Emperor Huizong of Song*[5] wrote *Treatise on Tea*.

Ming Dynasty

22 Then, in the Ming Dynasty(1368 – 1644), tea culture, which had been set back by Mongolians, underwent a renaissance with the familiar dark tea, green tea, and Oolong tea developed during this time.

23 Zhu Yuanzhang (reigned 1368 – 1398), the first Ming Emperor, oversaw a change from roll tea to lose tea, and this tradition has been retained ever since.

24 As their understanding of tea improved, people were no longer content to harvest tea from the wild, but began to plant and cultivate tea trees, while at the same time processing techniques were improving, with different methods producing the six major types of tea.

Manners of Tea Drinking

25 There are also detailed requirements of the drinkers. Meanwhile, with the popularization of tea, people in different regions and of different nationalities developed their own unique customs of taking tea.

26 In Guangdong, for example, people like drinking morning tea, in Fujian they prefer Kongfu tea, Hunan has Lei tea, Sichuan people love "covered-bowl tea", while people of the Bai nationality treat their guests with "Three-Course Tea". Tibetan people prefer buttered tea and those from Inner Mongolia like milk tea.

27 These various tea customs constitute the rich and profound Chinese tea culture.

28 Many traditional Chinese families drink tea after dinner or when greeting visitors. This is not only a healthy habit but also reflects rich culture and history. Chinese people can chat with a friend for a whole afternoon over a pot of good tea.

Notes

1. Lu Ton 卢仝 Lu Tong(795－835) was a Chinese poet of the Tang Dynasty, known for his lifelong study of the tea culture. He never became an official, and is better known for his love of tea than his poetry.

2. Bai Juyi 白居易 Bai Juyi(772－846)was a renowned Chinese poet and Tang Dynasty government official. Many of his poems concern his career or observations made about everyday life, including as governor of three different provinces. He achieved fame as a writer of verse in a low-key, near vernacular style that was popular throughout China, in Korea and Japan.

3. Lu Yu 陆羽 Lu Yu (733－804) was a Chinese tea master and writer. He is respected as the "Sage of Tea" for his contribution to Chinese tea culture. He is best known for his monumental book *The Classic of Tea*, the first definitive work on cultivating, making and drinking tea.

4. Cai Xiang 蔡襄 Cai Xiang (1012－1067) was a Chinese calligrapher, politician, structural engineer, and poet. He had the reputation as the greatest calligrapher in the Song Dynasty.

5. Emperor Huizong of Song 宋徽宗 Emperor Huizong of Song (1082－1135), personal name Zhao Ji, was the eighth emperor of the Song Dynasty in China. He was also a very well-known calligrapher. Emperor Huizong was also a great tea enthusiast. He wrote the *Treatise on Tea*, the most detailed and masterful description of the Song sophisticated style of tea ceremony.

• Reading Comprehension

1. **Directions**: *Discuss the following questions with your classmates.*

1) What is the main function of tea?
2) What do green tea, black tea, Oolong tea, and dark tea stand for respectively?
3) Who, according to the Chinese legend, was the first person to discover the effects of tea?
4) When had the function of tea to refresh the body and clear the mind gradually replaced its function as medicine?
5) What was the first definitive publication about tea in China?
6) What kind of tea do Chinese people prefer in the different regions of China?

2. **Directions**: *Read the following statements carefully, and decide whether they are true (T) or false (F) according to the text.*

( )1) Green tea, mild and reserved, is regarded as rather ladylike.

( )2) Oolong tea, with its lingering aftertaste, symbolizes the wisdom of the elderly.

( )3) Drinking tea first started to become popular in the Tang and Song Dynasties, and has continued into contemporary times.

( )4) By the Han Dynasties, the function of tea to refresh the body and clear the mind had gradually replaced its function as medicine.

( )5) Tea drinking is appropriate for a joyous occasion; while is best suited to tranquility.

( )6) It was also in the Tang Dynasty that teahouses in their true sense came into being.

( )7) The author of *The Classic of Tea*, Lu Tong, was consequently dubbed the "Sage of Tea" by later generations.

( )8) In the Ming Dynasty, tea culture, which had been set back by Mongolians, underwent a renaissance with the familiar dark tea, green tea, and Oolong tea all developing during this time.

Part Three

Topic-Related Activities

1. Case Study

While studying in the United States, Lin Jun made a few American friends. One day he invited two of them to his apartment and cooked them a meal. When his friends said they would like some coffee, he started boiling some water. Without asking them any questions, he made three cups of 3-in-1 coffee, the way he usually took it. Both friends tasted the coffee and frowned. One said she always took coffee black. The other said he preferred to have less sugar in his coffee. They also told him that the spoon is for stirring the coffee, not to drink like he did. Lin Jun was embarrassed. He had thought that everyone drank coffee the same way as he did.

Questions

1) What was Lin Jun's problem in treating his American friends with coffee?

2) What does Lin Jun's inappropriate way of stirring the coffee convey?

2. Team Project

Directions: *Watch the film* ***The GuaSha Treatment***, *and try to explore the Chinese values and the American values behind it.*

3. Translation

Directions: *Translate the passage into English.*

“你要茶还是咖啡?”是用餐人常被问到的问题。许多西方人会选咖啡,而中国人则会选茶。相传,中国的一位帝王于五千年前发现了茶,并用来治病。在明清期间,茶馆遍布全国。饮茶在6世纪传到日本,但直到18世纪才传到欧美。如今,茶是世界上最流行的饮料之一。茶是中国的瑰宝,也是中国传统和文化的重要组成部分。

Unit Twelve

Music

Part One

Lead-in

Without music, life would be a mistake.
—Friedrich Nietzsche

Music is a widely enjoyed human experience. It is, therefore, natural that we have wanted to describe, document, analyze and, somehow, grasp it in language. Throughout the history, music has always been an indispensible part of our life. With music, we gather our strength to stand up in the face of injustice; with music, we heal our wounds when defeated in battles; with music, we celebrate our joy with the beloved ones. Music has long been the backdrop of our life, which has influenced the history and even shaped the culture. Music is also called the universal language without border and it is one of the most dazzling fruits of human civilization. However, the difference between traditional Chinese music and Western music came to existence as they reflected different civilizations and different cultural spirits.

Part Two

In-Class Reading

Warm-up questions:

1. Do you like music?
2. What kind of music do you like best?

American Music

1 What is music? For some a **blissful** experience to be enjoyed along with a glass of the finest red, for some a distraction during a boring **treadmill** session. Some would consider **Beethoven's**[1] piano **sonatas** a copyrighted property of the **lullaby** channel and some would **mock** Indian classical music, the oldest surviving school of music, as sheer **wailing**.

2 Sounds never **evoke** the same emotions in different people. Thus, a comprehensive and universal definition of music is **practically** nonexistent. Some would consider it an exercise in **futility** to go ahead and try to define a list of musical **genres**. Fortunately, while some maintain that sounds such as a car horn and a crash of a falling plate constitute genres in themselves, the rest of the world has been sensible enough to **discern** musical genres from mere noise.

Country and Folk Music

3 Folk music can be broadly classified into two groups—traditional folk and folk revival. The actual folk songs are something that are **indigenous** to a culture, **popularized** at events and passed down mostly orally. The other group can be collectively called folk music or folk revival music. It is commercially successful, credible to artists who exist and are relatively new. The sound is derived from the old folk songs and the lyrics are created wholly by the artist or drawn from the folk song itself.

4 The people living in the **Appalachian Mountains**[2] are sometimes called "hillbillies". The first settlers there came from the British Isles, and they brought their folk music with them. This music, mixed with the blues, became **hillbilly** music.

5 Later, as hillbilly music became more popular, it was called country music. Like blues music, country music emerged from folk songs of the Southern US in the early 1920s. Immigrants in the Appalachian Mountains area, who had brought along instruments from their own countries, **merged** their art to form the famous genre of country music. Hence, it

contained elements from various countries such as Ireland, Italy, Germany and numerous African countries. Many of the early instruments in country music were string instruments, with the notable exception of the **harmonica**. Country songs are often sad stories of love and broken hearts. Not all country people were farmers. Many worked in the mines and factories. They also loved country music and it became the music of the working people.

6 During the 1930s America had many economic problems. Workers expressed their troubles in the folk music of the time. Folk songs are like country songs but they are more traditional and more serious.

7 They don't just talk about love, they tell about the lives of ordinary people. Woodie Guthrie was a folk song writer during the 1930s. He traveled around the country and wrote songs about the poor people.

8 During the 1950s folk music became popular again. **Martin Luther King**[3] wanted to improve the lives of black Americans. He led peaceful marches to change the laws in the US. The marchers sang old folk songs like *We Shall Overcome*.

9 In the 1960s many people were against the war in Vietnam. Folk singers like Bob Dylan and Joan Baez wrote anti-war songs like Dylan's *Blowin' in the Wind* and other songs about the problems of American society. Folk music continued to be the most political of all music in America.

Rock 'n' Roll

10 The origins of rock music are as **foggy** as the genre is popular. The term was **coined** in 1955 by Alan Freed, a disc jockey from Ohio. The oldest form of rock music was a mixture of R&B, country and rockabilly, only it was faster, louder and more dangerous. The man at the **forefront** of this genre was **Elvis Presley**[4], followed by personalities Chuck Berry and Litter Richard. The rock scene in the 1950s was more about shock value, which included fashion statements, sexually-oriented **lyrics** and dance moves catering to young audience in particular.

11 The 1950s were an exciting time for music in America. The economic problems of the 30s and the war of the 40s were over. America was rich again. A new group of people became important—American teenagers. For the first time in history young people had money to spend. They had a new way of dressing, new hairstyles and new dances.

12 In the early 50s slow romantic songs were still popular. But teenagers wanted dance music with a good **beat**, and so they began to listen to R&B (rhythm and blues) on the black radio stations. Rock and roll music had a strong dance beat. The musicians played electric guitars and the music was loud and fast. American teenagers loved it. About the same time, the owner of Sun Record Company, Sam Phillips said "If I could find a white man who had the Negro (black) sound and the Negro feel, I could make $1 billion." He found his wish in

Elvis Presley, the king of rock and roll. Elvis became a new American hero and young people copied his hairstyle, his dress, and his music.

Blues

13 The reason why blues became so popular can only be understood when you look at its time of creation. The origin of blues is too unclear to **pinpoint** to one artist or one year. For sake of historic importance, it's believed that the blues music was created in the late 19th century, by the black slaves that were forced to work in the cotton fields. Blues has firm roots in African traditional music. But above all else, the purpose of making blues is always the same, the expression of intense emotions. It is one reason why this genre had such a profound effect on America and eventually the world. Blues is usually **categorized** by the location of a style, because everywhere the blues went, it caught a different feel.

Soul, Disco and Rap

14 After World War II a large number of black people moved from the South to the big industrial cities like New York, Detroit, and Philadelphia. Many black people lived in poor parts of the city such as Harlem in New York. Musicians wrote and sang about life in the big cities. Life was hard but music and dancing made it a little easier.

15 Popular black music had a strong beat for dancing. At first this music was called rhythm and blues. By the 1960s it was called soul.

16 Soul music was always dance music but in the 1970s a new dance music became popular—disco. Disco is a kind of soul music, often with Latin rhythms. Discos opened up all over America. At discos, the music was on records (discs), not live. Many of the disco musicians were black, but disco dancing was popular with most Americans.

17 In the 1980s a number of black musicians became superstars, for example: **Prince**[5], **Michael Jackson**[6] and Whitney Houston. Some old stars like Tina Turner and Aretha Franklin made new hit records.

18 Rap is a very skillful kind of fast street talk, with a strong rhythm. It began with young black people in the big cities. When rap talking is combined with music it is called rap music. Rap music became very popular in the 1980s.

Jazz

19 Jazz is the second genre born from African traditional music. It is considered to be America's first indigenous form of music. It is believed to have started after the Civil War, when the black people were free to travel and seek employment. Similar to blues, the jazz styles are also classified according to time and location.

R&B

20 R&B, which stands for rhythm and blues, was a name coined due to need rather than

style. During the 1940s, any music created by the African-American populace was termed "black music" or "race music". The term was quite **offensive** and therefore **stunted** the growth and popularity of the artists. In order to make it sound more upbeat, Billboard reporter Jerry Wexler coined R&B and the phrase has stuck since then.

New and Old

21 By the 1970s rock music had become complex, with long guitar passages. It was not easy to dance to this music. Dance music was mostly disco, but many young people were bored with this. They preferred a new kind of rock music. It was loud and simple with a strong beat. This music was called Punk or New Wave.

22 In 1981 a new TV station MTV was started. Twenty-four hours a day this station played music videos. These videos became very popular. Soon every hit song needed a video to go with it.

23 The 1980s was a time of new trends, but more traditional rock music also continued to be important. Heavy metal groups, with their long hair and loud music, looked and sounded a lot like the groups of 20 years before.

24 In the 1980s, like in the 1960s, musicians and music fans became concerned about many problems in the world. They were worried about the environment and about starving people. Videos like "Live Aid" were made by musicians to help solve world problems.

Music of Today

25 Today we rely so much on technology for everything and music is no exception. There is a variety of music but the central genre is pop. There are hundreds of artists in pop music, which is why the genre is so diverse. Music of today uses technology for basically everything, even buying/downloading music. We have computers with us constantly, laptops, phones, iPods, etc. Our society is built on computers.

26 In the present, music is written all to do with love; falling in love, breaking up, suggesting things, and an occasional other subject. Some songs have no meaning at all and are just for pleasure of dance or listening, like Lady Gaga's *Just Dance*.

27 A lot of people listen to music; few actually hear what it is saying. Going back to technology, in some songs it is used so much that there's barely any singing. Some songs are created almost all on the computer. The Black Eyed Peas' *Just Can't Get Enough* has lots of technology involved in the song and other songs.

28 We have come very far in technology and taken a small step backward in song messages. Things will just keep getting more advanced and music will show us how.

29 Despite the **disproportionate publicity** given to the most radical experiments, the majority of leading composers working today continue along the **moderate** path established in

the late 1920s and 1930s. And, if one can rely on the lessons of history, the mainstream of music will continue to absorb those new techniques that contribute to expressiveness and communication while discarding that which is merely **novel** and **sensational**, so that music history will remain an **evolutionary** rather than a **revolutionary** process.

New Words and Expressions

blissful /ˈblɪsfl/ *adj.* completely happy and contented 极为幸福的

treadmill /ˈtredmɪl/ *n.* a dreary round or routine 单调的工作

sonata /səˈnɑːtə/ *n.* a piece of classical music written either for a single instrument, or for one instrument and a piano 奏鸣曲

lullaby /ˈlʌləbaɪ/ *n.* a quiet song intended to lull a child to sleep 摇篮曲;催眠曲

mock /mɒk/ *v.* treat with contempt 嘲笑,嘲弄

wailing /ˈweɪlɪŋ/ *n.* loud cries made while weeping 哭泣

evoke /ɪˈvəʊk/ *v.* call forth (emotions, feelings, and responses) 引起,唤起

practically /ˈpræktɪkli/ *adv.* virtually; almost 几乎
in actuality rather than in theory 实际上

futility /fjuːˈtɪləti/ *n.* lack of effectiveness or success 无用;徒劳

genre /ˈʒɒnrə/ *n.* a category of artistic composition, as in music or literature, characterized by similarities in form, style, or subject matter 体裁

discern /dɪˈsɜːn/ *v.* to recognize or perceive clearly 觉察出;识别

indigenous /ɪnˈdɪdʒənəs/ *adj.* originating or occurring naturally (in a country, region, etc.); native 本土的

popularize /ˈpɒpjələraɪz/ *v.* to make popular; make attractive to the general public 普及;推广

hillbilly /ˈhɪlbɪli/ *n.* old-fashioned term for country music 乡村音乐

merge /mɜːdʒ/ *v.* to blend or cause to blend 融入

harmonica /hɑːˈmɒnɪkə/ *n.* a small musical instrument, also called mouth organ 口琴

foggy /ˈfɒgi/ *adj.* stunned or confused and slow to react 模糊的

coin /kɔɪn/ *v.* make up 创造(新词,短语)

forefront /ˈfɔːfrʌnt/ *n.* the foremost part or place 最前线,最前部

lyric /ˈlɪrɪk/ *n.* the word of a song 歌词

beat /biːt/ *n.* the main rhythm that a piece of music has (音乐的)节奏

pinpoint /ˈpɪnpɔɪnt/ *v.* locate exactly 给……准确定位

categorize /ˈkætəgəraɪz/ *v.* place into or assign to a category 分类

offensive /əˈfensɪv/ *adj.* unpleasant or disgusting, as to the senses 无礼的,冒犯的

stunt /stʌnt/ *v.* check the growth or development of 阻碍……的正常生长或发展

disproportionate /ˌdɪsprəˈpɔːʃənət/ *adj.* out of proportion 不成比例的

publicity /pʌbˈlɪsəti/ *n.* the quality of being open to public view 公众的关注

moderate /ˈmɒdərət/ *adj.* not extreme 不偏激的,温和的

novel /ˈnɒvl/ *adj.* original and of a kind not seen before 新颖的

sensational /senˈseɪʃənl/ *adj.* causing intense interest, curiosity, or emotion 轰动的,激动人心的

evolutionary /ˌiːvəˈluːʃənri; ˌevəˈluːʃənri/ *adj.* of or relating to or produced by evolution 演变的,逐步发展的

revolutionary /ˌrevəˈluːʃənəri/ *adj.* markedly new or introducing radical change 革命性的,突破性的

Notes

1. Beethoven 贝多芬 Beethoven (1770 – 1827), German composer, who greatly extended the form and scope of symphonic and chamber music, bridging the classical and romantic traditions. His works include nine symphonies, 32 piano sonatas, 16 string quartets, five piano concertos, a violin concerto, two masses, the opera *Fidelio* (1805), and choral music.

2. Appalachian Mountains 阿巴拉契亚山脉 often called the Appalachians, area system of mountains in eastern North America.

3. Martin Luther King 马丁·路德·金 United States charismatic civil rights leader and Baptist minister who campaigned against the segregation of Blacks (1929 – 1968)

4. Elvis Presley 埃尔维斯·普雷斯利 Elvis Presley (January 8, 1935 – August 16, 1977) was an American singer and actor. Regarded as one of the most significant cultural icons of the 20th century, he is often referred to as the "King of Rock and Roll" or simply "the King".

5. Prince 普林斯 Prince (June 7, 1958 – April 21, 2016) was an American singer, songwriter, musician, record producer, dancer, actor, and director. He is widely regarded as one of the greatest musicians of his generation.

6. Michael Jackson 迈克尔·杰克逊 Michael Jackson (August 29, 1958-June 25, 2009) was an American singer, songwriter, and dancer. Dubbed the "King of Pop", he is regarded as one of the most significant cultural figures of the 20th century.

- **Reading Comprehension**

1. **Directions**: *Discuss the following questions with your classmates.*

   1) What are the genres of American music?

   2) How did immigrants in the Appalachian Mountains area form the genre of country music?

   3) Who coined the term rock 'n' roll? What was the oldest form of rock music?

   4) Who did Sam Phillips, the owner of Sun Record Company, find his wish in? What was his wish?

   5) In the 1960s many people were against the war in Vietnam including some folk singers. Can you list some of them according to the text?

   6) How will music history remain an evolutionary rather than a revolutionary process?

2. **Directions**: *Read the following statements carefully, and decide whether they are true (T) or false (F) according to the text.*

   (   ) 1) A comprehensive and universal definition of music is actually existent.

   (   ) 2) Folk songs don't just talk about the lives of ordinary people, and they tell about love.

   (   ) 3) Folk music continued to be the most political of all music in America.

   (   ) 4) Blues had a strong dance beat. The musicians played electric guitars and the music was loud and fast. American teenagers loved it.

   (   ) 5) Rock and roll music had a strong dance beat, and the musicians played electric guitars and the music was loud and fast.

   (   ) 6) It's believed that rap was created in the late 19th century by the black slaves that were forced to work in the cotton fields.

   (   ) 7) Blues is the second genre born from African traditional music. It is considered to be America's first indigenous form of music.

   (   ) 8) Billboard reporter Jerry Wexler coined R&B and the phrase has stuck since then.

   (   ) 9) Country and folk music is a very skillful kind of fast street talk, with a strong rhythm.

   (   ) 10) When many young people were bored with dance music, mostly disco, they preferred a new kind of rock music called Punk or New Wave by the 1970s.

After-Class Reading

Warm-up questions:

1. What do you think is the most impressive feature of Chinese music?
2. What do you know about ancient Chinese musical instruments?

Chinese Music

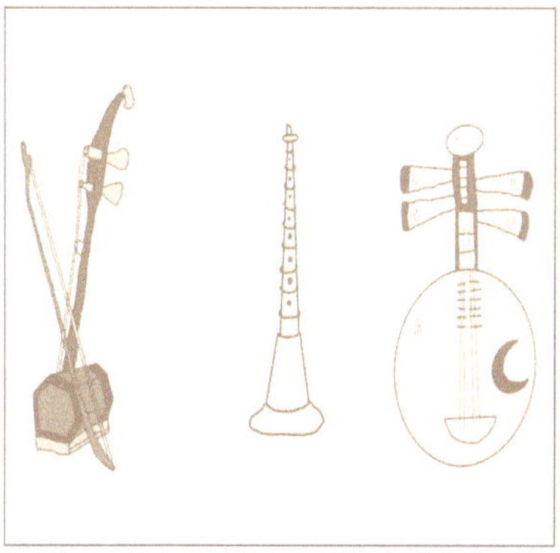

1 Traditional Chinese music can be traced back 7,000 – 8,000 years based on the discovery of a bone flute made in the **Neolithic Age**[1]. In the Xia, Shang and Zhou Dynasties, only royal families and dignitary officials enjoyed music, which was made on chimes and bells. During the Tang Dynasty, dancing and singing entered the mainstream, spreading from the royal court to the common people. With the introduction of foreign religions such as **Buddhism**[2] and **Islam**[3], exotic and religious melodies were absorbed into Chinese music and were enjoyed by the Chinese people at fairs organized by religious temples.

2 In the Song Dynasty, original opera such as *Zaju* and *Nanxi* was performed in tearooms, theatres, and showplaces. Writers and artists liked it so much that ci, a new type of literature resembling lyrics, thrived. During the Yuan Dynasty, *qu*, another type of literature based on music became popular. This was also a period when many traditional musical instruments were developed such as the pipa, the flute, and the **zither**[4].

3 During the Ming (1368 – 1644) and Qing Dynasties (1616 – 1911), the art of traditional opera developed rapidly and diversely in different regions. When these distinctive opera styles were performed at the capital (now called Beijing), artists combined the essence of the different styles and created Beijing opera, one of three cornerstones of Chinese culture (the other two being Chinese medicine and traditional Chinese painting) which continue to be appreciated even in modern times.

4 Besides these types of music, Chinese peasants were clever enough to compose folk songs, which also developed independently with local flavor. Folk songs described working and daily life such as fishing, farming, and herding and were very popular among the common people.

Traditional Musical Instruments

5 Traditional Chinese musical instruments can be divided into four categories: stringed

instruments, percussion instruments, plucked instruments, and wind instruments[5]. The following are just a few of them:

Horse-Headed Fiddle

6 The horse-headed fiddle is a bowed stringed instrument with a scroll carved like a horse's head. It is popular in Mongolian music. With a history of over 1,300 years, it even influenced European string music when Marco Polo brought one back from his travels through Asia. Its wide tonal range and deep, hazy tone color express the joy or pathos of a melody to its fullest.

7 The Mongolian people bestowed upon their beloved horse-headed fiddle a fantastic legend: during horse-racing at the Nadam Fair—their featured grand festival—a hero, Su He, and his white horse ran the fastest, which incurred the envy and wrath of the duke. The cruel duke shot the horse dead, and Su He grieved so much that he met his horse in a dream. In the dream, the horse told Su He to make a fiddle from wood and the hair of a horse's tail, and to carve the head of the fiddle in the shape of a horse's head. The lad followed the horse's advice and when he finished, the fiddle produced an extremely vivid sound. From then on, people loved this instrument and composed many songs for it.

Lute (Pipa)

8 Originally named after the loquat fruit, the earliest pipa known was found to have been made in the Qin Dynasty (221 BC – 206 BC). By the Tang Dynasty (618 – 907), the pipa had reached its summit. It was loved by everyone—from the royal court to the common folk—and it occupied the predominant place in the orchestra. Many well-known writers and poets created poems and mentioned it in their works. **Bai Juyi**[5], the master poet, vividly depicted the performance like this: rapid and soft notes mingled were just like big and small pearls dropping onto the jade plates.

9 Afterwards, the pipa underwent improvement in playing techniques and structure. Players then changed from holding the pipa transversely to holding it vertically, and from using a pick to using the fingers to pluck the strings directly. In modern times, the volume and resonance has also been improved. The traditional music work *Spring Moonlight on the Flowers by the River*, which has a history of over one hundred years, has brought harmony and a sense of beauty to untold numbers of people.

Erhu

10 The Erhu, also called "Huqin", was introduced from the Western Regions during the Tang Dynasty. During the Song Dynasty (960 – 1279), it was refined and improved and new variations appeared. It was also an important instrument for playing the melody of Beijing opera.

11 When playing, the player usually stands the Erhu on his lap, and moves the bow across the vertical strings. The well-known music *Two Springs Reflect the Moon* was created by the blind folk artist Hua Yanjun, also named A Bing by the people. Though he could not see anything of the world, he played his Erhu using his heart and imagination. This melody conjures up a poetic night scene under the moonlight and expresses the composer's desolation and hope.

Flute

12 The earliest flute was made from bone over 7,000 years ago. In the times since then, most flutes were made of bamboo, which allowed even common people to play it. By covering the holes and blowing through the side hole while moving the fingers flexibly between the six holes, a sound will be produced that is leisurely and mellifluous like sound from far away. This always reminds people of a pastoral picture of a farmer riding on a bull while playing a flute.

Notes

1. Neolithic Age 新石器时代 latest part of the Stone Age beginning about 10,000 BC in the Middle East (but later elsewhere)

2. Buddhism 佛教 a religious teaching propagated by the Buddha and his followers, which declares that by destroying greed, hatred, and delusion, which are the causes of all suffering, man can attain perfect enlightenment.

3. Islam 伊斯兰教 a monotheistic religion characterized by the doctrine of absolute submission to God and by reverence for Muhammad as the chief and last prophet of God.

4. zither 古筝 a musical stringed instrument with strings stretched over a flat sounding box; it is laid flat and played with a plectrum and with fingers.

5. Bai Juyi 白居易 a renowned Chinese poet and government official in the Tang Dynasty. Many of his poems concern his career or observations made about everyday life, including as governor of three different provinces. He achieved fame as a writer of verse in a low-key, near vernacular style that was popular throughout China, in Korea and Japan.

Reading Comprehension

1. Directions: *Discuss the following questions with your classmates.*

1) When can traditional Chinese music be traced back?
2) How were exotic and religious melodies absorbed into Chinese music and enjoyed by the Chinese people?
3) How were writers and artists inspired to create ci, a new type of literature resembling lyrics, in the Song Dynasty?

4) What are the three cornerstones of Chinese culture?

5) What categories can traditional Chinese musical instruments be divided into?

6) What traditional Chinese musical instruments are featured in the text?

2. **Directions**: *Read the following statements carefully, and decide whether they are true (T) or false (F) according to the text.*

( )1) Traditional Chinese music can be traced back 7,000 - 8,000 years based on the discovery of a bone flute made in the Neolithic Age.

( )2) In the Xia, Shang and Zhou Dynasties, only royal families and dignitary officials enjoyed music, which was made on wood and bones.

( )3) In the Song Dynasty, original opera such as *ci* and *qu* was performed in tearooms, theatres, and showplaces.

( )4) Folk songs described working and daily life such as fishing, farming, and herding and were very popular among the common people.

( )5) The horse-headed fiddle is a wind instrument with a scroll carved like a horse's head.

( )6) In the dream, the horse told Su He to make a fiddle from bones and the hair of a horse's tail, and to carve the head of the fiddle in the shape of a horse's head.

( )7) Originally named after the loquat fruit, the earliest pipa known was found to have been made in the Tang Dynasty.

( )8) The horse-headed fiddle was an important instrument for playing the melody of Beijing Opera.

( )9) When playing, the player usually stands the pipa on his lap, and moves the bow across the vertical strings.

( )10) The earliest flute was made from bone over 7,000 years ago.

Part Three

Topic-Related Activities

1. Case Study

Peter's First Day in China

Yesterday was Peter's first day in China. He decided to go to a park, and there he met several Chinese students, and he was happy to find a chance to practice speaking in Chinese. At first, they asked him some pretty easy questions. But then the questions started getting more complicated and hard to understand; also sometimes when Peter was struggling to answer, the students would laugh. That bothered him, and he felt like they were making fun of him. Then one student said something a little weird: "*Women zuo pengyou ba.*" But he didn't expect someone he hardly knew to just say "Let's be friends!" That seemed a little strange and rather pushy. So he made an excuse and left.

Questions

1) How can you interpret the story and offer possible explanations on your knowledge and understanding of cultures?

2) Can you offer some constructive suggestions?

2. Team Project

Directions: *Watch the film* ***A Grandson from America*** *and try to explore the Chinese values and the American values behind it.*

3. Translation

Directions: *Translate the passage into English.*

当古典音乐(classical music)流泻而出的一刹那,你可以清楚地看到在空气中流动的是高山、是流水、是丝竹、是冬雪、是千古的生命(eternal life)。那份说不出、道不尽的感动,就是中国古典音乐之美。古乐器一般都具有双重功能——表现性和实用性,即这些乐器既是表现音乐的工具,又是劳动生产的工具,或是生活用具(daily utensils)。中国音乐是光辉灿烂的中国文化的一个重要组成部分。历经数千年的漫长岁月,以其多姿多彩的品种和内涵丰富的体系闻名于世。

Key to Exercises

Unit One

In-Class Reading

• **Reading Comprehension**

1. **Directions**: *Discuss the following questions with your classmates.*

1) Why food was defined by a very small geographic zone?

Where there were wars, food was modified. Arabs conquered Europe; cane sugar went with them. The Chinese entered Japan and the soybean entered the Japanese diet. Immigration left a mark, too. Jews fleeing Portugal brought chocolate to southwestern France. African slaves brought frying and okra to the Caribbean and the American South. It seemed every time a royal marriage was arranged in France, the cuisine gained a few ingredients and dishes.

2) Can you give any examples to elaborate how the development of transportation sped up the changes of food in the 19th century?

Every day organic vegetables from California, freshly caught turbots packed in dry ice from France, fresh Portuguese sardines, New Zealand oysters and smelly durian from Asia land in the airports of the world.

3) How do you understand "food remains classist"?

The poor still eat mostly carbohydrates and fats, while the rich get the protein—something that can even be seen in the difference between airline meals in first class and economy.

4) Why do the rich resist the industrial farming, according to the author?

To see just how much resistance to industrial agriculture there is among the rich, travel to rural areas where wealthy urbanites have their vacation homes and watch them pay fees for the privilege of stooping in the field to harvest a crop.

5) What facts are covered by the seemingly thriving picture of French cooking?

The creativity of great French chefs belies the fact that there is less and less cooking going on in the average French home, almost none of it in any way resembling the food of restaurants.

6) What is the most important opportunity provided by the GM food?

Genetically modified food offers many opportunities, not the least of which is crops that are so insect repellent they need no pesticides.

7) How do you understand the famous dictum, "Tell me what you eat and I will tell you who you are"?

Our identities are closely related to what we eat and how we eat. Tell me what you eat and I will tell you who you are, where you live, where you stand on political issues, who your neighbors are, how your economy functions, your country's history and foreign relations, and the state of the environment. By looking at food, the age we live in is better understood.

8) How can climate change our food?

Water is becoming not only warmer but less salty. The oceans, however, have been assaulted with not only climate change, but with pollution and destructive industrial fishing. The only certainty is that the survival of the ocean's fish can no longer be assumed—something that portends not just a crisis for biology, but one of the most dramatic shifts in food consumption ever seen.

2. **Directions**: *Read the following statements carefully, and decide whether they are true(T) or false(F) according to the text.*

1) T 2) F 3) F 4) T 5) F 6) T

3. **Directions**: *Fill in the form based on the information provided in Paragraph 2.*

Causes	Who	Food Involved	From	To
War	Arabs	cane sugar	Arabia	Europe
Immigration	Chinese	soybean	China	Japan
	Jews	chocolate	Portugal	France
	African slaves	frying and okra	Africa	Caribbean and the American South
Royal Marriage	Catherine de' Medici	artichoke	Italy	Paris
	Marie Antoinette	sauerkraut	Lorraine	Paris

After-Class Reading

• Reading Comprehension

1. **Directions**: *Read the passage quickly and match each of the dishes with the school of cuisine it belongs to.*

D H A E B G F C

2. **Directions**: *Complete the following table with the missing information based on the text.*

Schools of cuisine	Materials	Cooking methods	Characteristics
Shandong	domestic animals, birds, vegetables and seafood	stewing, roasting, boiling, quick frying, quick frying with flour, and crystallizing with honey	wide selection of materials and use of diverse cooking methods
Sichuan	garlic, chili pepper, and the unique Sichuan pepper	stir-frying, steaming, braising, baking and quick frying	bold flavors, particularly the pungency and spiciness
Jiangsu	natural materials that maintain clarity, freshness, and mildness of the ingredients	stewing, braising, simmering, and boiling	be presented colorfully and artistically
Guangdong	fresh seafood and a wide variety of meat, including pork, beef, chicken, goose, duck, etc.	Many cooking methods are used, but steaming and stir-frying are the most favored. Other methods include shallow frying, double steaming, braising and deep-frying	Spices are used in modest amounts to avoid overwhelming the flavors of primary ingredients
Fujian	diverse seafood and woodland delicacies	braising, stewing, steaming and boiling	light, soft and tender, with particular emphasis on an umami taste
Zhejiang	sugar, beans, rice, and wheat	sautéing, braising and stewing	fresh and soft, with the flavor of mellow fragrance
Hunan	chili peppers, shallots and garlic	stewing, frying, pot-roasting, braising and smoking	spicy flavors, fresh aroma and deep colors
Anhui	wild herbs, fungi and mushrooms from the local mountains	chiefly braising and stewing	They are particular about controlling cooking time and temperature

Topic-Related Activities

1. Case Study

Questions

1) What is the difference in terms of food culture?

In America, hosts show the hospitality by offering their own American specialty , hoping that their guests would enjoy the food , while Chinese guests don't like those food or want to keep polite and well-mannered, so they just eat little ,however, American feel the Chinese don't have a good time. In China, in order not to lose face, hosts show the hospitality by offering much more Chinese food than guests could eat, so they are always busy with cooking, but which makes American couple feel disappointed since they hope the guests can sit down and communicate with them.

2) What is the Chinese understanding of the host-guest relationship?

According to Chinese, a good host-guest relationship means human emotion, showing their hospitality by serving much food, sharing most aspects of their life to guests. Usually, they use non-verbal strategies. Therefore, Liu and Yang cooked much more food than American guests could eat, and they didn't talk too much with the guests, just turning on the TV to show them all its high-tech features.

3) What is the American couple's attitude towards friendship?

They think friendship depends on frequent interaction with each other, spending time together. Although they are not willing to talk about their privacy, refusing to answer the price of their objects, they would like to say something about their families and jobs and ask Chinese couples about theirs.

4) Can you give some advice to both couples to help them further their friendship?

A: Both couples should try to respect and learn new culture by all means and adapt all aspects of each other's culture, including the new foods, habits.

B: Liu and Yang can provide more emotional support for the American couples.

C: The Chinese couples had better not ask privacy and have more conversation with their friends.

D: Since George and Janice have lived in China, they need to integrate fully and take on all parts of the Chinese culture.

2. Critical Thinking & Cultural Exploration

Step Two

Directions: *Please work in pairs and match the food in Column A with relevant holidays in Column B.*

Column A		Column B
zongzi		Mid-autumn Day
moon cake		The Double Seventh Festival
dumpling		The Dragon Boat Festival
tangyuan		The Spring Festival
chocolate		The Lantern Festival
turkey and pudding		Thanksgiving Day
egg		Christmas
candy		Valentine's Day
turkey and pumpkin pie		Easter
chocolate		Halloween

Step Three

Directions: *Is there any folklore behind the holidays and the traditional food? Choose one you are interested in and make a presentation about it.*

Dragon Boat Festival, one of the oldest Chinese traditions, is May 5 on Chinese lunar calendar. According to the prevailing sayings among Chinese folklore, the festival is used to memorize a great patriotic poet—Qu Yuan who wrote influential works like *Li Sao* in Chinese literature.

Qu Yuan was a high official of Chu state during the Spring and Period Annals in ancient China. He put forward policies and encouraged the king of Chu to make his state stronger. But his action was rejected by noble men of Chu state. Then he was entrapped by evil (speaking) and dismissed by the king. At the following time, he wrote a number of famous literary works to express deep worry about his state. Later on, the territory of the Chu state was invaded and occupied by Qin—another strong state at that time. Qu Yuan saw that. With extreme grief and indignation, he committed suicide by jumping into a river on May 5. The mass of the Chu were touched by his patriotic action. They used their ways to offer mourning to Qu Yuan after his death. The date and the ways were developed into a custom and a festival.

3. Translation

Directions: *Translate the passage into English.*

【参考译文】Most people like Chinese food. In China, cooking is not only considered as a skill but also an art. The well-prepared Chinese food is both delicious and good-looking. Although cooking methods and food ingredients vary wildly in different places of China, it is common for good cuisine to take color, flavor, taste and nutrition into account. Since food is crucial to health, a good chef is insistently trying to seek balance between cereal, meat and vegetables, and accordingly Chinese food is delicious as well as healthy.

Unit Two

In-Class Reading

1. **Directions**: *Discuss the following questions with your classmates.*

1) What is the difference between college and university?

Often people use the word college to refer to a small school that does not offer graduate degrees, and university for large schools that offer both undergraduate and graduate degrees.

2) What is the difference between public and private schools in the United States?

American public schools are free and open to all at the elementary and secondary level, but public universities charge tuition and have competitive entrance requirements. About 10 percent students choose to attend private schools that are associated with particular churches and receive financial support from them, though parents must also pay tuition. They believe that these schools are safer and have higher academic standards than the public schools. There are also some elite private schools which serve mainly upper-class children.

3) Are there any areas of inequality in the American education system? Illustrate your points with instances.

Yes. Elite private schools do conflict with the American ideal of equality opportunity. These schools often give an extra educational and social advantage to the young people whose families have the money to allow them to attend. There is another area of inequality in the American education system. Because of the way that schools are funded, the quality of education that American students receive in public schools varies greatly.

4) Why the middle-class family suffers the most from the rising tuition costs?

The family income may be too high to qualify for financial aid, but not high enough to afford the \$15,000 to \$35,000 per year (or more) needed for a private college education.

5) What other skills American schools emphasize besides intellectual skills? Why?

The development of social and interpersonal skills may be considered as important as the development of intellectual skills. So to help students develop these important skills, schools have added a large number of extracurricular activities (activities outside classroom studies) to daily life at school. It is by participating in these activities that students demonstrate their special talents, their level of maturity and responsibility, their leadership qualities, and their ability to get along with others.

6) What are the major characteristics of education in America?

Firstly, about 85% of American students attend public schools (schools supported by American taxpayers). The other 15% attend private schools, for which their families choose to pay special attendance fees. Four out of five private schools in the United States are run by churches, synagogues or other religious groups. In such schools, religious teachings are a part of the curriculum.

Secondly, Each of the 50 states in the United States has its own laws regulating education. From state to state, some laws are similar; others are not. Education in the United States was to remain in the hands of state and local governments.

Thirdly, Americans have a strong tendency to educate their children about major public concerns—problems such as environmental pollution, nuclear issues, neighborhood crime and drugs.

2. Directions: *Read the following statements carefully, and decide whether they are true (T) or false (F) according to the text.*

1) T 2) F 3) F 4) F 5) T 6) F

3. Directions: *Choose the correct answer to each of the following questions.*

1) B 2) C 3) C 4) B 5) A 6) D

After-Class Reading

- **Reading Comprehension**

1. Directions: *Complete the following table with the missing information based on the text.*

Notable Ancient China Academies

Names of Academy		Location	Time of Foundation
Chinese	English		
岳麓书院	Yuelu Academy	Changsha, Hunan	Northern Song
白鹿洞书院	White Deer Grotto Academy	Lushan Mountain, Jiangxi	Southern Tang
应天书院	Yingtian Academy	Shangqiu, Henan	Later Jin
嵩阳书院	Songyang Academy	Dengfeng, Henan	Northern Wei

2. Directions: *Translate the following passage into English.*

【参考译文】Confucius (551 - 479 BC) was the founder of Confucianism. He advocated a set of moral code on the basis of five merits: benevolence, righteousness, propriety, wisdom and trustworthiness. Among them, benevolence is considered as the cornerstone of his philosophy, which stands for faithfulness, filial piety, tolerance and kindness. He also requested people to keep in good harmony with each other and establish a community ruled by standard manners and behavior. One of his followers, Mencius (372 - 289 BC), repeatedly tried to convince rulers that the rulers should cultivate moral perfection in order to set a good example to the people and the rulers who governed benevolently would earn the respect of the people.

Topic-Related Activities

1. Case Study

Questions

1) What do you think of Chinese students' behavior in class?

A common cultural misunderstanding in classes involves conflicts between what is said to be direct communication style and indirect communication style. In American culture, people tend to say what is on their minds and to mean what they say. Therefore, students in class are expected to ask questions when they need clarification. However, Chinese students generally prefer indirect communication style, and therefore they tend not to say what is on their minds and to rely more on implications and inference, so as to be polite and respectful and avoid losing face through any improper verbal behavior. As is mentioned in the case, to many Chinese students, numerous questions would show a disrespect for the teacher and would also reflect that the student has not studied hard enough. There is also the concept of losing face if one is seen as not knowing something the teacher is talking about.

2) Do you think Confucianism will affect Chinese students' verbal behavior in communication?

Confucius' primary concern with social relationships has strongly influenced communication in China at large. In general, it has strengthened communication patterns that help to build and maintain proper human relationships.

Social relations, according to Confucius, should be conducted so that everyone's face is maintained. Thus, intermediaries are used to initiate social contacts and avoid conflicts, indirect language is used to avoid embarrassing confrontations, and formality is used to maintain a heightened sense of politeness that preserves face.

Since the main function of communication under Confucian philosophy is to initiate, develop and maintain social relationships, there is a strong emphasis on the kind of communication that promotes such relationships. For instance, it is very important in China to engage in small talk before initiating business and to communicate personalized information, especially information that would help place each person in the proper context.

Communication in China may be very complex and differentiated according to social status, the degree of intimacy, age, sex, and the level of formality. These differentiations are manifested in both verbal and nonverbal behaviors and they result from Confucian ethical rules that place the highest value on proper human relationships and on propriety.

The Confucian legacy of consideration for others and concern for proper human relationships has led to the development of communication patterns that preserve one another's face. Indirect communication helps to prevent the embarrassment of rejection by the other person or disagreement among partners, leaving the relationship and each other's face intact. There are a number of means by which face can be defended, such as asking someone else to transmit the message, talking to a third person in the presence of the hearer, and conveying one's message as being from someone else, which are all indirect forms of communication.

As a matter of fact, Confucius advocated what he said "clumsy word" for people when communicating with each other. He seemed to believe that the use of superb language skills instead of "clumsy word" to get an upper hand would, more often than not, lead to adverse consequences. Confucius deprecated "clever talk and a pretentious manner" in communication, for, according to him, "Clever talk confounds virtue." Therefore, he said, "I detest the clever talker out of fear that he becomes confused with the truth."

2. Critical Thinking & Cultural Exploration

Step Three

Directions: *Nowadays more and more people tend to send their children to a private academy for traditional education. What are the pros and cons of a private academy in your opinion? Discuss with your classmates about this issue and write a composition of more than 200 words to state your point of view.*

On Private Academy Education

People attach great importance to education all around the world. "Knowledge is power", as Sir Francis Bacon put it in a concisely accurate way. To receive good education means to be powered by great knowledge. No wonder Chinese parents are willing to exert every effort to grant their children opportunities to enter an excellent high school and then a top university for schooling. However, there are parents who would rather send their children to a private academy to receive traditional learning of Chinese classics. Why is it that they prefer traditional private teaching to modern public schooling?

In my point of view, a private academy enjoys many advantages compared to public schooling. In an academy, children are taught Chinese classics, such as works of Confucius, Mencius and Lao Tzu. There is no denying that such classical works embody the cream of traditional Chinese culture and convey great wisdom of Chinese philosophers. A serious learner may savor the thoughts inlaid in these enlightening books and obtain a tranquil perspective toward the world. Besides, the language of ancient Chinese classics is concise, elegant and profound. By reading philosophical works, novels and poetry, children will find their aesthetic senses highly refined. It is such works and learning that make us Chinese people what we are.

Of course, private academy education has its disadvantages, too. Above all, it cannot catch up with the times. In a globalized society, science and technology are valued as power of knowledge. Unfortunately, there is little advanced science or technology in ancient Chinese classics. If progress means keeping up with the developed countries, a private academy will never lead her students to a westernized way. This is why few people can stay in a private academy for long education. It is really an old-fashioned way of education.

Out of fashion or not, private academies attract people for their classic taste and nostalgic curriculum. They may never replace public schools, but they will survive modernized civilization by adhering to the core values of Chinese thought, which, no matter how times change, will never vanish in Chinese culture.

3. Translation

Directions: *Translate the passage into English.*

【参考译文】As China's economy booms, there is a dramatic increase in the number of people learning Chinese, which makes it become one of the most popular languages. In recent years, international ranks of Chinese universities rise significantly in world university ranking. Owing to the progress of Chinese education, it is not odd that China has become one of the most favorite destinations for oversea students studying abroad. In 2015, around four hundred thousand international students piled into China to study. What they learn is no more limited to the subjects of Chinese and Chinese culture; they also learn science and engineering. In the global education market, America and Britain still play dominant roles, while China is catching up.

Unit Three

In-Class Reading

- **Reading Comprehension**

1. **Directions**: *Discuss the following questions with your classmates.*

1) What can be chosen to the Noah's Ark and how many of them?

Two of every sort of bird and cattle and of every sort of living thing which goes on the earth.

2) Give a brief description of the Noah's Ark.

The Noah's Ark is three hundred cubits long, fifty cubits wide, and thirty cubits high. And it has a window in the ark, a cubit from the roof, and a door in the side of it, and with a lower and second and third floors.

3) What happened on the earth and in the heaven in the six hundredth year of Noah's life?

In the six hundredth year of Noah's life, in the second month, on the seventeenth day of the month, all the fountains of the great deep came bursting through, and the windows of heaven were open.

4) What happened to the rest living creatures that weren't be chosen to the Noah's Ark?

And destruction came on every living thing moving on the earth, birds and cattle and beasts and everything which went on the earth, and every man. Everything on the dry land, in which was the breath of life, came to its end.

5) How many days did Noah's family stay in the Ark?

About 370 days. (In the six hundredth year of Noah's life, in the second month, on the seventeenth day of the month, all the fountains of the great deep came bursting through, and the windows of heaven were open; And in the six hundred and first year, on the first day of the first month, the waters were dry on the earth; And on the twenty-seventh day of the second month the earth was dry. And God said to Noah,Go out of the ark.)

6) At the second time what did the dove come back with in her mouth and what does it mean?

And the dove came back at evening, and in her mouth was an olive-leaf broken off: so Noah was certain that the waters had gone down on the earth.

7) When the sweet smell came up to the Lord, what did he do?

The Lord said in his heart, "I will not again put a curse on the earth because of man, for the thoughts of man's heart are evil from his earliest days; never again will I send destruction on all living things as I have done."

2. Directions: *Read the following statements carefully, and decide whether they are true(T), false(F) or (N) not mentioned according to the text.*

1) F 2) F 3) F 4) T 5) N 6) T

3. Directions: *Fill in the blanks based on the information provided in the article (what happened on the date?).*

1) In the six hundredth year of Noah's life, in the second month, on the seventeenth day of the month, all the fountains of the great deep came bursting through, and the windows of heaven were open.

2) And for forty days the waters were over all the earth; and the waters were increased so that the ark was lifted up high over the earth. And the waters overcame everything and were increased greatly on the earth, and the ark was resting on the face of the waters...

3) And the waters were over the earth a hundred and fifty days. And God kept Noah in mind, and all the living things and the cattle which were with him in the ark: and God sent a wind over the earth, and the waters went down.

And the fountains of the deep and the windows of heaven were shut, and the rain from heaven was stopped.

And the waters went slowly back from the earth, and at the end of a hundred and fifty days the waters were lower.

4) On the seventeenth day of the seventh month the ark came to rest on the mountains of Ararat. And still the waters went on falling, till on the first day of the tenth month the tops of the mountains were seen. Then,

after forty days, through the open window of the ark which he had made, Noah sent out a raven, which went this way and that till the waters were gone from the earth. And he sent out a dove, to see if the waters had gone from the face of the earth.

5) In the six hundred and first year, on the first day of the first month, the waters were dry on the earth: and Noah took the cover off the ark and saw that the face of the earth was dry.

After-Class Reading

- **Reading Comprehension**

1. Directions: *Read the following statements carefully, and decide whether they are true(T) or false(F) according to the text.*

1) F 2) F 3) F 4) F 5) T 6) F

2. Directions: *Fill in the blank according to the passage about Niu Lang and Weaving Girl.*

1. kind-hearted 2. driven out 3. privileged but secluded 4. longed for 5. a lovely boy 6. moderately but peacefully 7. in such a wrath 8. Fearing that 9. Magpies 10. brief reunion

Topic-Related Activities

1. Case Study

Questions

1) Can you name the 12 gods of Greek and Rome separately? Who are they? Is there any difference from that you thought before?

(Reference to the matching game)

2) Why the gods have the same shortcomings as human beings in the Western mythology?

Cruel and fickle, passionate and vindictive, jealous and insecure, petty and insane: the inhabitants of Mount Olympus represent an attempt by the ancient Greeks to explain the chaos of the universe through human nature.

3) Have you noticed that some gods' names sound like some planets? Can you give some examples?

水星 Mercury, 金星 Venus, 火星 Mars, 木星 Jupiter, 土星 Saturn, 天王星 Uranus, 海王星 Neptune, 冥王星 Pluto

4) Try to make a comparison between the gods from Western and Chinese mythology.

2. A Matching Game

Directions: *Please work in pairs and match the gods in Column A and Column B. Search on the internet and find out their differences.*

Greek		Rome
Zeus		Minerva
Poseidon		Pluto, Orcus
Hermes		Apollo
Hera		Mercury
Hades		Venus
Dionysus		Neptune
Demeter		Mars
Apollo		Jupiter
Ares		Diana
Artemis		Bacchus
Athena		Juno
Aphrodite		Ceres

3. Translation

Directions: *Translate the passage into English.*

【参考译文】After the flames of war had spread for ten years before the walls of Troy, a prophet foretold that Troy could never be expected to fall as long as the Palladium was treasured by its people. In order to steal it out, Odysseus and Diomedes slipped into the capital one night in disguise, known to none but Hellen. The bad woman took them out to Hecuba, the queen of Troy, at whose feet Odysseus immediately bowed down and asked for mercy. The queen granted their request, and with the help of Helen, they successfully brought the image back to the Greek camp at dawn.

Unit Four

- **Reading Comprehension**

1. **Directions**: *Discuss the following questions with your classmates.*

1) Try to describe the Ancient Olympic Games with some words in the text.

full of blood, passion, extraordinary feats

2) How long did the Ancient Olympic Games last?

About 1200 years.

3) Why the Ancient Greece held the Games?

In order to fight against the Persians.

4) Who is Kyniska and what did she do in the Games?

Kyniska, daughter of a Spartan king, took advantage of a loophole to this misogynistic rule—chariot owners, not riders, were declared Olympic champions and anyone could own a chariot, claiming victory wreaths in 396BC and 392BC.

5) Where is the Olympia and why the ancient Greek held the Games there?

Olympia is situated in the north-western Peloponnese. Pock-marked by olive trees, from which the victory wreaths were cut, and featuring an altar to Zeus, it was a hugely scared spot.

6) How many facts do you know about the Games and what are they?

All athletes competed naked. Wrestlers and pankration (a sort of mixed martial art which combined boxing and wrestling) competitors fought covered in oil. Corporal punishment awaited those guilty of a false start on the track.

2. **Directions**: *Read the following statements carefully and decide whether they are true (T) or false (F) according to the text.*

1) T 2) F 3) F 4) F 5) T 6) F

After-Class Reading

- **Reading Comprehension**

1. **Directions**: *Discuss the following questions with your classmates.*

1) How many players are there in each Cuju team?

12 to 16 players each.

2) What is Wushu, and can you define it?

Wushu actually means martial arts in Chinese: Wu means military or martial, and Shu means art. The sport of Wushu was developed from Chinese martial arts in the 1940s. The goal was to standardize the practice of traditional martial arts.

3) What is the difference between Taolu and Sanda?

Taolu consists of basic movements: stances, kicks, punches, balances, jumps, and throws.

Contemporary Taolu may be done with bare hands, short weapons, or long weapons.

Sanda (sometimes called Sanshou) is a contemporary fighting style influenced by Chinese boxing. Sanda is more like Muay Thai, but it has grappling techniques.

4) Archery was one of the Six Noble Arts, and what are the other five arts?

The six arts included courtesy, music, archery, riding, writing and math.

5) How to play the lion dance?

In the dance usually two people act as a lion: one waving the lion head and the other waving the lion body and tail; or one performer acts as a cub, while the other holds a silk ball to play with it. They dance in tempo to the musical melody.

6) Why do the Chinese people hold the dragon boat racing on Duanwu Jie?

Because they want to commemorate Qu Yuan, a "poet" or "Chinese minister" who committed suicide by throwing himself into a river.

2. Directions: *Item I is the title of each part of the text. Item II is the idea mentioned in each part of the text. Match the idea with the title.*

C E A G B D F

Topic-Related Activities

1. Case Study

Questions

1) Why has the United States been a powerhouse in the world sports for a long time?

Maybe because the United States is powerful in economy and technology which provide their people with rich nutrition to build body and advanced facilities to train the athletes.

2) Which country held the 2018 FIFA World Cup?

Russia.

3) Which country is the champion of the 1998 FIFA World Cup?

France.

4) Which country is the home to many sports?

United Kingdom.

5) What is the most popular national sport in Australia?

Cricket.

2. Critical Thinking & Cultural Exploration

Step Two

Directions: *Please work in pairs and match the nation in Column A with relevant players in Column B and talk about their achievements.*

Column A		Column B
USA		Andrey Sergeyevich Arshavin
Russia		Raymond Kopa
United Kingdom		Michael Jordan
France		Dawn Fraser
Australia		David Beckham

Unit Five

In-Class Reading

• Reading Comprehension

1. **Directions**: *Discuss the following questions with your classmates.*

1) Who will benefit from doing the inquiries of the body language?

Such inquiries become invaluable to those engaged in professional pursuits involving human behavior: social workers, psychologists, and teachers in general and counselors in particular.

2) How does the school counselor obtain information that will help him or her assess the client?

The school counselor uses the verbal interview for obtaining information that will help him or her assess the client and develop a plan of action. In the physical setting of the counseling process, the counselor is aware of appearance, esthetic quality, comfort and privacy or lack of privacy and comfort, and general climate. The counselor also receives other messages from the client in the form of nonverbal communication or body language.

3) What did anthropologists learn according to Sapir in 1940s?

Anthropologists learned that body motions were not random but learned like a language.

4) What are the five disciplines that give birth to communication research?

Flora Davis, in her book *Inside Intuition: What We Know About Non-verbal Communication*, states that communication research is the off-spring of five different disciplines: psychology, psychiatry, anthropology, sociology, and ethology.

5) What is human ethology?

Human ethology studies how people court, raise the young, dominate others or signal submission, quarrel and make up. This very physical behavior can then be compared with the way monkeys and apes handle the same relationship.

6) Why is non-verbal communication the basic, primitive form of conveying information?

It has been estimated that in a normal communication between two people, only one-third of the meaning is transmitted on a verbal level, and nearly two-thirds on a non-verbal level.

2. **Directions**: *Read the following statements carefully, and decide whether they are true(T) or false(F) according to the text.*

1) T 2) F 3) T 4) F 5) T 6) T

3. **Directions**: *List as many as possible the examples of body language according to the text.*

eye contact	smiling	walking gestures	shoulder position
shaking hands	clenched fists	physique	posture
body odor	dress	facial expressions	behavior
silence or speech	tone and quality of voice	gestures	movements

After-Class Reading

• Reading Comprehension

1. **Directions**: *Read the passage quickly and match each of the body language with its appropriate meaning.*

1) B 2) C 3) A

2. **Directions**: *Complete the following table with the missing information based on the text.*

Body Language	Tapping fingers	Slapping the forehead	Turning up the corners of the mouth	Shaking the head up and down
Illustration	impatience	forgetfulness	happiness	yes (but in India it means no)

Topic-Related Activities

1. Case Study

1) What is the judgment of beauty in the United States?

That is the notion of leanness and trimness as sign of attractiveness.

2) Why is the judgment of beauty in many parts of Africa opposite to that in the United States ?

Because slimness is evidence of unhappiness, disease, or mistreatment at the hands of one's husband while plumpness is considered a sign of beauty, health, and wealth.

3) What is female's attractiveness in China?

According to Wenzhong and Grove, it is a kind of female attractiveness in China that many women keep their hairstyle simple (often one or two braids) and make little attempt to draw attention to themselves through self-decoration such as colorful scarves, jewelry, or makeup.

4) Why does judgment of beauty differ in different regions?

Judgment of beauty differs in different regions because people in those regions have distinct living environments (inclusive of geographic features, economic conditions, influence of foreign communication, etc.), traditions and customs.

2. Critical Thinking & Cultural Exploration (teacher-guided and student-centered activity)

3. Translation

Directions: *Translate the passage into English.*

【参考译文】Hanfu, the traditional costume of Han Chinese, also known as Han costume, Han clothing, Huafu (Chinese dress), was originated from the time when Huangdi took his throne and had been popular through the history of China until the middle of the 17th century. Based on Huaxia (China)-Han Chinese culture and etiquette, Han Chinese clothing, which is evidently different from the style of traditional garment and fittings of other ethnic groups in China, was formed naturally in history, having the distinctive feature and personality of Han Chinese. It reflects culture of China as a well-dressed, courteous nation as well as a country of beautiful silk garments. It involves the excellent techniques of Han Chinese tie-dying, weaving, and embroidering, etc., preserving more than 30 non-material cultural heritages of China and handing down the protected historical Chinese arts and crafts.

Unit Six

In-Class Reading

- **Reading Comprehension**

1. **Directions**: *Discuss the following questions with your classmates.*

1) What values are Americans bestowed with?

Americans are bestowed with such values as personal control over the environment/responsibility, change seen as natural and positive, time and its control, equality/fairness, individualism/independence, self-help initiative, competition, future orientation, action/work orientation, informality, directness/openness/honesty, practicality/efficiency and materialism/acquisitiveness.

2) What "to be fatalistic" is viewed as in the American context?

Americans do not believe in the power of fate, and they look at people who do as being backward, primitive, or naive. In the American context, to be "fatalistic" is to be superstitious, lazy, or unwilling to take initiative.

3) Why are Americans to be extremely productive?

Time is of utmost importance to most Americans. Americans are more concerned with getting things accomplished on time than they are with developing interpersonal relations. This philosophy has enabled Americans to be extremely productive, and productivity is highly valued in their country.

4) How prevalent is individualism in America?

Americans view themselves as highly individualistic in their thoughts and actions. It is not uncommon for Americans to say, and almost to believe: "If I don't have half an hour a day to myself, I go stark-raving mad!"

5) What are the traits of workaholics?

Workaholics are addicted to, and often wholly identify with, their job or profession.

6) Do Americans give a higher priority to obtaining, maintaining, and protecting material objects or to developing and enjoying relationships with people?

By any standard, Americans are materialistic. They give a higher priority to obtaining, maintaining, and protecting material objects than they do in developing and enjoying relationships with people.

2. Directions: *Read the following statements carefully, and decide whether they are true (T) or false (F) according to the text.*

1) F 2) T 3) F 4) T 5) F 6) F 7) T 8) F 9) T 10) F

After-Class Reading

• Reading Comprehension

1. Directions: *Please work in pairs and match the Chinese values in Column A with relevant traits or examples in Column B.*

Column A		**Column B**
connections		When dealing with a Chinese company or agency, try to find out if it has unfulfilled obligation that could affect your proposal.
reciprocal obligation		In a family of many children, younger siblings can never call their older siblings by name.
collective before individuals		At a banquet, guests are met at the door and escorted to the banquet room or to their seats.
respect for hierarchy		Compared to most Western societies, and especially the American society, Chinese are very group-oriented.
saving face		Possibly the most important possession to have in China is guanxi.
protocol and ceremony		A decision might be affected by the need to save face for an important person.

2. **Directions**: *Read the following statements carefully, and decide whether they are true (T) or false (F) according to the text.*

1) F 2) T 3) F 4) T 5) F 6) T 7) F 8) T

Topic-Related Activities

1. Case Study

Questions

1) How can you explain the fact that the foreigners shrugged and one or two of them even frowned a little in the end?

Wu Fa was trying to be helpful at the buffet. Even though a buffet means that everyone could pick his/her own food, she felt that she should take care of the foreign participants. The Chinese often say "no" when people offer them something, just to be polite, thus Wu Fa did not really take the rejection to her first offer to help seriously. Western people are familiar with buffets, and one of the rules they are taught is not to take more than they can eat. Wu Fa's effort at kindness, which she couched in the terms, "I can't eat this much food myself", came across as being silly and greedy. If she could not eat as much as she took, why did she take it?

Western people will sometimes say "no" to be polite, too. It can be difficult to know if someone is just being polite or if they truly mean "no". However, Western people usually don't hesitate to accept food at table they want more helpings. Furthermore, once can easily help oneself during a buffet, so their "no" should be taken as "no".

2) What do you think is the best solution to Wu Fa's dilemma?

Americans prefer the direct approach. They are likely to be completely honest in delivering their negative evaluations, and to consider, anything other than the most direct and open approach to be "dishonest" and "insincere". So, the best solution for Wu Fa to get out of the dilemma is to be honest with the foreigners about why she did so.

2. Team Project

(略)

3. Translation

Directions: *Translate the passage into English.*

【参考译文】Confucianism is the largest Chinese school of thoughts and the mainstream consciousness of the ancient China. Confucianism had been one of the ruling doctrines of the feudal ruling class since the Han Dynasty. The core of Confucianism is actually a kind of humanism. It advocates self-cultivation, and believes that human beings are teachable and improvable. A grand goal of Confucianism is to achieve a harmonious society in which each individual plays his or her part well, and maintains a good relationship with others.

Unit Seven

In-Class Reading

• Reading Comprehension

1. **Directions**: *Discuss the following questions with your classmates.*

1) What is Hollywood's status at the end of the first decade of the twenty-first century?

At the end of the first decade of the twenty-first century, Hollywood remains the dominant force in global cinema, a status it has held since the era of World War I, having been challenged seriously in that role only briefly in the 1920s and then again in the early to mid-1960s.

2) What happened to movie production in the early twenty-first century?

Hollywood has changed enormously since its beginnings. The studios that remain are mere shells of what they once were. All of them are now subsidiaries of giant media corporations in which moviemaking is but a single, relatively small, portion of their business. These large media corporations are just as likely to be owned by financial interests from outside the United States as from within.

3) Why does the author say the public consumption of movies has increasingly become a private matter?

Going out to a movie theater was a public act, but the social decorum of movie-watching in a theater demanded there be no conversation. Watching a movie in a private space at home—with someone else or others—may facilitate more conversation and human interaction.

4) Haven't the new digital technologies that have developed since the early 1990s completely taken over motion picture production?

No. Technology may influence certain artistic choices, but technology neither defines nor determines the art of film, or any of its constituent crafts. For editing, sound, and cinematography, the primary creative tools for filmmakers are as they've always been—the eye and the ear.

5) Why characters on the screen are important?

Because movies depend on storytelling, and the most engaging stories are about people and the relationships between them. Storytelling in movies nearly always combines elements that simultaneously are literary and theatrical.

6) What is cinema according to the author?

We understand it as a system that expands into spheres of culture, economics, ideologies, and social practice, but cinema may be best understood and appreciated as an artistic system unto itself.

7) Where does the total art of movies exist?

The total art of movies exists in a financial and business system of production, distribution, and exhibition.

8) What are the most reliably effective movie stories about?

The answer is that stories in movies may be about almost anything.

2. Directions: *Read the following statements carefully, and decide whether they are true(T) or false(F) according to the text.*

1) F 2) F 3) T 4) T 5) F 6) F

3. Directions: *Choose the correct answer to each of the following questions.*

1) A 2) B 3) D 4) C 5) D 6) A

After-Class Reading

- **Reading Comprehension**

1. Directions: *Read the following statements carefully, and decide whether they are true(T) or false(F) according to the text.*

1) F 2) T 3) F 4) T 5) F 6) T

2. Directions: *Please work in pairs and match the film in Column A with its translation in Column B.*

Column A		ColumnB
Cold War		《泰坦尼克号》
CZ12		《泰囧》
Lost in Thailand		《贫民窟的百万富翁》
Titanic		《西游·降魔篇》
Crouching Tiger, Hidden Dragon		《钢铁侠3》
Life of Pi		《十二生肖》
Slumdog Millionaire		《寒战》
Journey to the West: Conquering the Demons		《卧虎藏龙》
Iron Man 3		《少年派的奇幻漂流》

Topic-Related Activities

1. Case Study

Questions

1) What is the cultural conflict reflected in the film?

Cross-cultural communication (also frequently referred to as intercultural communication, which is also used in a difference sense, though) is a field of study that looks at how people from differing cultural backgrounds communicate, in similar and different ways among themselves, and how they endeavor to communicate cross-cultures. From the definition we can have a clear sense that different cultural background is the main reason leading to the difficulty in cross-cultural communication. As we can see in the film, because of the huge differences between Chinese and American culture, it's hard for people from the two countries to come to a consensus in almost every aspect, especially in accepting Traditional Chinese Medicine (TCM).

Guasha is a traditional Chinese medical treatment. It has more than 2,000 years' history in China. Literally, it is used to scrape away fever in TCM. With guasha, you can stimulate and increase flow of blood itself and it is beneficial to the blood circulation. Guasha involves repeated pressured strokes over lubricated skin with a smooth edge.

However, guasha is not recognized as legal form of treatment in the USA. So the doctors mistakenly consider guasha a kind of child abuse, causing many troubles. The fortune we inherited from ancestors is just accepted only in a small circle of all countries in the world. Because the Westerners already possess a complete and effective system of Western medicine, therefore it's difficult for them to accept TCM as a way of treating diseases. TCM is the splendid culture originated from China, so there's no doubt that Chinese has highly systematic professional expressions of TCM. While in the Western countries, they do not have such a comprehensive language of TCM, thus it would not be easy for them to understand the theory.

Quarrel on hitting Dennis and face, Xu's love toward Dennis, and filial piety towards his father, John's testimony in the court...are the cases that show the cultural conflicts.

2) What is the reason for the clash?

The film reflects the difference of value and culture views between Western society and Chinese society. China has been influenced by Confucianism for thousands of years. Confucianism is known as paying regard to human relationship and ethic. Piety, courtesy and loyalty are important ethics. But in Western culture more emphasis is placed on individualism, independence and equality. So conflicts in cross-culture communication are unavoidable.

Guasha treatment case is a trigger of clashes in the movie. Guasha treatment is an ancient oriental medical practice, which is an assistant treatment of TCM. TCM aims at keeping the balance of Qi, blood, yin and yang through meridians and collaterals, which can adjust the relationship between the human body and nature. Herbal medicine is the mainstream treatment of TCM. Acupuncture and cupping follow the principle of adjusting qi, blood and yin-yang. And TCM is rather experiential, individual and ambiguous, which makes it too hard to be described and understood for foreigners. TCM is based on the Chinese philosophy of wholeness of man and nature—the ideal harmony. The law of philosophy makes Chinese often opt for the golden mean, while the history of Western medicine indicates that Western biomedicine concentrates on clarity and confirmation. Western people are accustomed to viewing the whole world by analyzing, attaching great importance to objective verifying and microcosmic view of science.

The main reason for the clash is the difference between the individualism and collectivism among Americans and Chinese reflected in the movie, especially opinions about family and friendship of both races. In China, the kinship is more important, and the best illustration is filial piety. The Chinese ethic-centered society decides that Chinese pay much attention to relationship and concern face to a very high degree, while the members of Western families are generally more independent, free and equal. Relationship among friends is more unfixed. Thus, the value most closely identified with American culture is individualism, while with Chinese culture is collectivism.

The root of the cultural clashes reflected in the movie is cultural centralism. The symbol in the movie is the Monkey King. In the East and the West, there are still people who are sticking to outdated concepts and misunderstandings in the attitudes toward other cultures. Only abandoning cultural centralism can we achieve the world of "datong" that the director wants to convey to us. Abandoning the cultural centralism, promoting effective communication and building a completely new and highly developed socialism culture can be done by our efforts.

2. **Critical Thinking & Cultural Exploration**

Step Four

Directions: *Winners may have one minute to deliver an acceptance speech.*

Thank you to the Academy, thank you to all of you in this room. I have to congratulate the other incredible nominees this year. *The Revenant* was the product of the tireless efforts of an unbelievable cast and crew. First off, to my brother in this endeavor, Mr. Tom Hardy. Tom, your talent on screen can only be surpassed by your friendship off screen...thank you for creating a transcendent cinematic experience. Thank you to everybody at Fox and New Regency...my entire team. I have to thank everyone from the very onset of my career...To my parents, none of this would be possible without you. And to my friends, I love you dearly, you know who you are. And lastly I just want to say this: Making *The Revenant* was about man's relationship to the natural world. A world that we collectively felt in 2015 as the hottest year in recorded history. Our production needed to move to the southern tip of this planet just to be able to find snow. Climate change is real, it is happening right now. It is the most urgent threat facing our entire species, and we need to work collectively together and stop procrastinating. We need to support leaders around the world who do not speak for the big polluters, but who speak for all of humanity, for the indigenous people of the world, for the billions and billions of underprivileged people out there who would be most affected by this. For our children's children and for those people out there whose voices have been drowned out by the politics of greed. I thank you all for this amazing award tonight. Let us not take this planet for granted. I do not take tonight for granted. Thank you so very much.

Unit Eight

In-Class Reading

• Reading Comprehension

1. **Directions**: *Discuss the following questions with your classmates.*

1) Why is blue warmly welcome by most banks, corporations and brands?

Most banks, corporations and brands use the colour blue to evoke a feeling of reassurance and reliability to the customers.

2) Why do most sportsmen and thrill-seekers prefer orange apparel and accessories for their professions and hobbies?

Because it represents adventure and risk-taking and like red, it evokes confidence and enthusiasm.

3) How is white interpreted in colour psychology?

In colour psychology, it is known as a colour of fresh starts and new creations, acting as a blank canvas.

4) How do Western cultures and Eastern cultures view purple?

Western cultures believe purple is a colour of royalty and spirituality, while most Eastern cultures think purple is a colour of sorrow, wealth and mourning.

5) Why do restaurants tend to prefer red?

Restaurants often use red because of its ability to stimulate one's appetite.

6) How is yellow conveyed in the Greek and the French cultures?

Some cultures find yellow to have a negative meaning, like the Greek and the French, who perceive it to be related to sadness, envy and jealousy, respectively.

7) What does black symbolize in Western cultures and Eastern cultures?

In Western cultures, black is represented as a colour of power, danger, death and rebellion while in Eastern cultures black is seen more as a symbol of wealth, elegance and prosperity.

8) Which color has the soothing function?

Green is a cool, soothing colour that provides emotional and mental balance.

2. **Directions**: *Read the following statements carefully, and decide whether they are true (T) or false (F) according to the text.*

1) T 2) F 3) T 4) F 5) F 6) T 7) F 8) T

After-Class Reading

• Reading Comprehension

1. **Directions**: *Please work in pairs and fill in the blanks.*

Color	Symbolism in Chinese Culture
Red	auspicious color, symbolic of luck, happiness, joy, vitality, celebration and fertility
Yellow	imperial color, symbolic of power, royalty, prosperity and pornography in publications as well
Black	destruction, evil, profundity, disasters, cruelty, sadness and suffering, bad luck, irregularity and illegality
White	purity and death

Color	Symbolism in Chinese Culture
Blue	spring, immortality and advancement
Gold	wealth and riches
Green	clean and contamination free; used to describe organic things; "a man said to wear a green hat" means he has an unfaithful wife
Purple	divinity and immortality; used to represent love or romance in China in modern times

2. Directions: *Read the following statements carefully, and decide whether they are true (T) or false (F) according to the text.*

1) T 2) F 3) F 4) T 5) F 6) F 7) F 8) T

Topic-Related Activities

1. Case Study

Questions

1) How can you explain the fact that most of the Chinese of his father's age laughed at the sight of Jim in a green hat?

In Chinese culture, if a guy is wearing a green hat, it means that his wife has cheated on him. Jim, as an American born Chinese, obviously has no clue about the Chinese culture. So he was laughed at by the Chinese at the party who must have been informed of or familiar with the Chinese culture.

2) What's the symbolism of the color green in Western culture and Eastern culture?

Most Western cultures see green as the colour of luck and nature, while most Eastern cultures see green as a sign of regeneration, hope and fertility. The Japanese culture regards green as the colour of eternal life.

3. Translation

Directions: *Translate the passage into English.*

【参考译文】In Chinese culture, red symbolizes good luck, longevity and happiness. Therefore, red can be seen everywhere on the Spring Festival and other happy occasions. Cash is often enclosed in a red envelope when given as a gift to family members and close friends. Another reason why red is popular in China is that people connect it with China's revolution and the Communist Party. However, red does not always equal good luck and joy. Instead, red was previously used to write the names of the deceased so it is seen as an offence to write Chinese people's names in red ink.

Unit Nine

In-Class Reading

• Reading Comprehension

1. Directions: *Discuss the following questions with your classmates.*

1) What is the religious origin of Christmas?

Christians celebrate Christmas Day as the anniversary of the birth of Jesus of Nazareth, a spiritual leader whose teachings form the basis of their religion.

2) What are the popular customs of Christmas?

Popular customs include exchanging gifts, decorating Christmas trees, attending church, sharing meals with family and friends and, of course, waiting for Santa Claus to arrive.

3) What are the major Christmas decorative items?

In England, decorating Christmas trees has been widely popular. Some houses are decorated with evergreens (plants which do not lose their leaves in winter); a wreath of holly on the front door and garlands of holly, ivy and fir indoors. Bunches of mistletoe are often hung above doorways.

4) What is the traditional Christmas dinner in England?

The traditional Christmas dinner in England is a mouth-watering affair with the main dish being roasted turkey with vegetables and sauces. The dessert is usually a rich, fruity Christmas pudding with brandy sauce.

5) Where do children find their Christmas gifts?

Father Christmas is said to leave presents for children in their stockings (or pillowcases) that they hang at the end of their beds on Christmas Eve.

6) What is the special Christmas pantomime for children?

In London and the provinces, a number of theatres traditionally organize for kids a special Christmas pantomime based on some popular children's stories such as *Little Red Riding Hood* and *Aladdin*, with a deliberately made subtle connection to the festival.

7) What is the origin of Boxing Day?

It is named so because it was the day when the rich people gave presents to servants, tradesmen and poor people, which could be money or food. They would put them in a small box, which was smashed open when it was full.

8) What special activities are held in the US?

Customs such as Mumming take place in some communities. In the Southwest, there are some special customs which have some similarities to those in parts of Mexico.

2. Directions: *Read the following statements carefully, and decide whether they are true (T) or false (F) according to the text.*

1) F 2) T 3) F 4) F 5) T 6) F

3. Directions: *Fill in the form based on the information of Christmas meals provided in the text.*

Nation	Food
Estonians	blood-pudding
Finland	rice porridge, stockfish
Greece/Germany	pork
Canada	tourtiere meat pies, Christmas turkeys
England	pork, Christmas turkeys, plum pudding
France	oysters, caviar, foie gras, turkeys, geese
Denmark	rice porridge, geese, ducks
America	turkey or ham with cranberry sauce, cabbage dishes, and soups

After-Class Reading

- **Reading Comprehension**

1. Directions: *Match the Chinese names of the 24 solar terms in the left column with their English* *translations in the right column and talk about their meanings.*

	Chinese	English
K	立春	A. Spring Equinox
J	雨水	B. Pure Brightness
P	惊蛰	C. White Dew
A	春分	D. Beginning of Summer
B	清明	E. Lesser Heat
F	谷雨	F. Grain Rain
D	立夏	G. Beginning of Autumn
H	小满	H. Lesser Fullness of Grain
N	芒种	I. Summer Solstice
I	夏至	J. Rain Water
E	小暑	K. Beginning of Spring
M	大暑	L. Beginning of Winter
G	立秋	M. Greater Heat
S	处暑	N. Grain in Beard
C	白露	O. Cold Dew
Q	秋分	P. Waking of Insects
O	寒露	Q. Autumn Equinox
R	霜降	R. Frost's Descent
L	立冬	S. End of Heat
U	小雪	T. Lesser Cold
V	大雪	U. Lesser Snow
W	冬至	V. Greater Snow
T	小寒	W. Winter Solstice
X	大寒	X. Greater Cold

2. **Directions**: *Choose the best answer from the following choices.*

1) B 2) A 3) A 4) B 5) A 6) D

Topic-Related Activities

1. Case Study

Question: What surprised me?

1) In China, a visit to home always includes a meal. And guests always bring relatively expensive gifts to hosts. Gifts should be well wrapped or untouched.

2) In the West, a visit to home only means a meeting, not necessarily including a meal. And gifts are not

as important as they are in China.

3) I acted in a way that was based on Chinese customs, so I found the American way interesting (unusual).

2. Critical Thinking & Cultural Exploration

Step Three

Directions: *A handwritten letter or card of thanks is one of the most meaningful ways to express gratitude. Write your own thank-you message to whoever has recently helped you.*

Dear Mr. and Mrs. Smith,

I am back to China safe and sound. In this letter I would like to convey my heartfelt thanks to you and your lovely children for your kindness and hospitality to host me when I was in New York. Your generous help and tender care made me feel warmly welcomed and transformed my first American trip into a beautiful memory.

I do hope that your whole family pay a visit to China in future, so that I could have the opportunity to repay your friendship. I assure you that you would enjoy visiting here as I did at your home.

I feel obliged to thank you once more.

Love,

Li Ming

3. Translation

Directions: *Translate the passage into English.*

【参考译文】Chongyang Festival, falling on the ninth day of the ninth lunar month, is also named as the Double-ninth Festival and has a history of some 2,000 years. As an important festival in ancient China, Chongyang Festival was celebrated by holding various activities, such as climbing mountains, appreciating chrysanthemums, wearing cornel and eating Chongyang cakes. Climbing mountains is a major custom in Chongyang Festival. Ancient people thought climbing mountains on this day could help them avoid misfortune and prevent disasters. In recent years, a new meaning has been given to the old festival, and it gradually becomes an annual Seniors' Day, on which various activities are held in honor of senior people.

Unit Ten

In-Class Reading

• Reading Comprehension

1. Directions: *Discuss the following questions with your classmates.*

1) When did Prince Charles met Diana according to the text? Where did Prince Charles and Diana get married? And when did they get divorced?

The couple met when Diana was only a teenager. At St. Paul's Cathedral. In 1992.

2) What happened to Prince Charles the night before?

Prince Charles reportedly cried the night before the wedding because he was still torn over his feelings for former girlfriend Camilla Parker-Bowles.

3) Where do the royal weddings usually take place?

At Westminster Abbey.

4) How many people were there trying to catch a glimpse of Prince Charles and the bride-to-be on their special day?

The streets of London were flooded with around 600,000 people trying to catch a glimpse of Prince Charles and the bride-to-be on their special day.

5) What's the difference between Princess Diana's vows and previous ones?

She was the first royal to omit the word "obey" from her wedding vows.

6) Why did Princess Diana choose the ring from the Garrard jewelry collection catalogue?

Because it reminded her of her mother's wedding ring.

2. **Directions**: *Read the following statements carefully, and decide whether they are true(T) or false(F) according to the text.*

1) F 2) F 3) F 4) T 5) F 6) T

After-Class Reading

• Reading Comprehension

1. **Directions**: *Read the passage quickly and match each of the activities with the Three Letters and Six Etiquette it belongs to.*

E G I H C B F D A

2. **Directions**: *Fill the blanks according to the passage.*

selected good fortune bridal bed untouched respectively take a shower special meaning Three days roasted pigs and gifts a couple of

Topic-Related Activities

1. Case Study

Questions

1) What are the differences between Chinese and American wedding customs? Can you give any examples?

There are many differences between the two customs. Firstly, the choice of the color. In China, the red color always represents happiness and prosperity. The new couple is supposed to dress in red and their bridal room should be decorated in red. In America, they choose the white color which is holy and pure. Secondly, Chinese people usually set the fireworks before the ceremony and the Americans choose to sing a song or play a piece of music.

2) Do you think the customs are somewhat superstitious? And why?

Of course, some customs are superstitious. For example, "throwing rice at weddings". In America, it shows that the guests wish fertility, prosperity, and long-lasting happiness for the newly married couple. But scientifically, we know that the rice has nothing to do with fertility, prosperity, and long-lasting happiness. And in some regions of China, there is the same custom but bears another meaning "to protect the bride from being bitten by the chicken". Maybe this is the original purpose but gradually people give the action a meaning of best wishes.

3) What's your opinion about the wedding customs?

Open-ended.

4) Which wedding custom do you like, the Chinese or the American?

Open-ended.

3. Translation

Directions: *Translate the passage into English.*

Marriage is a major event in life. The saying goes, "When a son is grown, he takes a wife, and when a girl is old enough, she goes to her husband." Wedding ceremony, originally named "dusk ceremony", is one of the essences of the traditional culture of the Han nationality, as well as an important part of Chinese culture. The ancients thought that dusk was the auspicious time, so the ceremony to take a wife would be held at dusk. In traditional Chinese wedding customs, a wedding consisted of the three stages of before-wedding ceremony, in-wedding ceremony, and after-wedding ceremony, all of which originated from "Six Etiquette" (Request for Marrying the Bride, Request for Bride and Groom's Birthdates, Birthdates Matching, Presenting Betrothal Gifts, Wedding Date Fixing, Wedding Day) of the Zhou Dynasty.

Unit Eleven

In-Class Reading

• Reading Comprehension

1. Directions: *Discuss the following questions with your classmates.*

1) According to the Ethiopian legend, how did the goat herder Kaldi discover coffee?

The story goes that Kaldi discovered coffee after he noticed that after eating the berries from a certain tree, his goats became so energetic that they did not want to sleep at night.

2) What did patrons do in coffee houses across the Near East?

Not only did the patrons drink coffee and engage in conversation, but they also listened to music, watched performers, played chess and kept current on the news.

3) How did some people react to the unusual dark black beverage when it was brought back to Europe?

Some people reacted to this new beverage with suspicion or fear, calling it the "bitter invention of Satan".

4) Why were coffee houses called "penny universities" in England?

Because for the price of a penny one could purchase a cup of coffee and engage in stimulating conversation.

5) What incident that happened in the New World would forever change the American drinking preference to coffee?

The revolt, known as the Boston Tea Party, would forever change the American drinking preference to coffee.

6) How did Gabriel de Clieu manage to transport the young coffee plant safely to Martinique during his challenging voyage?

Despite a challenging voyage—complete with horrendous weather, a saboteur who tried to destroy the seedling, and a pirate attack—he managed to transport it safely to Martinique.

2. Directions: *Choose the best answer for each blank.*

1) B 2) C 3) B 4) A 5) C 6) B 7) B 8) C

After-Class Reading

• Reading Comprehension

1. Directions: *Discuss the following questions with your classmates.*

1) What is the main function of tea?

It is said to aid meditation and self-reflection and to induce tranquility, even perhaps inspiring imagination.

2) What do green tea, black tea, Oolong tea, and dark tea stand for respectively?

Green tea, simple and light, stands for the scholasticism of south China; black tea, mild and reserved, is regarded as rather ladylike; Oolong tea, warm and persistent, resembles the perseverance of philosophers; dark tea, with its lingering aftertaste, symbolizes the wisdom of the elderly.

3) Who, according to the Chinese legend, was the first person to discover the effects of tea?

It is said that the first person to discover the effects of tea was Sheng Nong—the father of agriculture and herbal medicine in China.

4) When had the function of tea to refresh the body and clear the mind gradually replaced its function as medicine?

By the Zhou Dynasty (1046 – 256 BC).

5) What was the first definitive publication about tea in China?

The Classic of Tea, which was the first of its kind in the world.

6) What kind of tea do Chinese people prefer in the different regions of China?

In Guangdong, for example, people like drinking morning tea, in Fujian they prefer Kongfu tea, Hunan has Lei tea, Sichuan people love "covered-bowl tea", while people of the Bai nationality treat their guests with "Three-Course Tea". Tibetan people prefer buttered tea and those from Inner Mongolia like milk tea.

2. Directions: *Read the following statements carefully, and decide whether they are true (T) or false (F) according to the text.*

1) F 2) F 3) T 4) F 5) F 6) T 7) F 8) T

Topic-Related Activities

3. Translation

Directions: *Translate the passage into English.*

【参考译文】"Tea or Coffee?" is a question frequently brought forth to dinners. Coffee is usually the Westerners' first choice, while tea is the preference given to by the Chinese. Legend has it that tea was found by one Chinese emperor, who lived 5,000 years ago. At that time, tea was used to heal sickness. During Ming-Qing Dynasties, teahouses were distributed across the country. Tea drinking was introduced to Japan as early as in the 6th century, yet it did not spread into Europe and America until the 18th century. Nowadays, tea is one of the most popular beverages all over the world. Tea is the treasure of China and the important component of Chinese tradition and culture.

Unit Twelve

In-Class Reading

• Reading Comprehension

1. Directions: *Discuss the following questions with your classmates.*

1) What are the genres of American music?

Genres of American music include country and folk Music, rock 'n' roll, blues, soul, disco and rap, jazz, R&B and so on.

2) How did immigrants in the Appalachian Mountains area form the genre of country music?

Immigrants in the Appalachian Mountains area, who had brought along instruments from their own countries, merged their art to form the famous genre of country music.

3) Who coined the term rock 'n' roll? What was the oldest form of rock music?

The term was coined in 1955 by Alan Freed, a disc jockey from Ohio. The oldest form of rock music was a mixture of R&B, country and rockabilly, only it was faster, louder and more dangerous.

4) Who did Sam Phillips, the owner of Sun Record Company, find his wish in? What was his wish?

The owner of Sun Record Company, Sam Phillips said "If I could find a white man who had the Negro (black) sound and the Negro feel, I could make $1 billion." He found his wish in Elvis Presley, the king of rock and roll.

5) In the 1960s many people were against the war in Vietnam including some folk singers. Can you list some of them according to the text?

Folk singers like Bob Dylan and Joan Baez wrote anti-war songs like Dylan's *Blowin' in the Wind* and other songs about the problems of American society.

6) How will music history remain an evolutionary rather than a revolutionary process?

If one can rely on the lessons of history, the mainstream of music will continue to absorb those new techniques that contribute to expressiveness and communication while discarding that which is merely novel and sensational, so that music history will remain an evolutionary rather than a revolutionary process.

2. Directions: *Read the following statements carefully, and decide whether they are true (T) or false (F) according to the text.*

1) F 2) F 3) T 4) F 5) T 6) F 7. F 8) T 9) F 10) T

After-Class Reading

- **Reading Comprehension**

1. Directions: *Discuss the following questions with your classmates.*

1) When can traditional Chinese music be traced back?

Traditional Chinese music can be traced back 7,000 – 8,000 years based on the discovery of a bone flute made in the Neolithic Age.

2) How were exotic and religious melodies absorbed into Chinese music and enjoyed by the Chinese people?

With the introduction of foreign religions such as Buddhism and Islam, exotic and religious melodies were absorbed into Chinese music and were enjoyed by the Chinese people at fairs organized by religious temples.

3) How were writers and artists inspired to create *ci*, a new type of literature resembling lyrics, in the Song Dynasty?

In the Song Dynasty, original opera such as Zaju and Nanxi was performed in tearooms, theatres, and showplaces. Writers and artists liked it so much that *ci*, a new type of literature resembling lyrics, thrived.

4) What are the three cornerstones of Chinese culture?

Beijing opera, Chinese medicine and traditional Chinese painting.

5) What categories can traditional Chinese musical instruments be divided into?

Traditional Chinese musical instruments can be divided into four categories: stringed instruments, percussion instruments, plucked instruments, and wind instruments.

6) What traditional Chinese musical instruments are featured in the text?

Horse-headed fiddle, lute (pipa), Erhu and flute.

2. Directions: *Read the following statements carefully, and decide whether they are true (T) or false (F) according to the text.*

1) T 2) F 3) F 4) T 5) F 6) F 7) F 8) F 9) F 10) T

Topic-Related Activities

1. Case Study

Questions:

1) How can you interpret the story and offer possible explanations on your knowledge and understanding of cultures?

Peter's first day in China is rather awkward and upsetting, probably because he doesn't know Chinese and Chinese culture well. First, about the laughing, it is possible that these students enjoy listening to him to struggle to speak in Chinese. He might have made some funny mistakes or said something sounding pretty funny in Chinese. They might laugh with him instead of laughing at him. Second, regarding cultural differences, Chinese often try to get rid of embarrassing situations by wearing a smiling face, while Westerners do it by looking guilty.

2) Can you offer some constructive suggestions?

Suggestions for Peter: He may keep practicing his Chinese and learn more about Chinese people and culture, and not to jump to conclusions with just initial contacts.

3. Translation

Directions: *Translate the passage into English.*

【参考译文】The very instant that the classical music gets hold of you, one can clearly visualize the mountain ranges, the running streams, the elegant bamboos, the winter snow and the eternal life flowing in the air. That kind of emotion, unable to be clearly articulated, epitomizes the serenity of Chinese classical music. Traditional musical instruments usually serve as a dual role, both entertainment and pragmatic use. Not only are they the instruments to play music, but also they are often tools of laboring or daily utensils. Chinese music is an integral part of China's rich and profound culture. Having developed for thousands of years, it becomes famous all around the world due to its rich varieties and systems of abundant connotations.